MW00356389

Murder in the Shenandoah

On July 4, 1791, the fifteenth anniversary of American independence, John Crane, a descendant of prominent Virginian families, killed his neighbor's harvest worker. *Murder in the Shenandoah* traces the story of this early murder case as it entangled powerful Virginians and addressed the question that everyone in the state was heatedly debating: what would it mean to have equality before the law – and a world where "law is king"? By retelling the story of the case, called *Commonwealth v. Crane*, through the eyes of its witnesses, families, fighters, victims, judges, and juries, Jessica K. Lowe reveals how revolutionary debates about justice gripped the new nation, transforming ideas about law, punishment, and popular government.

Jessica K. Lowe teaches at the University of Virginia School of Law.

See the Studies in Legal History series website at
http://studiesinlegalhistory.org/

Studies in Legal History

EDITORS

Sarah Barringer Gordon, University of Pennsylvania
Holly Brewer, University of Maryland, College Park
Michael Lobban, London School of Economics and Political Science
Reuel Schiller, University of California, Hastings College of the Law

Other books in the series

Martha S. Jones, *Birthright Citizens: A History of Race and Rights in Antebellum America*

Cynthia Nicoletti, *Secession on Trial: The Treason Prosecution of Jefferson Davis*

Edward James Kolla, *Sovereignty, International Law, and the French Revolution*

Assaf Likhovski, *Tax Law and Social Norms in Mandatory Palestine and Israel*

Robert W. Gordon, *Taming the Past: Essays on Law and History and History in Law*

Paul Garfinkel, *Criminal Law in Liberal and Fascist Italy*

Michelle A. McKinley, *Fractional Freedoms: Slavery, Intimacy, and Legal Mobilization in Colonial Lima, 1600–1700*

Mitra Sharafi, *Law and Identity in Colonial South Asia: Parsi Legal Culture, 1772–1947*

Karen M. Tani, *States of Dependency: Welfare, Rights, and American Governance, 1935–1972*

Stefan Jurasinski, *The Old English Penitentials and Anglo-Saxon Law*

Felice Batlan, *Women and Justice for the Poor: A History of Legal Aid, 1863–1945*

Sophia Z. Lee, *The Workplace Constitution from the New Deal to the New Right*

Michael A. Livingston, *The Fascists and the Jews of Italy: Mussolini's Race Laws, 1938–1943*

The Valley of the Shenandoah, from Jefferson's Rock, 1838, by William Henry Bartlett

Murder in the Shenandoah

Making Law Sovereign in Revolutionary Virginia

JESSICA K. LOWE
University of Virginia

CAMBRIDGE
UNIVERSITY PRESS

CAMBRIDGE
UNIVERSITY PRESS

University Printing House, Cambridge CB2 8BS, United Kingdom

One Liberty Plaza, 20th Floor, New York, NY 10006, USA

477 Williamstown Road, Port Melbourne, VIC 3207, Australia

314–321, 3rd Floor, Plot 3, Splendor Forum, Jasola District Centre, New Delhi – 110025, India

79 Anson Road, #06-04/06, Singapore 079906

Cambridge University Press is part of the University of Cambridge.

It furthers the University's mission by disseminating knowledge in the pursuit of education, learning, and research at the highest international levels of excellence.

www.cambridge.org
Information on this title: www.cambridge.org/9781108421782
DOI: 10.1017/9781108377812

© Jessica K. Lowe 2019

First published 2019

Printed and bound in Great Britain by Clays Ltd, Elcograf S.p.A.

A catalogue record for this publication is available from the British Library.

Library of Congress Cataloging-in-Publication Data
Names: Lowe, Jessica K., author.
Title: Murder in the Shenandoah : making law sovereign in revolutionary Virginia / Jessica K. Lowe, University of Virginia.
Description: Cambridge [UK]; New York, NY: Cambridge University Press, 2019. |
Series: Studies in legal history | Includes index.
Identifiers: LCCN 2018003790 | ISBN 9781108421782 (hardback)
Subjects: LCSH: Crane, John, Jr. –1792 – Trials, litigation, etc. | Trials (Murder) – Virginia. |
Murder – Virginia – Shenandoah – History – 18th century. | Equality before the law – United States – History. | LCGFT: Trial and arbitral proceedings.
Classification: LCC KF223.C685L69 2019 | DDC 345.755/02523–dc23
LC record available at https://lccn.loc.gov/2018003790

ISBN 978-1-108-42178-2 Hardback

To Mom and Dad with thanks,
and to the Honorable Robert B. King, for introducing me to
West Virginia history

Contents

Figures

Acknowledgments

Many people have contributed to this manuscript. In seminars, at conferences, in personal conversations, and on social media, numerous friends, colleagues, mentors, and family members have shared their knowledge and insights.

A few individuals merit special mention. Along with my advisor Dirk Hartog, the other members of my dissertation committee – Dan Rodgers, Bill Nelson, Stan Katz, and Peter Onuf – all engaged substantially with the manuscript well beyond the confines of the defense. Dan Rodgers asked a critical question at my very first presentation of Crane's story in 2009, one that I came back to over and over at every stage of the manuscript's development. Bill Nelson, an outside reader, read the full manuscript twice, and provided copies of his related in-progress work to help mine along. Stan Katz gave extensively of his own time and wisdom, serving as a constant example of scholarly generosity. Peter Onuf, who had previously been my undergraduate advisor (making me an incredibly fortunate undergraduate), spent valuable time coaching me through the final stages of completing the dissertation; it was he who suggested that I give Tucker a larger role in the book. Each of these distinguished and very senior scholars made me feel like a colleague, for which I am deeply grateful. They are models not just of good scholars but of good people.

Several other people also made important contributions to this story and its author. My wonderful graduate school colleagues, especially Annie Twitty, spent hours – years, really – discussing John Crane and St. George Tucker, legal history, the South, and much else. These friends – Annie Twitty, Dael Norwood, Chris Moses, Laura Weinrib, Sarah Milov, Lo Faber, and more – made graduate school some of the most fun I've ever had. William Chester Jordan, despite a failed quest to make me a medievalist, nonetheless loyally listened to at least five presentations of the Crane material, and offered helpful thoughts about moving forward. Sean Wilentz enthusiastically attended more than his share of Crane talks, managed to appear interested at each one, and gave valuable advice and encouragement, especially about writing narrative history. Barbara Oberg and the staff of the Jefferson Papers at Princeton were always supportive and provided helpful feedback on drafts and presentations. Through Princeton's Program in Law and Public Affairs, Kim Lane Scheppele provided abundant forums for graduate student work and invested much time in our progress.

At Virginia, my colleagues in the Law School and in the Corcoran Department of History enthusiastically offered their expertise from the very first presentation. Risa Goluboff believed in me and in the project, and worked to open doors for both. Her careful and attentive feedback on my written work took each version of the project to a new level. Cynthia Nicoletti, a longtime friend and classmate and now colleague, gave me fantastic comments and support, and engaged in long discussions of the book and field of legal history in general. Ted White, Dick Howard, Julia Mahoney, Max Edelson, Chuck McCurdy, Paul Halliday, and more, all at various points lent me their valuable time and wisdom. Brandon Garrett read three separate introduction drafts, offering a fresh eye when I very much needed one. Alan Taylor read a late draft of the book and offered critical advice for the final manuscript. My fantastic faculty assistant, Delores Clatterbuck, provided expert help at every stage. And portions of the book benefited from previous editing for publication in *Law and Social Inquiry*, under the direction of Howard Erlanger, and in Sally Hadden and Patti Minter's *Signposts: New Directions in Southern Legal History*.

This book was also made possible by some amazing archivists, librarians, and other specialists. The University of Virginia Law School library staff is unparalleled, and the reference librarians, especially Kent Olson, bent rules and beat bushes to find what I needed. Their assistance, including results of their research work (especially by Cathy Palombi and Kristin Glover), is evident throughout these pages. Loren Moulds and Jim Ambuske took on image gathering and permissions like the book was their own, and Jim first discovered the map that became the cover image. Rick Britton created two stunning, meticulous maps. Outside of the University of Virginia community, the Berkeley County Historical Society's late Don Wood gave me my start on uncovering Crane's story. The staffs at the Library of Virginia, the Handley Regional Library in Winchester, the West Virginia Culture Center, and Charles Town Library were always ready to help, as were the many West Virginians I met along the way, including the Honorable Thomas Steptoe, who offered his knowledge of the Crane family. At the Tucker-Coleman Papers at the College of William and Mary, Susan Riggs and Margaret Cook were generous with their vast knowledge of the papers and incredibly supportive of my work, as was Chuck Hobson, editor of Tucker's law papers. Chuck discovered Tucker's heated exchange with Charles Lee early in my research and brought it to my attention, changing the direction of the book. And his truly comprehensive knowledge of the early Virginia legal profession answered many of my questions along the way. Erich Kimbrough generously gave me permission to reproduce Frances Bland Randolph Tucker's portrait from his personal collection, and he and Deborah Llewellyn used their own time and resources to create an appropriate digital image. Bill Beiswanger offered me access to his amazing collection of books on early national Virginia, which allowed me to locate the John Marshall image used in Chapter 8. And my friend Mary Carlson cheerfully offered her time and skills to help design the cover.

Many, many people have read drafts of Crane-related material, or provided feedback at seminars or conferences. I have presented versions of the Crane story at the McNeil Center for Early American Studies, the Virginia Forum, the Law and Society Association, the Hurst Summer Institute in Legal History, Mount Holyoke College, the Omohundro Institute of Early American History and Culture, the Society for Historians of the Early American Republic (SHEAR), the St. George Tucker Society, and the Golieb Seminar at the New York University School of Law. Philip Morgan and Tom Green read early drafts of a Crane-related article. Various forums at Princeton University (the Modern America Workshop, the Program in Law and Public Affairs, and the Center for Human Values especially) helped to shape and improve the Crane story. Once I returned to my alma mater, the University of Virginia, to teach in 2012, audiences both at the Law School and at the Early American Seminar raised meaningful questions and provided important advice.

At the University of Virginia School of Law, several research assistants also made key contributions. John Gunter, Sarah Rafie, Sarah Ulmer, and Wes Sudduth all helped at critical moments. Amelia Nemitz's comprehensive, thoughtful research shows up throughout the book, and especially in the chapter on pardons. Over at least three years, Joseph Stuart checked sources at the Library of Virginia, copyedited, formatted, and checked all my footnotes, and photographed hundreds of documents to aid my research. In all this, he provided outstanding assistance.

At Cambridge, Holly Brewer, Sally Gordon, and Debbie Gershenowitz enthusiastically took on the project and helped it through the submission and publication processes. Having Holly's scholarly expertise as lead editor was especially invaluable, and her feedback made this a much better book.

Dirk Hartog has lived with this project – and my need to think out loud about it – since at least 2009. He first suggested looking at Tucker in 2006, during my first year at Princeton. In all the time since, he has listened to lofty dreams, quasi-rants about historiography, and excited recitations of dry genealogical finds, all with plausible enthusiasm. His scholarly example, thoughtful guidance, and deep caring for his students have been a privilege to experience.

Finally, this manuscript would not have been possible without my parents. When personal circumstances made it necessary, they came out of retirement to help on research and conference trips, and during one rainy day even spent a few hours in the archive themselves, using their considerable genealogy skills to help track down the people of *Commonwealth v. Crane*. I am grateful for their love and support.

Introduction

July 4, 1791

It was July 4, 1791, the fifteenth anniversary of American independence, and there was much work to be done. Around the country, proud citizens celebrated; they organized parades, listened to sermons, and even sparked a few riots.[1] But in Berkeley County, Virginia, just a few miles north of Winchester, two groups of sweaty, angry men – exhausted from a long day harvesting wheat in John Crane's and Thomas Campbell's adjoining fields – stared each other down across a fence. Their gazes threatened, their words taunted; they were ready to fight.[2]

John Crane, who stood his ground on his own side of the fence, was new to the neighborhood, but everyone knew who he was. The twenty-four-year-old Crane came from one of the county's most important families. His father had, until recently, been Berkeley's deputy sheriff; his wife, the former Catherine Whiting, was from one of Virginia's oldest and most powerful families – and

---

[1] For independence celebrations across the nation, see "Philadelphia, July 6," *Gazette of the United States* (New York City, NY), July 6, 1791; "New York," July 9, 1791," *Weekly Museum* (New York City, NY), July 9, 1791; "Boston, Monday, July 11, 1791," *Boston Gazette* (Boston, MA), July 11, 1791; "Baltimore, July 5," *Federal Gazette* (Baltimore, MD), July 8, 1791; "Elizabethtown, July 6," *New York Journal* (New York City, NY), July 9, 1791; "Worcester, July 7," *Massachusetts Spy* (Boston and Worcester, MA), July 7, 1791; "Providence, July 6, 1791," *United States Chronicle* (Providence, RI), July 7, 1791; "Portsmouth, July 7," *New Hampshire Gazette* (Portsmouth, NH), July 7, 1791; "Boston, Monday, July 11, 1791," *Boston Gazette* (Boston, MA), July 11, 1791; "Philadelphia, July 6," *Boston Gazette* (Boston, MA), July 18, 1791; "Philadelphia, July 13," *The Pennsylvania Gazette* (Philadelphia, PA), July 13, 1791. I am grateful to Amelia Nemitz for retrieving this information.
[2] See Commonwealth v. John Crane, the Younger, 3 Va. 10 (1791); "Deposition of Hugh McDonald, October 1, 1791," *Calendar of Virginia State Papers and Other Manuscripts*, vol. 5: *From July 2, 1789 to August 10, 1792*, ed. William P. Palmer and Sherwin McRae (Richmond, VA: Virginia State Library, 1885), 371–372.

one of Berkeley's richest.[3] But despite their privilege, on this July 4, John and Catherine had been working all day to bring in their first harvest on 200 acres of land – a decent amount of property, but small next to the thousands of acres some Shenandoah Valley landlords, such as Catherine's family, owned.[4]

And for this harvest, of course, the Cranes had help. First there were the enslaved people they owned – two adults and two teenagers, probably (like the land) a gift from family.[5] Several white men had also pitched in for the day. Thirty-one-year-old John Dawkins, the Cranes' neighbor, had offered his strong back and long experience to help the young landowners harvest their crop. Dawkins had lived in the area for years, maybe all his life, but in 1791 his parents had just sold their land, and his family was on its way to Kentucky (in those days still Virginia's westernmost region).[6] Dawkins knew the men in Campbell's field well; now, he stood with Crane at the fence, facing Campbell's angry reapers.[7]

---

[3] For a detailed discussion of both John and Catherine Whiting Crane's families and backgrounds, see Chapter 1.

[4] "John Crane Jun." appears on the Berkeley land tax records for the first time in 1790, owning 200 acres, but as a personal property owner in 1791. See Berkeley County Land Tax, East 1790, Berkeley County Historical Society, Martinsburg, WV (hereafter BCHS); Berkeley County Personal Property Tax Records, East 1791, BCHS. Entries from a family Bible that appears to have belonged to Catherine Whiting Crane, John's wife, list his birth date as December 30, 1766, although the printed source citing the Bible reports that the date is of dubious legibility. See Dakota Best Brown, *Data on Some Virginia Families* (Berryville, VA: Virginia Book Company, 1979), 251. For settlement patterns, see Warren Hofstra, *A Separate Place: The Formation of Clarke County, Virginia* (Madison, WI: Madison House Publishers, 1999), 27. James Crane had obtained land grants for property that, because of its location, seems to have been among what John Crane farmed. See grant to James Crane of "34 acres adjoining John Dawkins and George Hyots heirs," Northern Neck Grants U, 1789–1790, 455–456 (Reel 300), The Library of Virginia, Richmond, VA (hereafter Library of Virginia); grant to James Crane of "106 acres near and on the east side of Opeckon Creek," Northern Neck Grants U, 1789–1790, 453–455 (Reel 300), Library of Virginia. (The Crane family owned other Berkeley property not included in these grants.) Additionally, the Cranes had grants for land further west, including John Crane's 1785 grant for 400 acres in Monongalia County. Land Office Grants P, 1784–1785, 487 (Reel 56), Library of Virginia.

[5] Berkeley County Personal Property Tax Records, East 1791, BCHS.

[6] See land grant to James Crane, March 2, 1790, for 34 acres "adjoining John Dawkins and George Hyots heirs," Northern Neck Grants U, 1789–1790, 455–456; John Dawkins is listed in the Berkeley County tax records as owning 150 acres. See, e.g., Berkeley County Land Tax Records, East 1790, BCHS. The Dawkins family identifies the John Dawkins of the Crane case as John Dawkins Jr. See Lela Wolfe Prewitt, *The Dawkins and Stewart Families of Virginia and Kentucky* (n.p.: 1968), 5–6. Dawkins appears as a significant figure in the ultimate verdict in *Commonwealth v. Crane*, as a witness in court documents, and in other materials related to the case. See, e.g., *Crane*, 3 Va. at 10–13; "Deposition of Hugh McDonald, October 1, 1791," *Calendar of Virginia State Papers*, 5:371–372.

[7] Dawkins's father had posted security for the will of Campbell's reaper Isaac Merchant's father, who died in 1772. See entry "June 16, 1772," Berkeley County Minute Book, BCHS, giving £500 security with David Lewis and Priscilla Merchant on the will of William Merchant.

The men across the fence, on the lands of Crane's neighbor Thomas Campbell, were itching for a fight.[8] These young white men lived in the area and had been working for Campbell all day; they were only steps away from Crane, but in some ways worlds apart. One was Isaac Merchant whose old Quaker family had fallen on hard times, and no longer followed the faith; Isaac had worked hard to purchase some land and was now reestablishing himself as a Valley landowner even as he helped Campbell with his harvest.[9] Others of Campbell's workers owned no land, including two young men named Abraham and Joseph Vanhorn, whose father lived nearby.[10] Abraham drove a team for a living, and now lived in Winchester – only a few miles to the south.[11]

It was summer, but on this Independence Day, as the men faced off at the fence, the normally hot July weather topped out in the low sixties.[12] The sweaty men felt the chill as night fell and the temperature dropped. Harvest time made for a long, grueling day, and their bodies ached from the work. They had also been drinking. And as they stared each other down at the fence between Crane's and Campbell's fields, they were agitated – not the normal frustrations of a long day, but something deeper, more urgent.

These two groups of men, threatening each other amidst the rolling hills of the Shenandoah Valley, in many ways embodied the history and demographics of the place where they stood. Berkeley County – stretching in 1791 from just north of Winchester to the confluence of the Shenandoah and Potomac rivers at Harpers Ferry – was both old and new, diverse and alike, settled and quickly changing. White settlers had been in the area since around 1730, when the first wave of Berkeley pioneers had come from the North – from Pennsylvania, New Jersey, and New York. These recent immigrants came from Dutch, German, Welsh, or Scottish backgrounds, and they settled on grants made to them by Virginia's colonial government.[13] But Lord Thomas Fairfax had his own claims. Fairfax, a British peer and descendant of the Culpeper family, held the Culpepers' old proprietary charter from

---

[8] "Deposition of Hugh McDonald, October 1, 1791," *Calendar of Virginia State Papers*, 5:371–372.

[9] Isaac Merchant is discussed at length in Chapter 3.

[10] See discussion of Vanhorn and his (probable) parentage in Chapter 1.

[11] *ClayPoole's Daily Advertiser* (Philadelphia, PA), July 19, 1791, 2. For the Winchester connection, see William Greenway Russell, *What I Know About Winchester*, ed. Garland R. Quarles and Lewis N. Barton (Staunton, VA: McClure Publishing Co., 1953), 47, n. 59.

[12] Letter from Thomas Mann Randolph Jr. to Thomas Jefferson, Monticello, July 7, 1791, in *The Papers of Thomas Jefferson*, vol. 20: *1 April–4 August 1791*, ed. Julian P. Boyd (Princeton, NJ: Princeton University Press, 1982), 607.

[13] See John Walter Wayland, *The German Element in the Shenandoah Valley* (Charlottesville, VA: Michie Co., Printers, 1907); A. H. and M. H. Gardiner, *Chronicles of Old Berkeley* (Durham, NC: Seeman Press, 1938); William Thomas Doherty, *Berkeley County, U.S.A.: A Bicentennial History of a Virginia and West Virginia County, 1772–1972* (Parsons, WV: McClain Publishers, 1972); Don Wood, *A Documented History of Martinsburg and Berkeley County* (Martinsburg, WV: Berkeley County Historical Society, 2004).

the Crown, which entitled them to large portions of Virginia; he too claimed parts of the Berkeley area. Competing with the colonial government for control of the area, in the early eighteenth century Fairfax's land agent, Virginian Robert "King" Carter, had granted huge swaths of land to himself, his heirs, and other Tidewater Virginians, concentrating large amounts of choice land in the hands of some of Virginia's most elite families.[14] In the old days, these wealthy Virginians had usually managed their Berkeley and Frederick land as absentee landlords, but by the 1780s, their heirs began to move to the fertile Valley. There they thrived. As one eastern Virginian remarked with astonishment, "the men who have moved from Gloucester to Frederick make near five times as much there as they did down here."[15] As they moved, they began to push land prices up and some older settlers farther west – to Kentucky especially, and soon to Ohio as well. Observing the exodus from Berkeley and Frederick to the west, one resident commented, "The emigration of inhabitants is … astonishing."[16]

Berkeley was desirable country. Bounded on the south by Frederick and its bustling county seat of Winchester and on the north by the Potomac River, Berkeley offered beautiful, abundant land and easy transportation for people and goods. Maryland was visible just across the Potomac, and in the northernmost part of the county, near the resort town of Bath (otherwise known as Berkeley Springs). Pennsylvania also lay only a few miles away, to the north.[17] The county was an economic mix, with mills dotting the landscape on abundant rivers that ran alongside farms and plantations. Wagons and wagon-drivers transported goods to market on the Great Wagon Road, which ran through Winchester and up to Philadelphia.[18] By 1760, thousands of settlers per year traveled south on that road, some stopping in Winchester and others continuing on, to North Carolina or Kentucky, making Winchester one of the busiest towns in Virginia.[19] This made the Valley bustling and extremely diverse by eighteenth-century standards. As Methodist circuit rider Frances Asbury complained about Winchester in the 1780s, the "inhabitants are much

[14] There was a debate over how much of the area Fairfax's patent covered. See Stuart E. Brown *Virginia Baron: The Story of Thomas, 6th Lord Fairfax* (Baltimore, MD: Clearfield Company, 2003). For an excellent discussion of the dynamics of east versus west in the Valley, see Hofstra, *A Separate Place.*
[15] The writer was John Page of Rosewell, as quoted ibid., 11.
[16] Ibid., 26.
[17] See, e.g., Wood, *Documented History of Martinsburg and Berkeley County*, 207–209, 234–237.
[18] See Harry M. Ward, *Major General Adam Stephen and the Cause of American Liberty* (Charlottesville, VA: University of Virginia Press, 1989), 94, 103; A. D. Kenamond, *Prominent Men of Shepherdstown, 1762–1962* (Charles Town, WV: Jefferson County Historical Society, 1962), 11. See also Warren Hofstra and Karl Raitz, eds., *The Great Valley Road of Virginia* (Charlottesville, VA: University of Virginia Press, 2010).
[19] Hofstra, *A Separate Place*, 32.

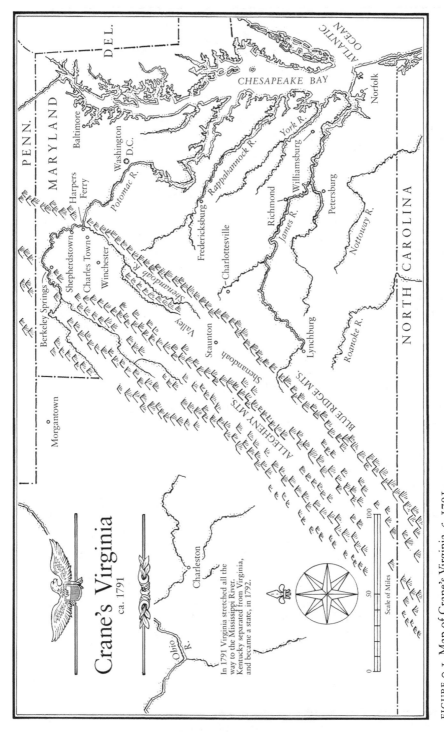

FIGURE 0.1 Map of Crane's Virginia, c. 1791

Crane's Virginia
ca. 1791

In 1791 Virginia stretched all the way to the Mississippi River. Kentucky separated from Virginia, and became a state, in 1792.

Scale of Miles
0   50   100

PENN.

MARYLAND

DEL.

Morgantown

Charleston

Ohio R.

Berkeley Springs

Shepherdstown

Charles Town

Winchester

Harpers Ferry

Baltimore

Washington D.C.

Potomac R.

Shenandoah R.

Valley

Staunton

Lynchburg

Shenandoah

ALLEGHENY MTS.

BLUE RIDGE MTS.

Fredericksburg

Charlottesville

Richmond

James R.

Petersburg

Williamsburg

York R.

Rappahannock R.

Nottoway R.

Roanoke R.

Norfolk

CHESAPEAKE BAY

ATLANTIC OCEAN

NORTH CAROLINA

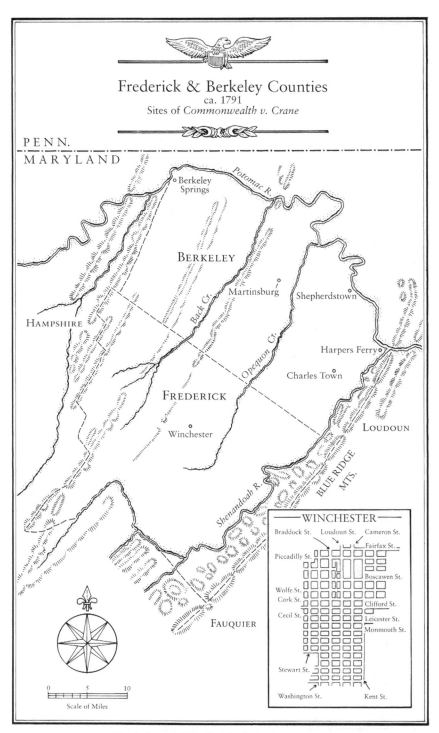

FIGURE 0.2 Map of Berkeley and Frederick Counties, *c.* 1791

divided, made up, as they are, of different nations, and speaking different languages," agreeing "scarcely in any thing [sic] except it be to sin against God."[20]

On July 4, 1791, as the two groups of men reaped wheat in adjoining fields in the southern part of Berkeley County, they embodied this diversity and these changes, both their promise and their peril. They were settlers from eastern Virginia, Dutch farmers, Quakers, enslaved African Americans, slaveholders and those who eschewed the system. And as Americans around the country celebrated the Fourth of July, these men worked – sharing some grog in between.[21]

The grog may have made conflict more likely. By nightfall, the men fought, wrestling each other down to the ground near the fence between Crane's and Campbell's fields. As the melee cleared, Abraham Vanhorn lay mortally wounded – stabbed, crying, "my guts are out!"[22] Some witnesses claimed John Crane had delivered the fatal blow. Crane insisted on his innocence. Had he done it? And if so, why?

For the next twelve months, Crane's friends and neighbors would debate exactly that: what had happened at the line between Crane's and Campbell's fields? In time, the fight became the center of a sensational case – a case that, like the knife that gutted Vanhorn, sliced to the core of postrevolutionary Virginia.

When I first began reading through collections of early Virginia cases, I anticipated a different project. I had planned on a sweeping study of the development of Virginia's criminal law between the Revolution and the 1830s – one that would examine, through shifting ideas about crime and its punishment, Virginia's transition from colony to nation and from nation to self-consciously Southern state. As the first colony, the mother of so many founders and early presidents, and later the capital of the Confederacy, Virginia seemed an ideal vehicle for this study.

On the way, I stumbled across John Crane's case. Its drama and complexity leapt out at me. For one thing, Crane's jury had been unable to decide on a verdict, and had left a long, detailed special verdict instead – one included in the case report. That verdict gave a careful description of the fatal fight and left the legal decision (murder or manslaughter?) to the court. To twenty-first-century eyes, that seemed odd. After all, the jury had passed the buck to the judge in a murder case, allowing him to determine whether a defendant lived or died. At any time, this would be striking, but in the era of the American Revolution, when the right to a jury had been a key tenet of the revolutionary struggle, it stood out. Moreover, the jury's verdict contradicted a basic truism of American legal

---

[20] Entry marked "June 21, 1783," *The Journal of the Rev. Francis Asbury, Bishop of the Methodist Episcopal Church, from August 7, 1771, to December 7, 1815 …*, vol. 1 (New York, NY: N. Bangs and T. Mason, 1821), 357.

[21] "Deposition of Hugh McDonald, October 1, 1791," *Calendar of Virginia State Papers*, 5:372.

[22] "American Intelligence: Winchester, Virginia, July 9," *Western Star* (Stockbridge, MA), August 2, 1791; *Crane*, 3 Va. at 13.

history: that in the late eighteenth and early nineteenth centuries, special verdicts were a device of *judges*, used to take cases away from juries.[23] Crane's, however, seemed to originate with the jurors themselves – to the judge's consternation.

I was also drawn in by the story, by the characters – not the founders or writers or politicians who can so easily populate tales of the past. Instead, these people had ordinary lives, of the type hard to detect in surviving historical records. Their stories had been made extraordinary, and thrust into the historical record, by a single day's violence. Who were John Crane, Abraham Vanhorn, and the others who argued in the fields that day? What had happened at the line between Crane's and Campbell's fields? What about in the court process that followed? These questions took me to the farmlands of what is now Jefferson County, West Virginia, where the site of the fatal fight is still a scene of rolling, grassy fields; to the streets of Winchester, Virginia, where Crane was tried; and to Charles Town, West Virginia, where I traced the deed to the Crane family's town home, pacing out its instructions on the town's historic streets and locating it in relation to the homes of others who participated in the case. My journey took me to archives in Charleston, Charles Town, and Martinsburg, West Virginia; Williamsburg, Richmond, and finally Charlottesville, Virginia; Washington, DC; also on brief incursions into Pennsylvania, Kentucky, and even into Bermuda history. It at times spanned decades, even centuries, as members of the families materialized in records, in tales, or sometimes in person during archival trips and secondary research.

While some participants in the case were common folk, the man who served as Crane's trial judge was St. George Tucker, one of the most important jurists and legal scholars in early America. A native of Bermuda who had studied law at the College of William and Mary and then married into Virginia's gentry, Tucker was in 1791 not only serving as a judge of Virginia's General Court but also teaching law at the College of William and Mary and annotating William Blackstone's famous *Commentaries on the Laws of England* for an American audience. In 1803 he would publish his work as the first American edition of Blackstone, and his treatise would become the most widely used American legal text until the 1830s.[24] At the time of *Commonwealth v. Crane*, Tucker had immersed himself in Virginia's effort to revise its laws. The fact that Tucker served as the judge on Crane's sensational case meant that John Crane's legal proceedings intersected with the very heart of Virginia's tense and passionate discussion about what it meant to have law in a republic – or, as Judge Tucker would have put it, a "Govt. of the People."[25]

[23] Morton Horwitz, *The Transformation of American Law, 1780–1860* (Cambridge, MA: Harvard University Press, 1977).

[24] See Davison M. Douglas, "Foreword: The Legacy of St. George Tucker," *William and Mary Law Review* 47, no. 4 (2006): 1111–1121, 1114–1115; Charles F. Hobson, "St. George Tucker's Law Papers," *William and Mary Law Review* 47, no. 4 (2006): 1245–1278, 1246–1247.

[25] "Republican" is a fraught term in the historiography, and has been a subject of much excellent scholarship and disagreement. For a thorough introduction to the literature on republicanism,

Criminal law provided a linchpin for that discussion. Early Americans, much like Americans today, loved to talk about crime. Stories of both shocking and mundane crimes, many of them gruesome, spread quickly up and down the East Coast and were printed and reprinted in newspapers throughout the country.[26] Crowds gathered eagerly to listen to condemned felons say their last words before hanging, pamphlets told the scandalous stories of their crimes, and anonymous composers produced ballads to mark execution day. Popular gossip about sensational crimes ranged from fascination with macabre details to "astute attention to ... procedural norms."[27] In the words of historian Steven Wilf, in the late eighteenth century criminal law was the "most talked about legalism in ... America's coffee houses and cobblestone streets."[28]

But criminal law was also about more than talk or entertainment. It was – as any good student of the Enlightenment knew – a key indicator of the nature of a society's government. In the days before written constitutions, to think about constitutional questions was to think about the interchange between power and liberty, and criminal law provided the paradigmatic example of the state's power over the citizen.[29] Could the state take a life? What did it mean for the law to treat a criminal as a citizen, instead of as a subject? The most important political theorists, such as Locke and Montesquieu, paid special attention to this problem. Free governments, everyone agreed, required new, different criminal laws from those of the Old World monarchies – including the English common law, with its many hangings, its judge-made law, and its frequent pardons.

---

see Daniel T. Rodgers, "Republicanism: The Career of a Concept," *Journal of American History* 79, no. 1 (1992): 11–38. In a much simpler vein, Tucker explained it to his law students this way: in America, a republic was "synonymous" with democracy; it was to be "considered as a Govt. of the People; as a Pure Democracy ... Whenever the body of the people are divested of the supreme power it is no longer a pure republic." St. George Tucker, "Ten Notebooks of Law Lectures," Notebook 1, 1, Tucker-Coleman Papers, Swem Library, The College of William and Mary, Williamsburg, VA (hereafter Tucker-Coleman Papers). The term "republicanism" is used here because it is the term that Tucker and his contemporaries used, without intending to resurrect or rehash this complex discussion – except to note that Tucker early identified "republic" with democracy in his law lectures which, though undated, span the early 1790s to 1804, when he resigned the post. See Charles F. Hobson, ed., *St. George Tucker's Law Reports and Selected Papers, 1782–1825* (Chapel Hill, NC: University of North Carolina Press, 2013), vol. 1, 9–13.

[26] In *Body in the Reservoir: Murder and Sensationalism in the South* (Chapel Hill, NC: University of North Carolina Press, 2008), Michael Ayers Trotti examines newspaper reports in depth, and concludes that most sensationalized coverage was in Northern papers until the turn of the nineteenth century.

[27] Steven Wilf, *Law's Imagined Republic: Popular Politics and Criminal Justice in Revolutionary America* (New York, NY: Cambridge University Press, 2010), 1–4.

[28] Wilf, *Law's Imagined Republic*, 1.

[29] As Bernard Bailyn explains, eighteenth-century constitutional thought focused on the interchange between power and liberty, presenting the two as in constant tension. Bernard Bailyn, *Ideological Origins of the American Revolution* (Cambridge, MA: Belknap, 1992 [first printing 1967]). See also Gordon Wood, *The Creation of the American Republic, 1776–1787* (Chapel Hill, NC: University of North Carolina Press, 1998), 18–28.

The American revolutionaries had absorbed this lesson. After all, monarchies and despotic governments differed from republics – and a republic was what the newly independent colonies aspired to be. In a republic there was, as Tucker instructed his grand juries, "no sovereign but the laws."[30] Or, as Thomas Paine put it in *Common Sense*, "In America, THE LAW IS KING."[31] As Paine confidently asserted, "the nearer any government approaches to a Republic, the less business there is for a King." He explained, "in absolute governments the King is law," and the opposite should be true as well: "in free countries the law *ought* to be King; and there ought to be no other."[32]

Paine made explicit what many felt: that the basis of authority, and the nature of law, had fundamentally changed. In keeping with this, after independence the states began to revise their laws to reflect the new republican reality. Virginia was at the forefront of this effort. In 1776, leading revolutionaries embarked on ambitious "revisals," as they called them, of colonial laws, meant to purge the remnants of monarchy and create a republican legal order. This was not merely a technicality, a passing necessity of a new government. Instead, as St. George Tucker later explained, Virginia's effort to revise its laws was born of "political experiment," and aimed to make those laws "conform to the newly adopted principles of republican government."[33] It was, as Thomas Jefferson put it, the "whole object of the present controversy."[34]

Americans had the sense that the whole world's eyes were upon them, and they were right. Some years later, after the states began to enact reforms, France would even dispatch a representative to examine criminal punishment in America.[35] It was a time, as Massachusetts's John Adams remarked to his Virginian friend George Wythe, "when the greatest lawgivers of antiquity would have wished to have lived."[36]

Ideas were one thing, but putting those ideas into practice – and seeing how (and whether) they worked – was more complicated. In the years after the Revolution, theory began to change as ideas were hammered out, by trial

---

[30] St. George Tucker, Grand Jury Charge, filed with General Court Docket 1793, Tucker-Coleman Papers.

[31] Thomas Paine, *Common Sense, Addressed to the Inhabitants of America …*, 6th edn. (Providence, RI: John Carter, 1776), 26.

[32] Ibid., at 15, 26.

[33] St. George Tucker, *Blackstone's Commentaries with Notes of Reference to the Constitution and Laws of the Federal Government of the United States; and of the Commonwealth of Virginia*, vol. 1 (Philadelphia, PA: William Young Birch and Abraham Small, 1803), editor's preface, x.

[34] Quoted in David John Mays, *Edmund Pendleton* (Cambridge, MA: Harvard University Press, 1952), 1:138.

[35] Alexis de Tocqueville and Gustave de Beaumont, *On the Penitentiary System in the United States and its Application in France; with an Appendix on Penal Colonies and also Statistical Notes* (Philadelphia, PA: Carey, 1833).

[36] John Adams, "Thoughts on Government" [April 1776], *Founding Fathers: Digital Editions of the Papers of the Winthrops and Adamses*, ed. C. James Taylor (Boston: Massachusetts Historical Society, 2018).

and error, in practice – particularly in the often difficult or mundane cases that came before the courts. Over time, some Virginians began to doubt, or at least modify, the old assumptions about "republican" law, about discretion, common law, and where power could be most safely deposited. And as John Crane's case moved through the courts from July 1791 to July 1792, it would highlight three aspects of this emerging postrevolutionary legal order – three places where Virginians were struggling over what it meant to "make law king."

First, the case would take place right in the middle of Virginia's unfinished law reform. In 1776, Thomas Jefferson had drafted a new criminal code, in his capacity as a revisor of the law, but the Virginia legislature had deadlocked over its enactment. This left the old colonial "bloody code" in place, and important questions on the table. What should criminal punishment be? Were pardons proper in a republican government? What power should a judge hold, as opposed to the legislature or the jury? Should the new "republican" law privilege the legislature and strict interpretation of the written word, or would common-law traditions continue?

Second, Crane's case would also press on the fault lines of class and privilege that threatened to explode postrevolutionary Virginia. Virginia's laws, at least in theory, operated "without regard to the Circumstances of the Offender," as Judge Tucker charged his grand juries.[37] But in reality, class mattered. The years after the Revolution were full of tensions between rich and poor, high and low. The struggle for independence had unintentionally opened doors for "new men" and empowered some who had previously found themselves subject to Virginia's powerful gentry.[38] Additionally, some citizens balked at the burdens of debt and taxes which, they complained, mainly helped the rich. It was one thing for people like Jefferson or Tucker to talk about equality – but what would that mean, in practice?

Finally, even in this process of rapid change, one thing – a third essential characteristic – remained constant: Virginians' deep commitment to the rule of law. Examining Crane's case explores how ordinary Virginians acted in day-to-day cases and disputes, how they engaged in practice with the many ideas that were being thrown about in theory. In fact, putting the legal aspects and the social background of the case together upends a key lesson of the traditional historiography about law in the American South: namely, that Southerners – especially typical Southerners "on the ground" – favored extra-legal, interpersonal ways to resolve their problems.

For over a generation, scholars have seen the South as a region where honor dominated, not law. One frequently repeated anecdote lays out this perspective. When France's Alexis de Tocqueville traveled through America in the 1830s,

---

[37] St. George Tucker, Grand Jury Charge, filed with General Court Docket 1793, Tucker-Coleman Papers.

[38] See Rhys Isaac, *The Transformation of Virginia, 1740–1790* (Chapel Hill, NC: University of North Carolina Press for the Omohundro Institute of Early America History and Culture, 1982).

he reported a conversation with a young Alabama lawyer, who explained that "[t]here is no one here but carries arms under his clothes. At the slightest quarrel, knife or pistol comes to hand. These things happen continually; it is a semi-barbarous state of society." Tocqueville asked, "But when a man is killed like that, is his assassin not punished?" The lawyer replied, "He is always brought to trial, and always acquitted by the jury, unless there are greatly aggravating circumstances ... This violence has become accepted. Each juror feels that he might, upon leaving the court, find himself in the same position as the accused, and he acquits." The lawyer revealed several scars on his head from his own fighting; when Tocqueville inquired if he had gone to law for redress, the lawyer responded adamantly in the negative. "My God! No. I tried to give as good as I got."[39]

Historians have tended to think of the behavior described by Tocqueville as part of a Southern culture of honor, one in which a (white) man's worth was determined by the opinions of those around him and which required that wrongs be avenged personally in order for honor to be preserved.[40] Bertram Wyatt-Brown provided the major exposition on this culture, and argued that it provided the structuring ethic for Southern life.[41] Edward Ayers agreed but insisted that honor itself arose in essence from the slave system. And where honor dominated, it relegated law to the periphery. For, as Ayers explained, scholars have accepted that "honor and legalism, as students of other honor-bound societies have observed, are incompatible."[42]

Newer scholarship, this time associated with what historians and legal scholars call "legal pluralism," has shown a similar tendency. Recent work has argued that people in local communities had their own ideas about law in Crane's day, ideas that conflicted with those of state elites. According to these scholars, people in local courts and state courts came from different legal cultures and saw law differently. State elites desired reform and uniformity, but local people and their local courts – including local elites and justices of the peace – valued the traditional "keeping of the peace." "Keeping the peace" meant, in this usage, a process where local elders, represented by the justices of the peace, could dispense justice as they saw fit, according to local custom, religion, and discretion, regardless of official law.[43] This is important, because

---

[39] Alexis de Tocqueville, *Journey to America*, trans. George Lawrence, ed. J. P. Mayer (New Haven, CT: Yale University Press, 1960), 103, quoted in Edward L. Ayers, *Vengeance and Justice: Crime and Punishment in the Nineteenth Century American South* (New York, NY: Oxford University Press, 1984), 17.

[40] Bertram Wyatt-Brown, *Southern Honor: Ethics and Behavior in the Old South* (New York, NY: Oxford University Press, 1982).

[41] Wyatt-Brown, *Southern Honor*.

[42] Ayers, *Vengeance and Justice*, 18, 22–33.

[43] Laura F. Edwards, *The People and Their Peace: Legal Culture and the Transformation of Inequality in the Post-Revolutionary South* (Chapel Hill, NC: University of North Carolina Press, 2009), 12.

scholars had previously assumed that elite and popular ideas of law tend to be similar; in other words, that professional/elite (or "mandarin," as scholars call it) law is usually, in the words of legal scholar Robert Gordon, merely a "purified and formalized version" of popular law, and vice versa.[44] This new paradigm of "state legal culture" versus "localized legal culture" has become the accepted baseline for discussions of Southern law.[45]

But as I examined the world of *Commonwealth v. Crane*, I found something different. In late eighteenth-century Virginia, the very same people who brought cases and served as justices of the peace in local courts, also appeared in the state courts as litigants, jurors, grand jurors, and other officers. Rather than representing different legal cultures, both courts drew from the same pool of people. Moreover, in both types of courts, Virginians talked about law, agitated for law that would be to their benefit, and tried to use the law to their best advantage.

Indeed, the early Virginia that I discovered was a society steeped in law. There were, of course, conflicts over law. What, people debated, should the law be? How should it be administered? And by whom? But these were conflicts about politics and power – about *how* the law would function, and *who* it would help – not about the idea of law itself.

Significantly, this Virginian discussion had national implications. In this era, Virginia had the most people and the most territory of any state in the Union, by a large margin.[46] Virginia was so important that, during the recent struggle to ratify the federal constitution, the new government's proponents worried that if Virginia rejected the document the new federal union would fail, regardless of which other states ratified it.[47] Designing the new nation had fallen and would continue to fall largely on Virginians, making it the state that more than any other would shape early American government and law. Virginians had not only been the principal movers behind the new federal constitution, but they would continue to lead into the nineteenth century. Four of the first five presidents were Virginians, leading the nation – as historian Lorri Glover has noted – for thirty-two of its first thirty-six years.[48] In 1791, as the events that would become *Commonwealth v. Crane* began, George Washington was

---

[44] Robert W. Gordon, "Critical Legal Histories," *Stanford Law Review* 36 (1984): 57–125, 66.

[45] As legal historian Christopher Tomlins explains, Edwards "seems to me to indicate quite decisively that this is not the case." Instead, according to Edwards, popular ideas of law were "fundamentally incompatible at a base, conceptual level." Christopher Tomlins, "What is Left of the Law and Society Paradigm after Critique? Revisiting Gordon's 'Critical Legal Histories,'" *Law and Social Inquiry* 37, no. 1 (2012): 155–166, 163.

[46] Lorri Glover makes a thorough and convincing case for the preeminence of Virginia in *The Fate of the Revolution: Virginians Debate the Constitution* (Baltimore, MD: Johns Hopkins University Press, 2016), 4–5 and throughout.

[47] Ibid., 4. See also, generally, Michael Klarman, *Framers' Coup* (New York, NY: Oxford University Press, 2016).

[48] Glover, *The Fate of the Revolution*, 158.

President, Thomas Jefferson served as Washington's Secretary of State, and Crane's trial lawyer, Charles Lee, would soon become US Attorney General. Only a few years later Virginian John Marshall, Crane's appellate lawyer, would become the new Chief Justice of the United States. Along with Crane's judge, scholar, and legal commentator St. George Tucker, these men – and their sometimes conflicting ideas – would create America's legal culture, making *Commonwealth v. Crane* both a Virginian case, and an American one.

During my research, as I began to unearth the world of *Commonwealth v. Crane*, my aims for the project changed. Most of all, I wanted to tell the case's story, the story of John Crane, Abraham Vanhorn, Isaac Merchant, and St. George Tucker. And I wanted to tell that story not just for their sakes, but for what it reveals about law, about Virginia, and about how seeing a case as an experience, instead of an outcome, opens up the process of doing legal history. Writing narrative, I discovered, is hard. It is one thing to take a stack of documents and make an argument, another to reconstruct a world from a handful of discarded pieces of paper – newspaper articles, the remnants of a court file, and occasionally some tax records. But I have done so because it is only by recreating this story – only by following the people of *Commonwealth v. Crane* as they moved from court to court, and place to place, only by seeing the law in motion – that we can view the world that these Virginians themselves experienced.[49]

The narrative format is thus, behind the story, also a key part of the book's argument. In our modern world, we are accustomed to thinking of "law" narrowly, as a set of rules, promulgated by legislatures or handed down by judges. But most people who deal with law do so in real time – as defendants, litigants, or even lawyers or judges. They encounter law as a system and an experience as well as a rule or endpoint. Studying that larger encounter (the lived experience of the law) is essential for gaining an accurate impression of what the law is, now and at the time of *Commonwealth v. Crane*: how it functioned, who it harmed and helped, and what it meant to the people whom it claimed to both police and represent.[50] Law is in motion, and it is created as it moves. The people who examined and deliberated Crane's fate – the justices of the peace, the wealthy planters who sat on his grand jury, the judge who conducted his trial, the angry, partial witnesses who testified, and the jury that confronted his crime – all helped to create the law and the legal process that threatened Crane with death. But even as they themselves implicitly negotiated and produced the

---

[49] In *Law in American History*, G. Edward White eloquently describes a related way of thinking about historical writing: the "challenge to re-create the ways in which actors in a slice of time in the past experienced their world." G. Edward White, *Law in American History*, vol. 1: *From the Colonial Years through the Civil War* (New York, NY: Oxford University Press, 2012), 6.

[50] See, for instance, Hendrik Hartog, "Pigs and Positivism," *Wisconsin Law Review* (1985): 899–935.

law that pointed Crane towards the gallows – as they weighed what should happen to the man on whom they sat in judgment – they also turned to the law to decide his fate. This is a story of that dialogue, between popular participation and what Tucker called "legal science"; between class privilege and republican uniformity; between public events and private conflict, in a nation that was rapidly changing – the story of John Crane and his legal world.

The Facts of the Fight

By July 9, 1791, five days after his fight with Abraham Vanhorn, John Crane found himself pacing the confines of the small Berkeley County jail. The jail was "thirty-six feet long and thirty-six feet wide" with "three rooms on a floor." The walls were plank, but behind the plank was stone – solid, unyielding.[1]

The jail, in the county seat of Martinsburg, was probably the last place that Crane had ever expected to find himself. But now he was awaiting trial – well, not trial exactly, but an examination before the Berkeley County justices of the peace to determine whether he should then be sent to Winchester, to the state District Court, to be tried for the murder of Abraham Vanhorn.

Vanhorn had not died immediately. Instead, after he was stabbed on the night of July 4, the other men had carried him over to Thomas Campbell's home, where he lingered for two days while his abdominal wounds festered.[2] After Abraham finally died around 3 a.m. on July 7, the coroner's examination uncovered several large lacerations on his abdomen.[3] The "one that proved mortal" was under his ribs on his left side and "penetrated the chest about three inches – the greater part of the small intestines protruded immediately, which were also wounded."[4] And from the beginning, witnesses had claimed that John Crane was to blame.

[1] "November 19, 1772," Berkeley County Court Minutes, BCHS.
[2] "Shepherd's-Town July 11," *The Potowmack Guardian and Berkeley Advertiser* (Shepherdstown, VA), July 11, 1791. This account identifies David Campbell as the owner of the field; however, other materials from the case identify the owner as Thomas Campbell.
[3] William Greenway Russell, *What I Know About Winchester*, ed. Garland R. Quarles and Lewis N. Barton (Staunton, VA: McClure Publishing Co., 1953), 47, n. 59.
[4] "American Intelligence: Winchester, Virginia, July 9," *Western Star* (Stockbridge, MA), August 2, 1791.

It's not clear that Crane knew Vanhorn – at least, not before the fatal July 4 workday. Vanhorn was not an immediate neighbor, and in surviving historical records, he is a mere shadow. As one newspaper later reported, Vanhorn was a wagoner and, as tax records indicate, he lived in Winchester.[5] There is no definitive record of his age, or who his parents were; however, a "John Vanhorn & wife," maybe Abraham's parents, were summoned to court to testify in Crane's case, and lived in the town of Smithfield, just a few miles north of Crane's fields.[6] They were not landowners, at least according to records, but John Vanhorn did own three slaves aged over sixteen and ten horses – ample holdings.[7] (At the time of his death thirteen years later the senior Vanhorn would own lots in the town of Smithfield.[8]) There is also one more fact: in Winchester, Abraham Vanhorn had served on juries with men of vastly different circumstances.[9] This, along with his father's property holdings, probably indicates that the community generally considered him respectable, but it could also mean that judges had picked him from a pool of bystanders to fill out thin jury pools.[10]

Instead, Vanhorn's unremarkable life emerged most vividly in the many newspaper stories, printed all over the country, that accompanied his death. This was, in some ways, ironic – that his death brought attention, for the first time, to his life – but it was not surprising. After all, the lives of middling men like Vanhorn left little occasion for public attention except in remarkable circumstances, like murder. But after his death at the hands of the young and privileged John Crane, Abraham became news – the paragon of the virtuous,

---

[5] Frederic Morton, *The Story of Winchester in Virginia* (Strasburg, VA: Shenandoah Publishing House, 1925), 271.

[6] For instance, they had recently had a change in their household size, probably because Abraham had moved to Winchester, leaving only his brother Joseph at home. John Vanhorn was listed on Berkeley tax lists in 1789 as having two grown sons at home, but in 1791 only one son was still listed in the household, along with three slaves and ten horses. See Berkeley County Land Tax, East 1789, BCHS; Berkeley County Personal Property Tax Records, East 1791, BCHS. Russell's *What I Know About Winchester* lists Vanhorn as living in Winchester.

[7] Berkeley County Personal Property Tax Lists, East, 1791, BCHS. Conclusions about the relationship between John, Joseph, and Abraham Vanhorn are based on changing "tithables" in Berkeley property tax records, plus other information from the case. A William Vanhorn also appears in county records, and is mentioned in connection with the case in Russell's *What I Know About Winchester*, which states that a William Vanhorn filed the original complaint for Abraham's murder; unfortunately the case records referenced by Russell's editors seem to no longer exist.

[8] See will of John Vanhorn, decreeing that his lots in the town of Smithville be sold to pay expenses. Jefferson County Will Book 2, 142, dated April 26, 1814, probated May 23, 1814 and June 27, 1814 in Jefferson County Court, BCHS.

[9] November 1789, Frederick County Court Order Book 1789–1791, Reel 76, Library of Virginia (hereafter "Frederick County Court Order Book").

[10] St. George Tucker, *Blackstone's Commentaries with Notes of Reference to the Constitution and Laws of the Federal Government of the United States; and of the Commonwealth of Virginia*, vol. 4 (Philadelphia, PA: William Young Birch and Abraham Small, 1803), 64 (appendix).

industrious young man whose life had been prematurely and, as one report said, "dastardly" cut short.[11]

The earliest report of the fight originated at Winchester, but papers up the east coast reprinted its account. This report described a typical fight gone wrong.

Winchester, July 9

We learn from Berkeley County that on Monday last, a dispute arose between Abraham Vanhorne and John Crane, which terminated in an engagement – and the former is since dead of a wound he received during the conflict: – The following are the particulars of this unhappy affair, related by some of the persons who were present when it happened: –

The aggression originated with Crane, in a harvest field, as the deceased and some others, were going to dinner – that the same was renewed on their return from work a little before dark – that the deceased and Crane mutually agreed to box – that, a very short time after the commencement of the conflict, the deceased cried out – enough – and that his guts were out. There were several large wounds on the body of the deceased – but the one that proved mortal was received just below the ribs on the left side – it penetrated the chest about three inches – the greater part of the small intestines protruded immediately, which were also wounded.

Crane is committed to Martinsburg goal [sic]. The verdict of the jury of inquest is not yet come to hand. Vanhorn owned a team, and was held in high estimation by the merchants and others who had occasion for his services.[12]

This report stuck to the basics. Crane had provoked a fight in the early afternoon, which was renewed at nightfall; witnesses reported that they had agreed to fight, but that during the fight, Vanhorn had been stabbed, yelling that "his guts were out."[13]

Now the matter was in the hands of the inquest, which was its own type of legal proceeding. Typically, before the family moved or buried the victim, the county coroner summoned twenty-four freeholders, of whom twelve were chosen to view the body and determine the cause of death.[14] Vanhorn's inquest concluded on July 10, and Berkeley's own local paper, Shepherdstown's *Potowmac Guardian and Berkeley Advertiser*, reprinted the inquest's verdict, along with a new account of the fight.[15] This report added critical details about the fight to

[11] See "Shepherd's-Town July 11," *The Potowmack Guardian and Berkeley Advertiser* (Shepherdstown, VA), July 11, 1791.

[12] *ClayPoole's Daily Advertiser* (Philadelphia, PA), July 19, 1791.

[13] Ibid.

[14] Hugh F. Rankin, *Criminal Trial Proceedings in the General Court of Colonial Virginia* (Williamsburg, VA: Colonial Williamsburg, 1965), 68.

[15] "Shepherd's-Town July 11," *The Potowmack Guardian and Berkeley Advertiser* (Shepherdstown, VA), July 11, 1791. The county's old coroner's records seem to be lost (Berkeley's county clerk informed me that they were not available). But the first newspaper report, July 9, said that the

the public record. "The following melancholy transaction," as the paper called it, "took place on Tuesday last, a few miles from this town – Mr. Abraham Vanhorne and Mr. John Crane being in-company with a number of other persons in a harvest field ... some dispute arising between them, a recourse to blows was immediately had." But, according to the paper, Vanhorn had overpowered Crane: "the former proving too powerful for the latter, who, finding himself in a situation bordering on a defeat, drew from his pocket a knife, and in a most dastardly and barbarous manner thrust it into the body of Mr. Vanhorne, and wounded him in such a manner that he immediately fell!" Vanhorn had been taken to "Mr. Campbell's, where he lay in the most excruciating pain until Thursday morning, when he expired."[16] The coroner's inquest had now concluded. "[T]heir verdict," the paper relayed, was "willful murder."[17] The inquest's verdict meant that Crane would now have to face the justices of the Berkeley County Court, who would hold a hearing to decide if he should be tried for murder.[18]

But the reports omitted a critical fact – John Crane's identity. Crane was no ordinary defendant. His father, James Crane, "gentleman," had served as Berkeley County's deputy sheriff and as a founding trustee of Charles Town, the town that President Washington's brother Charles had established on his Berkeley County land.[19] The Cranes and the Washingtons had known each other from Spotsylvania County, where John Crane's grandfather had served as a justice of the peace with Charles Washington. Grandfather Crane had also served as Spotsylvania's high sheriff and colonel of the militia – positions of respect that, in the colonial era, were doled out according to rank, indicating the highest social standing.[20] Young John's uncle served as a justice of the

---

inquest was not completed, and the July 11 Berkeley report stated that the inquest had concluded, so it is reasonable to assume that it concluded on July 10.

[16] "Shepherd's-Town July 11," *The Potowmack Guardian and Berkeley Advertiser* (Shepherdstown, VA), July 11, 1791.

[17] Ibid.

[18] Although the county's old coroners' records are not available, Merchant would have been required to post bond at the inquest to ensure his appearance at the county court. See, e.g., Rankin, *Criminal Trial Proceedings*, 72 for the colonial practice of the recent past. The notes to the late nineteenth-century recollections of a local citizen, William Greenway Russell, indicate that some depositions related to the case were once in the custody of the Winchester Historical Society. See Russell, *What I Know About Winchester*. An exhaustive search by the Society's successor, the Handley Regional Library, could not locate the records, nor were they located in any potentially relevant collections at the Library of Virginia.

[19] For James Crane's service as deputy sheriff, see *Journal of the House of Delegates of the Commonwealth of Virginia* (Richmond, VA: Thomas W. White, 1828), 83. James Crane is mentioned as deputy sheriff to Henry Whiting in Berkeley County Court Minute Book, October 16, 1785, BCHS. For appointment of James Crane, "gentleman" as Charles Town trustee, see William Waller Hening, *The Statutes at Large ...*, vol. 12 (Richmond, VA: George Cochran, 1823), 371, and Millard Kessler Bushong, *A History of Jefferson County, West Virginia, 1719–1940* (Westminster, MD: Heritage Books, 1941), 17.

[20] For John Scanland Crane's service as a justice, see Virginia State Library, *Justices of the Peace of Colonial Virginia 1757–1775* (Richmond, VA: State of Virginia, 1922), 91. For his appointment

peace in Spotsylvania still, although he also owned land in Berkeley.[21] John's mother's people were also well connected: Lucy Minor Crane was the daughter of a wealthy Spotsylvania County man who owned at least two large plantations, and her relatives had held high posts in revolutionary Virginia's new government.[22]

Good as this heritage was, John had married even better. Catherine Whiting, his wife of five years, was the daughter of his uncle's Berkeley neighbor, Mathew Whiting; her kinsmen were not only among the wealthiest men in the area, they had served for generations in the House of Burgesses and on Virginia's elite governing Council.[23] Her mother was a Robinson, one of the colony's most distinguished families – one relative had been the bishop of London; another had been a founding trustee of the College of William and Mary and the Secretary for Foreign Plantations; and another served as the acting governor in the mid-eighteenth century.[24] A cousin, John Robinson had been the most powerful native

as high sheriff, see "November 19, 1772," Spotsylvania County Order Book, 1768–1774, Reel 45, Library of Virginia.

[21] Included in Judge St. George Tucker's 1793 General Court Docket Book is an August 17, 1790 summons for the General Court judges to sit as the Court of Appeals in the case of *Armistead v. Winslow*, because a substantial number of the Court of Appeals judges were interested in the case and had to recuse themselves. The summons lists as a defendant the senior John Crane and two others, "surviving justices of Spotsylvania County." See 1793 General Court Docket book, Tucker-Coleman Papers.

[22] Her father was Thomas Minor. The Minors were connected by marriage to, among others, Benjamin Waller, one of the most respected lawyers of colonial Virginia. Among other appointments, Benjamin Waller served as a judge in Virginia's newly created Court of Admiralty. For general information, see Colonial Williamsburg's biography, "Benjamin Waller," *Colonial Williamsburg*, accessed December 10, 2016, www.history.org/almanack/people/bios/biowallr. cfm. For Crane/Minor connection to the Wallers, see will of Thomas Minor, December 19, 1776, Spotsylvania County will Book E, Reel 28, Library of Virginia. Owen Minor's wife, Sarah Waller, is traditionally said to be the daughter of William Waller and Ann Standard; William Waller was the son of John Waller, clerk of Spotsylvania County and father of Benjamin Waller. See will of William Waller, died August 2, 1753, probated October 1, 1754, Spotsylvania County will Book B, Reel 26, Library of Virginia.

[23] According to Catherine's Bible, they were married on May 24, 1786. Dakota Best Brown, *Data on Some Virginia Families* (Berryville, VA: Virginia Book Company, 1979), 251. Slaves of Mathew Whiting were prosecuted for allegedly stealing Crane's hogs. See entry for January 19, 1773, Berkeley County Court Minute Book, BCHS. Mathew Whiting's exact relationship to the rest of the Whiting clan has long vexed local historians and genealogists, but there is a general consensus that he was related to the other Whitings in Berkeley and in other parts of Virginia – perhaps a brother or a cousin. All evidence points to Catherine being Mathew's daughter. For instance, what seems to have been her Bible, passed down in the Slaughter family after her second marriage to Smith Slaughter, records the death dates of Mathew Whiting and his son, suggesting that they were her father and brother, as well as information on both John Crane (birth and death dates) and the couple's infant daughter. See Brown, *Data on Some Virginia Families*, 262–264.

[24] See will of Major John Robinson, excerpted in "Some Virginia Colonial Records," *Virginia Magazine of History and Biography* 10, no. 4 (1903): 371–382, reprinted in, *inter alia*, Brown, *Data on Some Virginia Families*, 242. See also Mary Pollard Clarke, "Christopher Robinson, One of the First Trustees of William and Mary College: His Home, 'Hewick on the Rappahannock,'"

Virginian of the colonial era, serving as Treasurer and Speaker of the House until his death in 1766.[25] Some of Catherine's wealthy Robinson cousins had been prominent Loyalists during the late war.[26]

John and Catherine had married in May 1786; since then, they had had only one child, a daughter they named Lucy Whiting Crane – Lucy after John's mother, and Whiting to preserve their association with Catherine's family name. But, as Catherine carefully recorded in her Bible, Lucy had died at birth in April 1787.[27] In the past four years, there had been no more children. So perhaps, in July 1791, as Crane brought in his harvest on his 200-acre farm, life already was not turning out quite the way he (and Catherine) had expected it to.

John's background was one thing, but the stories that were emerging about his fight with Vanhorn were anything but gentlemanly. After the inquest, a new newspaper report offered a shocking account, perhaps with information gleaned from the inquest itself. Printed several times in various papers throughout the country, this report traced the fight to a conflict: one that centered on Vanhorn's horses.

The newspapers attributed the information to a "gentleman of veracity" and explained that Vanhorn worked as a wagon-driver; on July 4, he had just returned with his horses from a long journey:

Frederick-Town (Virg.), July 12

The following tragical circumstance (communicated to the Printer by a gentleman of veracity) took place Tuesday last, at Charleston, in Virginia, 28 miles from this town: — A Mr. Abraham Van Horne, an inhabitant of that neighborhood, who kept and drove a team for several years past, had just returned from a journey – his horses being fatigued, they were turned loose, in order to give them an opportunity to recreate themselves.

Two horses, however, "broke into a wheat field belonging to Mr. John Crane, and, without doubt, did some damage to the proprietor."[28]

The papers alleged that Crane had found the horses in his fields, and viciously attacked them. "Mr. Crane," the story reported, "having received intelligence

---

William and Mary Quarterly, 2nd Series, 1, no. 2 (1921), 134–136. On the prestige of the Robinsons, see also Alan Taylor, *The Internal Enemy: Slavery and War in Virginia 1772–1832* (New York, NY: W. W. Norton, 2013), 29.

[25] Brown, *Data on Some Virginia Families*, 251.

[26] Maya Jasanoff, *Liberty's Exiles: American Loyalists in the Revolutionary World* (New York, NY: Knopf, 2011), 36; Richard Channing Moore Page, *Genealogy of the Page Family in Virginia* (New York, NY: Jenkins and Thomas, 1883), 148. For the Berkeley Whitings and the Revolution, see "Francis Whiting pension application for service as a Lieutenant, First Regiment Light Dragoons," Library of Virginia, accessed December 10, 2016, http://image.lva.virginia.gov/cgi-bin/GetRev.pl?dir=0613/S0008&card=75.

[27] Brown, *Data on Some Virginia Families*, 252, 264.

[28] "Frederick-Town, July 12," *ClayPoole's Daily Advertiser* (Philadelphia, PA), July 27, 1791. Other papers carried the same report.

that the horses were in his field, immediately repaired thither – cut out the horses' eyes – tied a bunch of straw to each of their tails, set it on fire and drove them away." This was bad enough, but there was more. "Had the scene ended here," the papers reported, "happy would it have been for Mr. Crane! whose ungovernable disposition, heated by passion and resentment, knew no bounds, but pressed on, with eagle swiftness, the heart it surrounded to obtain a further satisfaction of the inoffensive owner of the beasts."

Predictably, the papers reported, Vanhorn had confronted Crane about his horses. "Mr. Vanhorne, on hearing of the fate of his horses, went to Crane and remonstrated with him on the impropriety of treating his property in the manner above mentioned – high words arose, and the consequence was, that Mr. Vanhorne received a wound in the lower part of his belly given by his adversary with a knife, which let out his bowels and he died immediately." The papers concluded with a sad summary: "Thus perished, in the bloom of life a young and useful member of society; particularly distinguished among his neighbors as a peaceable, inoffensive man, and lamented by all with whom he was acquainted."[29]

The report was damning. But was it true? After all, there were a few clear inaccuracies. First, Vanhorn had not died immediately, but had lingered for days. Second, all other accounts emphasized an extended back-and-forth, as well as an agreement to fight, before Crane had stabbed Vanhorn. Regardless, this report offered a new picture of Crane. No longer merely the story of a fight gone wrong, it was now about – as the papers put it – Crane's "ungovernable disposition."

Crane had a history of violent behavior. A few years earlier, in 1788, he had been brought before the Berkeley County Court for "breaking the peace"; the justices had ordered him to post a £100 bond, with two sureties of £50 apiece, to assure that he would keep the peace for at least a year.[30] And a recent fight with Ephraim Worthington – perhaps an in-law, because his wife's sister had married a Worthington – would soon result in an assault suit filed in the Winchester District Court.[31]

---

[29] Ibid.

[30] The record identifies only "John Crane," not whether it was the elder or younger, but given the latter's subsequent history and the information that emerged about him, it is likely that it was him. "December 17, 1788," Berkeley County Minute Book, BCHS.

[31] Ephraim Worthington v. John Crane, September 4, 1792, Superior Court Order Book, Reel 93, Frederick County Records, Winchester District Court Order Book, 1789–1793, Library of Virginia (hereafter Winchester District Court Order Book) (suit dismissed because of defendant's death). Ann Whiting, Catherine Crane's sister, married Robert Worthington; James Crane was a surety on the guardianship for Worthington's younger brother Thomas, who would one day be the governor of Ohio. When James Crane was appointed guardian for young Matthew Whiting, Edward Tiffin was appointed guardian for his brother, John Whiting; Tiffin, a physician, was Robert and Thomas Worthington's brother-in-law (married to their sister, Mary). He would also later be involved in John Crane's case, as a pardon petitioner, and relocated to Ohio, along with the Worthingtons later in the 1790s. For more on Ann Whiting and Robert Worthington's relationship, see *The History of Menard and Mason Counties, Illinois* ... (Chicago, IL: O. L. Baskin

But Crane was not the only Virginian with a penchant for fighting. In the late eighteenth century, Virginia was becoming infamous for its "no holts [sic] barred" fights, sometimes called "gouging." These were no ordinary fights – instead, men kicked, bit, and tore at each other's eyeballs, ears, and testicles.[32]

As English traveler Isaac Weld recalled of Virginia in the 1790s: "Whenever these people come to blows, they fight just like wild beasts, biting, kicking, and endeavoring to tear each other's eyes out with their nails. It is by no means uncommon to meet those who have lost an eye in combat, and there are men who pride themselves on the dexterity with which they can scoop one out."[33] Weld elaborated on how a gouging took place:

To perform the horrid operation, the combatant twists his forefingers in the side locks of his adversary's hair, and then applies his thumbs to the bottom of the eye, to force it out of the socket. If ever there is a battle, in which neither of those engaged loses an eye, their faces are however generally cut in a shocking manner. But what is worse than all, these wretches in their combat endeavor to their utmost to tear out each other's testicles.

These brutal fights were common. "Four or five instances," Weld reported, "came to my own observation, as I passed through Maryland and Virginia, of men being confined in their beds from the injuries which they had received of this nature in a fight."[34] Nor was this just a Virginian pastime: "in the Carolinas and Georgia," Weld explained, "I have been credibly assured, that the people are still more depraved in this respect than in Virginia."[35]

Even a minor insult could spark a brutal fight. According to Philip Vickers Fithian, a tutor for one of the branches of Virginia's wealthy Carter family, almost anything could provoke a vicious brawl. As Fithian scathingly recorded in his journal, perhaps one man had "mislaid the other's hat, or knocked a peach out of his Hand, or offered him a dram without wiping the mouth of the Bottle." All these, "and then thousand more quite as trifling and ridiculous are thought and accepted as just Causes of immediate Quarrels, in which every diabolical Stratagem for Mastery is allowed and practiced."[36]

& Co., Historical Publishers 1879), 705. See an image of the Robert Worthington House at "Robert Worthington House," *Wikipedia*, http://en.wikipedia.org/wiki/Robert_Worthington_House, accessed May 28, 2015. See also Surety for William Worthington as guardian of Thomas Worthington, orphan of Robert Worthington, along with Edward Tiffin, September 16, 1788, Berkeley County Orphan's Bond Book 1, 1776–1796, 76, BCHS.

[32] Translator's note, undated, in François-Jean, marquis de Chastellux, *Travels in North America in the Years 1780–81–82* (New York, NY: n.p., 1828), 293, n. Although the translator's name does not appear in the volume, the translation has been attributed by Hathi Trust to George Grieve or J. Kent Sabin.

[33] Isaac Weld, *Travels through the States of North America* (London: Printed for John Stockdale, 1799), 192.

[34] Ibid., 192–193.

[35] Ibid., 193.

[36] Phillip Vickers Fithian to John Peck, August 12, 1774, in Phillip Vickers Fithian, *Journals and Letters*, ed. Hunter Dickinson Farish (Williamsburg, VA: Colonial Williamsburg, 1943),

Crane's own Berkeley County was right in the middle of this mayhem, which stretched down to North Carolina and Georgia, north to Wheeling and west to Kentucky.[37] Recounting his experience in Leesburg, Virginia, less than thirty miles from where the fight between Crane and Vanhorn took place, one traveler recalled:

During a day's residence at Leesburg ... [w]hile we were seated round the spring, at the edge of a delightful wood, four or five countrymen arrived, headed by a veteran Cyclops, the terror of the neighborhood, ready on every occasion to risk his remaining eye. We soon found ourselves under the necessity of relinquishing our posts, and making our escape from these fellows, who evidently sought to provoke a quarrel.

His "friends," he learned at the end of the day, "thought they had exhibited great moderation in not exposing me, at the spring, to the effects of 'biting and gouging.' "[38]

Gouging was brutal, but it had rules. According to historian Elliott Gorn, before a fight, the men agreed to either fight "fair," according to the rules of English boxing, or to fight "rough and tumble." A "rough and tumble" fight was a gouging match where all techniques were permitted except one: weapons. Beyond that, the men could do what they wanted to each other "without interference, until one gave up or was incapacitated."[39] This ban on weapons explains why newspapers had described Crane's use of a knife so scathingly. They papers used similar language to report on a fight from nearby Frederick County: there, John Farrel and Thomas Regan had exchanged some "warm words" and "proceeded to blows, when the latter drew a knife out of his pocket, and cut his antagonist across the belly, in a manner too shocking to relate." But, unlike Vanhorn, here "a surgeon was sent for, who sewed up the wound, and we understand that Farrel is in a fair way of recovery." Nonetheless, Regan was "committed to prison, in this town, on said offence."[40] Crane – and Vanhorn – had not been so lucky.

The ban on weapons in Virginia's "rough and tumble" fights meant that although fighting was common, deaths from it were rare. Indeed, homicide in general was rare in Virginia, and this made Crane's case exceptional. As historian and sociologist Randolph Roth has concluded, America was one of the "least homicidal societies in the Western world in the mid-eighteenth and again in the early nineteenth centuries."[41] The homicide rate had begun dropping at the end of the seventeenth century, and had remained low – "by historical and

240–241. Quoted in Elliott T. Gorn, " 'Gouge, Bite, Pull Hair and Scratch': The Social Significance of Fighting in the Southern Backcountry," *American Historical Review* 90, no. 1 (1985): 18–43, 19.

[37] See Gorn, " 'Gouge, Bite, Pull Hair and Scratch'," 21.

[38] See footnote in Chastellux, *Travels in North America*, 293.

[39] Ibid., 20.

[40] "Winchester, July 28," *New York Packet* (New York, NY), August 12, 1790.

[41] Randolph Roth, *American Homicide* (Cambridge, MA: Harvard University Press, 2009), 13–14.

modern standards" – until the turmoil of the 1760s and 1770s.[42] In Virginia specifically, Roth notes that during the eighteenth century, Virginians increasingly used the courts to settle disputes, instead of interpersonal violence.[43] The American Revolution brought a burst of violence in other areas of the country, particularly Philadelphia and the northeast, but in the Shenandoah Valley the rate of lethal violence remained low.[44]

Virginia's surviving coroners' records for the period paint a similar picture.[45] As Roth notes, "Virginia courts held examinations or inquests into nearly every suspicious death (including lynchings), and preserved a record of nearly every homicide proceeding."[46] They found few homicides, despite investigating broadly. Some inquests involved violence against slaves by whites.[47] Others were pretty clearly not homicides at all – deaths

---

[42] Ibid., 61.

[43] Ibid., 88. This is similar to William Nelson's portrayal of both colonies as dominated by ideas of the rule of law in this same time period. See William E. Nelson, *The Common Law in Colonial America*, vol. 1: *The Chesapeake and New England, 1607–1660* (New York, NY: Oxford University Press, 2008).

[44] Roth attributes this to elites' support for the war, and thus less social conflict. Roth, *American Homicide*, 173.

[45] The inquests are available at the Library of Virginia, by county. I am grateful to my research assistants Joseph Stuart (for gathering the inquests and cataloging them for me) and Amelia Nemitz (for summarizing them).

[46] Roth, *American Homicide*, 483.

[47] For instance, the Amelia coroner investigated the death of Marklin, a slave of John Fowlkis, who was shot by "Simon Walton jun. ... tho agreeable to evidence did it not Desirably." Amelia County: Marklin, August 16, 1786, in Amelia County (VA) Coroners' Inquisitions, 1779–1830, Local Government Records Collections, Amelia County Court Records, Library of Virginia (hereafter Amelia County Coroners' Inquisitions). In 1782, the Amelia coroner had also investigated the death of Polydore, a "negro man belonging to the estate of Peter R. Bland," whose "death was occasioned by Abram Lockett and John Claybrooks beating him with a large stick and other ill usage." See Polydore, December 8, 1782, in Amelia County Coroners' Inquisitions. In Henry County, the coroner investigated the death of the slave Dick in 1791, who had been killed by Nathan Anderson, hit with a stick on the head; in 1786, Henry County's coroner also investigated the death of a slave named Major, who, the inquest determined, had been killed when a gun held by James Hubbard had, they put it cryptically, "exploded." See Dick, April 10, 1791, and Major, March 23, 1786, in Henry County (VA) Coroners' Inquisitions, 1779–1946, Local Government Records Collection, Henry County Court Records, Library of Virginia (hereafter Henry County Coroners' Inquisitions). In Louisa County, the coroner investigated in 1786 when the slave Jeny was whipped to death by an overseer, William Tuggle; a deposition affirmed that although Tuggle's family was "of good and honest character," Tuggle was called a "barbarous man to negroes." See Jeny, February 10, 1786, in Louisa County (VA) Coroners' Inquisitions, 1786–1904, Local Government Records Collection, Louisa County Court Records, Library of Virginia (hereafter Louisa County Coroners' Records). In Mecklenburg County, the coroner investigated in 1788 when the slave Emanuel was shot by his owner's "business manager" as he tried to run away – the inquest determined that the wrong type of "shot" had been loaded into the gun, so that the manager had killed when he thought he would only wound. See Emanuel, July 12, 1788, in Mecklenburg County (VA) Coroners' Inquisitions, 1785–1879,

that happened when the victim was seemingly alone, as when he or she was hit by a falling tree, fell off a horse, was run over by a wagon, or drowned.[48] In other cases, inquests determined that deaths were from natural causes, usually referred to as a "visitation from God."[49] Eight were

Local Government Record Collection, Mecklenburg County Court Records, Library of Virginia (hereafter Mecklenburg County Coroners' Inquisitions). And in 1785, the Charlotte County coroner investigated the death of a slave named Bob, who died of "a Blow given him about half an inch above his right eye & one other Blow near his right ear and many stripes on his body." See Bob, November 5, 1785, in Charlotte County (VA) Coroners' Inquisitions, 1785–1864, Local Government Records Collection, Charlotte County Court Records, Library of Virginia (hereafter Charlotte County Coroners' Inquisitions).

[48] *Amelia*: Ben (slave boy) "drowned by accident," July 7, 1787; Charles Doyal, "killed by a large limb that fell on him," December 7, 1786, in Amelia County Coroners' Inquisitions. *Botetourt*: George Clear, drowned by accident, March 5, 1790; John McCammon, accidental – flung by a horse against a tree, April 11, 1788, in Botetourt County (VA) Coroners' Inquisitions, 1785–1854, Local Government Records Collection, Botetourt County Court Records, Library of Virginia (hereafter Botetourt County Coroners' Inquisitions). *Frederick*: James Erwin, January 24, 1779 and David Ferguson, November 22, 1789, run over by his wagon; Jacob Hickman, June 4, 1789 and Philip Dick, June 7, 1789, killed by falling tree; Greenberry D. Craig, "came to his death in an accidental manner," November 22, 1788, in Frederick County (VA) Coroners' Inquisitions, 1779–1927, Local Government Records Collection, Frederick County Court Records, Library of Virginia (hereafter Frederick County Coroners' Inquisitions); *Goochland*: Unknown, Negro man, unknown to all, supposed accidental drowning, May 1789 in Goochland County (VA) Coroners' Inquisitions, 1787–1947, Local Government Records Collection, Goochland County Court Records, Library of Virginia (hereafter Goochland County Coroners' Inquisitions); *Henry*: John Jonas, accidentally fell from a house while building it, February 22, 1787; Unknown, killed by falling tree, February 15, 1788, in Henry County Coroners' Inquisitions. *Lunenburg*: Dunkin Smith, horse dragging him, June 28, 1761; Robert Waymark, tree fell on him, May 6, 1761; Thomas Adkins, accidentally drowned in river, October 30, 1752, in Lunenburg County (VA) Coroners' Inquisitions, 1752– 1924, Local Government Records Collection, Lunenburg County Court Records, Library of Virginia (hereafter Lunenburg County Coroners' Inquisitions). *Norfolk*: Kendall, slave man, "accident," May 2, 1774; Michael Simmons, accidentally drowned, August 10, 1774; Unknown, 1774: negro, accidentally drowned, February 23, 1774; William Bassett, accidentally drowned, September 28, 1774, in Norfolk County (VA) Coroners' Inquisitions, 1766–1909, Local Government Records Collection, Norfolk County Court Records, Library of Virginia (hereafter Norfolk County Coroners' Inquisitions). *Northampton*: Thomas Savage, drowned, June 1729, in Northampton County (VA) Coroners' Inquisitions, 1728–1868, Local Government Records Collection, Northampton County Court Records, Library of Virginia (hereafter Northampton County Coroners' Inquisitions). *Powhatan*: Daniel, fell from horse and was dragged for half a mile due to the "rope halter being tied around his arm," December 28, 1777; Golbert, slave, tree fell on him, October 21, 1790, in Powhatan County (VA) Coroners' Inquisitions, 1777–1904, Local Government Records Collection, Powhatan Court Records, Library of Virginia (hereafter Powhatan County Coroners' Inquisitions).

[49] *Amelia*: Davey (slave) dead in woods, "no marks of violence appearing on his body" and "died by the visitation of God, in a natural way," April 27, 1784; David Bailey, dead at house of Wm. Watson, "no marks of violence appearing upon his body," and "died by the visitation of God and in a natural way," September 30, 1784; Jacob (slave), "no marks of violence upon his body, and died of the visitation of God in a natural way" in "Mr. Bolling's quarter" (Bolling's slave), May 25, 1782; John Gunney, found dead no marks of violence, died by the "visitation

suicides.[50] And others were miscellaneous, such as the two men who died from overdrinking.[51] There were some regional variations – for instance, some areas, like Norfolk, tended to have more drownings.[52] But together, Virginia's records show both a breadth of investigations and a low number of violent deaths. For all the "rough and tumble" fighting in Virginia, it did not tend to result in death.

While coroner's inquests could have massaged the facts, making deaths appear innocent that were not, this does not seem to be the case, either. There are, of course, a few cases where the inquest seems to have fudged some facts. For instance, in the case of an enslaved man named Bob, the Charlotte coroner's jury claimed that, although his owner and the plantation he was on were known, they could not determine who had given him the "Blow ... about half an inch above his right eye & one other Blow near his right ear and many stripes on his body" – difficult to believe.[53] Similarly, a Powhatan County inquest might have been massaging the truth when it found that the slave Daniel had merely fallen from his horse before he was dragged for a half mile due to the "rope halter being tied around his arm."[54] But, given both the wide swath cut by coroner's investigations and the contents of those investigations, it seems unlikely that inquests systemically buried the real homicide rate, particularly from fights arising between white men.

of God," January 8, 1786 in Amelia County Coroners' Inquisitions. *Chesterfield*: Henry Bailey, no marks of violence, "died by visitation of God," February 1790; William Benstrod, "natural death," March 1784, in Chesterfield County (VA) Coroners' Inquisitions, 1783–1914, Local Government Records Collection, Chesterfield County Court Records, Library of Virginia (hereafter Chesterfield County Court Records). *Frederick*: George Ennis (free negro), natural – found dead with "no marks of violence appearing on his body," November 14, 1780 in Frederick County Coroners' Inquisitions; *Henry*: Mordecai Stewart, found dead on the road with no marks of violence, May 28, 1785, in Henry County Coroners' Inquisitions. *Louisa*: infant child of Jeanny Biby, natural causes, October 1790. Joe, Slave, found dead on road, no marks of violence, November 3, 1788, in Louisa County Coroners' Inquisitions. *Norfolk*: Unknown, died naturally in county jail, September 2, 1774, in Norfolk County Coroners' Inquisitions.

50 *Amelia*: Fellow (negro), "he hung himself," October 27, 1779, in Amelia County Coroners' Inquisitions. *Botetourt*: Phillip Love, hanged himself, September 26, 1789, in Botetourt County Coroners' Inquisitions; *Chesterfield*: Joseph Watkins, "shot himself with a gun in the head" because of an "unsound mind," October 1783; Lewis Kuro, drowned himself in James River – no "unsound mind," December 6, 1789; Wilson, hanged himself, October 7, 1786, in Chesterfield County Coroners' Inquisitions. *Frederick*: James Knight, August 5, 1779, suicide "with a small cord," and Martha Sherrard, July 8, 1781, "in a fit of lunacy" "by means of a cord," in Frederick County Coroners' Inquisitions; *Powhatan*: John Eggleston, suicide – cut his throat with a penknife, July 27, 1784, in Powhatan County Coroners' Inquisitions.

51 *Chesterfield*: John Cumpton, "died Drunk," April 1786, in Chesterfield County Coroners' Inquisitions; *Frederick*: James McAnnulty, October 20, 1790, in Frederick County Coroners' Inquisitions.

52 Three cases in the nine surviving pre-1791 inquests. See Norfolk County Coroners' Inquisitions.

53 See Bob, November 5, 1785, in Charlotte County Coroners' Inquisitions.

54 See Daniel, December 28, 1777, in Powhatan County Coroners' Inquisitions.

But if there was so much fighting – eye-gouging, testicle-pulling, ear-biting brawls – why did more men not die? There are two potential reasons. First, the ban on weapons may have indeed served to make fights vicious, but not deadly – keeping the homicide rate down and reflecting prevailing attitudes against lethal violence. Second, Gorn suggests that by the end of the eighteenth century, fewer men were fighting – that Virginia's gentlemen in general had become less likely to engage in brawling, cutting down on the overall incidence. These men moved away from rough displays of strength, instead imitating the English aristocracy with English "boxing" and dueling.[55]

The Southern homicide rate would start to rise later, but that would be in the nineteenth century. By the 1830s, travelers would remark on the laxity with which the legal system treated homicide.[56] As a result, it is easy to attribute this same behavior, a willingness to condone homicide and refusal to convict, to Southerners across time. But this was certainly not the reality that young John Crane encountered in 1791. And, given the stories circulating in American newspapers, Crane had reason to be worried.

But Crane also had a story of his own. As he waited in jail in 1791, one final tale made the rounds. This tale would not enter the official record until much later, but it hints at another view of what had happened at the line between Crane's and Campbell's fields – a view that was favorable to Crane. Hugh McDonald had been working for Crane on July 4, and he gave a very different account of the fight. He claimed that, on that fatal July 4, Crane had been on the defensive – that his neighbor John Dawkins, and Campbell's reaper Isaac Merchant, two local men who had known each other all their lives, had provoked the fight.[57]

According to McDonald, first "Mr. Crane and his hands, together with myself, went to dinner; after dinner we returned to work." After dinner, the trouble began:

A negro man of Mr. Cranes informed John Dawkins & the rest of us, that Mr. Campbell's hands had sent us a challenge to fight them; upon which Dawkins highly resented & said he would go and see Campbell's hands, for he was not afraid of any one man that was then in Campbell's field. After some little time, Mr. Crane came from his house to his field; John Dawkins then said to Mr. Crane that Campbell's hands had sent him & his hands a challenge. Mr. Crane made answer & said he did not know what harm he

[55] Gorn, "'Gouge, Bite, Pull Hair and Scratch'," 22.

[56] Alexis de Tocqueville, *Journey to America*, trans. George Lawrence, ed. J. P. Mayer (New Haven, CT: Yale University Press, 1960), 103; Edward L. Ayers, *Vengeance and Justice: Crime and Punishment in the Nineteenth Century American South* (New York, NY: Oxford University Press, 1984), 17.

[57] Dawkins's father had posted security for Isaac's own father's will when he died in 1772. See entry "June 16, 1772," Berkeley County Minute Book, BCHS, giving £500 security with David Lewis and Priscilla Merchant on the will of William Merchant.

had done to offend any of Mr. Campbell's hands, & said he would go and know the truth of it; which we all then went too [sic] Campbell's field to ask them what offence we had given them? They answered, none.[58]

This sounded like the fights so famous in Virginia, particularly in the Valley – a gang of men itching for a fight, and looking to provoke one for no good reason.[59]

Campbell's men had issued a challenge, but McDonald reported that after Crane spoke with Campbell's men, all seemed to be well. "Campbell then invited Crane & his harvest hands to take a drink of grog with him; which was done, and then Crane & his hands returned to Crane's field." Crane went back to his house. McDonald continued:

Mr. Crane was lying on his bed, when the noise of Campbell's hands approaching Crane's house, induced Crane to order them off his premises, & [he] threatened to shoot Vanhorn; & Merchant then assailed Crane, and in the fight Vanhorne [sic] was stabbed.[60]

This version painted Crane as a peaceful landowner, and accused the rough workers – the run-of-the-mill farmers and laborers – of starting the quarrel. McDonald claimed that Campbell's reapers had said that Crane had given them no "offense" – just like the men who had tried to provoke a fight with the English traveler at the spring in Leesburg, solely for the sake of fighting.[61] Most importantly, McDonald suggested that the brawl had been so chaotic that it was not clear *who* had stabbed Vanhorn.

But McDonald's story stood alone. It told a drastically different tale from the other accounts circulating the county and appearing in the papers. This prompted the question: what had *really* happened at the line between Crane's and Campbell's fields? It would be up to the courts to find out.

---

[58] "Deposition of Hugh McDonald, October 1, 1791," *Calendar of Virginia State Papers and Other Manuscripts*, vol. 5: *From July 2, 1789 to August 10, 1792*, ed. William P. Palmer and Sherwin McRae (Richmond, VA: Virginia State Library, 1885), 371–372

[59] Footnote in Chastellux, *Travels in North America*, 293.

[60] "Deposition of Hugh McDonald, October 1, 1791."

[61] Footnote in Chastellux, *Travels in North America*, 293.

2

The Making of a Republican Judge

As Crane languished in the Berkeley County jail, across the state Judge St. George Tucker was in Williamsburg, working long hours in the chilly study of his stately Market Square home. Although it was July, the weather was unseasonably cool – cool enough, according to one Virginian, to "render fires comfortable."[1]

The summer of 1791 had been a hard one for Tucker. Only a few days short of his thirty-ninth birthday, the judge – lanky, dark-haired, and handsome, a bit dashing even – normally counted himself in good health. But he suffered periodic bouts of a mysterious sickness that would leave him virtually deaf for periods of time and from other common ailments, and the summer of 1791 was no exception.[2] And, on top of ill health, he was very busy.

First there were his law students. Tucker had been appointed the College of William and Mary's "Professor of Law and Police" the previous year, taking over from his own mentor, George Wythe, who now served on the Court of Chancery and lived in Richmond. Because Tucker served as a judge himself – on Virginia's General Court, its highest court for cases "at law" (instead of in equity, which Wythe's chancery court heard) – he had to fit in his classes between court terms. The General Court sat in Richmond in November and June, but its judges also rode circuit around the Commonwealth in the fall

---

[1] Letter from Thomas Mann Randolph Jr. to Thomas Jefferson, July 7, 1791, in *The Papers of Thomas Jefferson*, vol. 20: *1 April–4 August 1791*, ed. Julian P. Boyd (Princeton, NJ: Princeton University Press, 1982), 607.

[2] Letter from St. George Tucker to John Randolph, August 18, 1791, Papers of John Randolph of Roanoke, Accession 3400, Special Collections, University of Virginia Library, Charlottesville, VA (hereafter UVA Special Collections); Charles F. Hobson, ed., *St. George Tucker's Law Reports and Selected Papers, 1782–1825*, vol. 1 (Chapel Hill, NC: University of North Carolina Press, 2013), 35–36.

and spring. This meant that Judge Tucker spent much of his year on the road. So in 1791, Tucker taught his courses in two terms: one in the summer, during the judicial recess, and the other during his winter vacation between circuits.[3] Pressed for time, he had prepared his lectures by jotting down annotations to a recent London edition of Blackstone's *Commentaries on the Laws of England*; despite his hurried initial preparation, one student later commented that Tucker was "more luminous on the subject of law than any man I ever saw."[4] However, another bemoaned Tucker's wide-ranging curriculum, complaining that "Bacon, Selden, Rolle, Plowden, Coke, & other fathers of nonsense & pedantry" were "trash" and of little practical use. The student complained that, rather than learning such "ancient law lore" from Tucker, he would have learned more "in an attorney's office."[5]

But as Tucker worked in his study in the twilight of July 4, 1791, he had more than teaching on his mind. In March, the judge had eagerly accepted an appointment to a committee created to revise Virginia's laws, something that successive committees of Virginia legislators, lawyers, and judges had been attempting do since 1776, with only partial success. The Virginia General Assembly had tasked them with the monumental effort of identifying what laws were in force and then with writing single statutes which would compile all the previous laws on a particular subject. They also needed to determine which English statutes were in force and suited to Virginia, which Virginia laws should be continued, which should be discarded, and "prepare marginal notes, and a full index to all the laws of this Commonwealth."[6] Tucker had enthusiastically accepted the post (although many others had tried to dodge the heavy responsibility) and in July 1791 he would spend three weeks meeting with the rest of the revisors in Williamsburg.[7]

On top of these responsibilities, Judge Tucker also had to prepare for a long, arduous journey west. He would depart in August for his assigned judicial circuit, a journey of almost 600 miles which included the far-flung district courts in Winchester and Monongalia.[8] The burdensome responsibilities of

---

[3] Hobson, "Biographical Overview," ibid., 29.

[4] Letter from William T. Berry to his brother, January 30, 1804, quoted in Charles T. Cullen, *St. George Tucker and Law in Virginia, 1772–1804* (New York, NY: Garland Publishing, 1987), 132.

[5] Letter from Garritt Minor to Joseph C. Cabell, 20 May 1801, Cabell Family Papers, UVA Special Collections; Hobson, "Biographical Overview," 1:10; Cullen, *St. George Tucker and Law in Virginia*, 134.

[6] See Charles T. Cullen, "Completing the Revisal of the Laws in Post-Revolutionary Virginia," *Virginia Magazine of History and Biography* 82, no. 1 (1974): 84–99.

[7] See letter from St. George Tucker to Governor Beverley Randolph, March 16, 1791, Dreer Collection of American Poets, Historical Society of Pennsylvania, Philadelphia, PA, and Cullen, "Completing the Revisal of the Laws," 91.

[8] See Cullen, *St. George Tucker and Law in Virginia*, Appendix C, for Tucker's District Court assignments, as well as Hobson, *St. George Tucker's Law Reports*, 1:32–33.

circuit-riding had nearly forced Tucker to resign. He complained that the long absences made him "almost a stranger to my own house," and lamented that he found himself "extremely anxious to see my poor babies again." His two-year-old daughter had even begun to refer to the children's tutor as "papa."[9]

By 1791, life – and law – had become hard. Tucker had arrived in Virginia in 1772, as a nineteen-year-old Bermuda immigrant sent to Williamsburg to study law with George Wythe. He had made friends, married well, and allied himself with Virginia's leading families. Then, after the war ended, he watched as his social and economic world crumbled. Soon his personal life fell apart, too, and in 1791 the young judge found himself a widower with three trouble-some teenaged stepsons and five young children of his own – forced to depend on law for his livelihood.[10] When he came to Virginia, law had been his hope; now it was his lifeboat.

When St. George Tucker first embarked for Virginia from Bermuda on October 14, 1771, it had been his first trip off the tiny but economically important island.[11] The Tuckers were an old and prominent Bermuda family; one ancestor had served as the island's second governor, from 1616 to 1619, and the current royal governor's daughter had married St. George's oldest brother, making him a relative by marriage.[12] St. George's father, Henry Tucker Sr., had been the speaker of the Bermuda assembly throughout the 1740s and 1750s as well as the colony's London agent. Henry Tucker Sr. was also one of the island's most successful merchants, running a shipping business that had thrived earlier in the century.[13] By the early eighteenth century, Bermuda had become the second big-gest carrier in British America, second only to Boston, and increasingly econom-ically independent from Britain.[14] But after the Seven Years War, the empire's postwar depression pummeled the island, while Bermudians also faced increas-ing competition from American vessels.[15] The Tuckers began to scramble. The next generation of the family, it seemed, would require new opportunities.[16]

The answer seemed to be in a professional education. First St. George's older brother, Thomas (Tommy) Tudor Tucker, went to Edinburgh to study medicine.

---

[9] Phillip Hamilton, *The Making and Unmaking of a Revolutionary Family: The Tuckers of Virginia, 1752–1830* (Charlottesville, VA: University of Virginia Press, 2003), 94.

[10] Hobson, *St. George Tucker's Law Reports*, 1:14.

[11] Cullen, *St. George Tucker and Law in Virginia*, 3.

[12] Hamilton, *Making and Unmaking of a Revolutionary Family*, 9, 17; Michael J. Jarvis, *In the Eye of All Trade: Bermuda, Bermudians, and the Maritime Atlantic World, 1680–1783* (Chapel Hill, NC: University of North Carolina Press for the Omohundro Institute of Early American History and Culture, 2010), 22, 390.

[13] Hamilton, *Making and Unmaking of a Revolutionary Family*, 10–17.

[14] Jarvis, *In the Eye of All Trade*, 115–133 (discussing the importance of unrecorded Bermuda shipping traffic).

[15] Ibid., 380–382.

[16] Hamilton, *Making and Unmaking of a Revolutionary Family*, 18–19.

It was a long, sometimes frustrating course of study. Tommy wrote home to St. George that some students stayed "as long as they think proper, from 4 or 5 to 8 or 10 years."[17] As a result, Henry Tucker Sr. began to look for cheaper ways to educate St. George, the family's youngest. The teenager had shown an interest in law, and his father had hoped to send him to the Inns of Court in London to study. But such an education surpassed the family's current means. Instead, St. George began work as a clerk for his uncle, Bermuda's Attorney General – an experience he loathed, for its tediousness and the difficulty of his uncle's temper, as well as the loneliness it brought.[18] His sister Eliza lamented his situation, "nothing but an utter incapacity can prevent this best of Fathers from doing every thing for the service of his Children that themselves could wish. But Fortune seems to take Pleasure in disappointing the Plans he makes for fixing them genteelly in life."[19]

A solution arrived in the form of a visiting Virginian, Bolling Sharp. Sharp told Henry Tucker about the cheap legal education available at Virginia's College of William and Mary, under the direction of Williamsburg lawyer George Wythe. The elder Tucker decided to send his son to Virginia, hopefully only to begin his education, which he would continue later in London.[20] So in October 1771, the young man left the island of Bermuda for the first time to begin his education in Virginia. He had, as his oldest brother, Henry Jr. reminded him, entered "the grand Theatre of the World."[21]

There was a lot riding on the nineteen-year-old St. George. His success depended not just on brainpower but on connections – relationships that his genteel Bermuda background could facilitate but could not guarantee. Kin and patronage, after all, dominated Virginia's dense, intricately connected ruling class. And the Tuckers had already learned that connections back home did not ensure success on the mainland. St. George's brother Tommy had only recently moved to South Carolina to start a medical practice, and Tommy's melancholy letters complained that his services had been engaged only by a "few Bermuda negroes." "I am quite a stranger here," he wrote, "and you know most people have some kind of Engagement or Attachment to a particular Physician which only Time or Accident can be expected to break."[22] He lamented that he had heard it said by people who had traveled the world that "there is not a

---

[17] Letter from Thomas Tudor Tucker to St. George, January 10, 1768, Series 1 (Correspondence), Box 1, Folder 2, Item 16, Tucker-Coleman Papers.

[18] Hamilton, *Making and Unmaking of a Revolutionary Family*, 24–26; Hobson, "Biographical Overview," 1:5; Cullen, *St. George Tucker and Law in Virginia*, 6.

[19] Letter from Elizabeth Tucker to St. George Tucker, *c.* August 12, 1770, Series 1 (Correspondence), Box 1, Folder 3, Item 39, Tucker-Coleman Papers.

[20] Cullen, *St. George Tucker and Law in Federal Virginia*, 6–9.

[21] Hamilton, *Making and Unmaking of a Revolutionary Family*, 8.

[22] Letter from Thomas Tudor Tucker to St. George Tucker, August 14, 1771, Series 1 (Correspondence), Box 1, Folder 5, Item 46, Tucker-Coleman Papers.

more healthy spot than Charleston," unfortunate for a man in his profession.[23] Making a living in Virginia would likewise require of St. George not just skill but social connections.

The Williamsburg that St. George encountered was an exciting place. It had a history of changing young men's worlds, even young Virginians, let alone that of an island teenager encountering the mainland for the first time. In the 1760s, a young Thomas Jefferson had found the colonial capital and its intellectual society pivotal in his intellectual and personal development. He later recalled that his friendships there, especially with George Wythe, had "the most salutary influence on the course of my life," and gave him the "incessant wish," he remembered, "that I could even become what they were." In their company, Jefferson recalled after a long, full life in public service and international society, he had heard "more good sense, more rational and philosophical conversation than in all my life besides."[24]

St. George's ambitions were perhaps more pragmatic, if only because of the pressing influence of his practical father and the family's mounting financial concerns. But he was also, by nature it seems, more focused on people and on networks than on academics alone. Or perhaps, as an outsider, he was less able to simply take those networks for granted. His letters to his anxious family were filled with people, including descriptions of who had received him and who showed promise of welcoming him into their social circles, each letter received with celebration and relief at home. His outgoing disposition served him well – even as his family worried about a tendency to perhaps be too familiar, too teasing. Their letters were full of caution and concern, particularly advice to watch his sense of humor. "Be Therefore always upon your guard not to offend in word or deed," his father instructed, "nor let ... wit get the better of prudence for a stroke of Satire sometimes wounds deeper than a two edged Sword, and what may be overlooked in your near friends and relations, by a Stranger may never be forgiven."[25] After all, his father gravely reminded him, "your future fortune and happiness depend upon your present conduct."[26]

St. George, however, quickly began to forge connections with important Virginians. First he contacted his uncle, Norfolk merchant Archibald Campbell, and then met with William and Mary's Rev. Thomas Gwatkin, who directed him to first undertake courses in natural and moral philosophy before embarking on the law (though the extra expense dismayed his father).[27] At the

---

[23] Letter from Thomas Tudor Tucker to St. George Tucker, December 22, 1771, Series 1 (Correspondence), Box 1, Folder 6, Item 62, Tucker-Coleman Papers.

[24] Quoted in Willard Sterne Randall, *Jefferson: A Life* (New York, NY: Harper-Perennial, 2014), 54–55.

[25] Letter from Henry Tucker, Sr. to St. George Tucker, November 30, 1771, Series 1 (Correspondence), Folder 5, Item 53, Tucker-Coleman Papers.

[26] Letter from Henry Tucker to St. George Tucker, August 1, 1772, Series 1 (Correspondence), Folder 10, Item 112, Tucker-Coleman Papers.

[27] Hamilton, *Making and Unmaking of a Revolutionary Family*, 26–27.

College, St. George joined the Flat Hat Club, which met in a local tavern and sometimes included laughter which "shook the house."[28] There he added the future Virginia lawyer James Innes and future Virginia Governor John Page to his circle of friends. He also created relationships with Thomas and William Nelson, the sons of William Nelson, Virginia's powerful Secretary of State. The senior Nelson's job included assigning the lucrative clerk positions in the county courts, the jobs sought after by young lawyers.[29] Tucker's acquaintance with the Nelsons proved key to integrating into Virginia's legal profession (as Tucker's father reminded him, the Secretary had "many pretty things in his gift").[30] For their part, the Nelsons were impressed with St. George. Secretary Nelson wrote to the senior Tucker in Bermuda, commenting on St. George's "good sense, cheerfulness of disposition, and goodness of heart" which had "recommended him ... to some of the most respectable persons among us."[31] For his part, Tucker provided his new friends with gifts from his native island, such as pineapples, turtles, and oranges.[32]

When St. George arrived in Williamsburg, the Virginia capital bubbled with the imperial crisis, offering not only a bookish but also a practical education. George Wythe, his new law teacher, was a longtime member of Virginia's House of Burgesses, and had been an early opponent of the 1765 Stamp Act; Wythe had drafted a remonstrance sent to the House of Commons to explain Virginia's position.[33] And the following years brought more trouble.[34]

One of the newest controversies, over the request of some in New York and New Jersey for the Church of England to extend the episcopacy to America, hit St. George's extended family directly. The controversy had divided William and Mary's faculty, and the Rev. Thomas Gwatkin, the professor who had advised St. George to take a general course of study before beginning law, was one of the chief opponents of the plan (Gwatkin and the Rev. Samuel Henley received official thanks from the House of Burgesses for their "wise and well-timed opposition").[35] St. George's uncle by marriage, the Rev. Samuel Auchmuty, rector of Trinity Church, New York, had another opinion. "Are their Character so bad," he wondered of the episcopate's opponents, "as to make them dread

---

[28] "The Flat Hat Club," *William and Mary College Quarterly Historical Magazine* 25, no. 3 (1917): 161–164.

[29] See Hobson, "General Introduction," in *St. George Tucker's Law Reports*, 1:6.

[30] Hamilton, *Making and Unmaking of a Revolutionary Family*, 28.

[31] Cullen, *St. George Tucker and Law in Virginia*, 13.

[32] Jarvis, *In the Eye of All Trade*, 326.

[33] "George Wythe," *Colonial Williamsburg Foundation*, accessed February 20, 2016, www.history.org/almanack/people/bios/biowythe.cfm; Virginia House of Burgesses; "Remonstrance to the House of Commons," *Wythepedia*, accessed August 30, 2016, http://lawlibrary.wm.edu/wythepedia/index.php/Remonstrance_to_the_House_of_Commons.

[34] Bernard Bailyn, *Ideological Origins of the American Revolution* (Cambridge, MA: Belknap, 1992 [first printing 1967]), 117–119.

[35] "Williamsburg – The Old Colonial Capital," ed. Lyon G. Tyler, *William and Mary College Quarterly Historical Magazine* 16 (1907): 1–65.

the Inspection of a Superior? Are they," he accused, "Presbyterians in their heart, and ready to accept of Lay Ordination if offered?" He wrote to his nephew asking for observations on the recalcitrants: "As we have not yet such a particular account of these protestors as we could wish, if you can afford any Anecdotes concerning them, you will oblige me. Your Name shall forever be concealed," he added conspiratorially. "I am told one or two of these conceited Cockscombs are professors in your College. A Blessed Church College indeed that harbors such Reptiles!"[36]

It seemed, however, that St. George enjoyed life among the "reptiles." Studying law with Wythe put him in the middle of Virginia's influential legal profession and the colony's ruling class. While some Virginians were, like St. George's brother, going abroad to learn medicine, by the late eighteenth century many stayed in the colony to study law, and Wythe was the man to study it with. Wythe's students were "under preparation for public life," as Thomas Jefferson put it.[37] They not only clerked in his office, but also received a more organized education. They pursued heavy reading assignments in their spare time, and prepared arguments for Wythe's moot courts, where they would present in front of other students. Wythe mentored his students with great dedication. He introduced them to members of the Bar, and had them attend sessions of the colony's General Court so that they could watch and take notes. Furthermore, Wythe charged no fee. Back in Bermuda, St. George's father determined that this was a very good education indeed, especially since "I am rightly informed no care is taken of you in the Inns of Court in London."[38]

The education also had other dimensions. Wythe was, as historian Alan Taylor has put it, "a liberal who lived by his principles."[39] He had antislavery convictions, and during his life Wythe would continue to maintain, contrary to other Virginians, that the races could live together; he freed his own slaves after his wife's death in 1787, and even adopted a young mixed-race boy and educated him as a gentleman, partly to make a point about the boy's potential.[40] In studying with Wythe, the young Tucker saw his moralism as well as

[36] Letter from Samuel Auchmuty (rector of Trinity Church, New York) to St. George Tucker, February 15, 1772, Series 1 (Correspondence), Folder 7, Item 67, Tucker-Coleman Papers. Auchmuty's stepdaughter was Frances Tucker Montresor, daughter of Thomas Tucker, who seems to have been St. George's uncle. See letter from Frances (Auchmuty) Montresor to St. George Tucker, August 1, 1772, Series 1, Box 1, Folder 10, Item 111, Tucker-Coleman Papers (writing about their grandmother's recent death). Her portrait was also painted by John Singleton Copley. "Mrs. John Montresor," *US Department of State*, accessed February 6, 2017, https://diplomaticrooms.state.gov/Pages/Item.aspx?item=93&rm=2.

[37] Letter from Thomas Jefferson to Richard Price, August 7, 1785, in *The Papers of Thomas Jefferson*, vol. 8: *25 February to 31 October 1785*, ed. Julian P. Boyd (Princeton, NJ: Princeton University Press, 1953), 357.

[38] Cullen, *St. George Tucker and Law in Virginia*, 9–10.

[39] Alan Taylor, *The Internal Enemy: Slavery and War in Virginia 1772–1832* (New York, NY: W. W. Norton, 2013), 105.

[40] Ibid., 104–105.

his republicanism; in Taylor's words, Tucker "sought to navigate between the allure of power as a Virginia gentleman, on the one hand, and the appeal of Wythe's self-denying principles, on the other."[41]

The world, it seemed, had begun to unfold at St. George's feet, but that had its costs. At first, his connection with the Nelsons paid off; Secretary Nelson appointed him to one of the coveted county court clerkships. But before Tucker could settle into his new post, Virginia's revolutionary leaders began closing the colony's courts. In 1774, the House of Burgesses allowed the Act setting the rate of court fees to expire, then failed to renew it before the royal governor dissolved the House of Burgesses.[42] Most county courts closed their dockets, which were dominated, conveniently, by debt suits, including the collection of British debts.[43] In March 1775, the new Virginia Convention – Virginia's extra-legal revolutionary legislature – called on litigants to delay their suits, asking creditors to be indulgent, debtors to pay to the extent of their ability, and for "judicious neighbours" to mediate where parties could not come to an accord themselves. Meanwhile "the people," they advised, should "observe a peaceable and orderly behavior."[44] This left the new lawyer without a livelihood. In 1775, Tucker obtained admission to the Bar of Virginia's still-open General Court. However, that court then itself closed almost immediately for the next three years.[45] In the short term, it seemed, his promising Virginia legal career had come to an end.

Out of work, St. George assessed his options. He considered proposing marriage to a young Philadelphia woman whom he had met on his first voyage to Virginia, but her main asset, he admitted to his family, was her "very considerable fortune," which might rescue him from "the Trouble of prosecuting the dry and tedious Study of Law."[46] Out of options and out of money, St. George reluctantly returned to Bermuda, which he called "that romantic spot ... where peace, health, and poverty have created their joint dominion."[47]

But the Tucker family was resourceful, and even in Bermuda they soon found a way to capitalize on the connections that St. George had made in Virginia. The Continental Congress's trade embargo threatened to starve the island; it cut off food imports, and the Bermuda salt industry, which exported chiefly to America, would collapse without trade. Faced with a looming crisis, an extralegal Bermudian council voted to send Henry Tucker, Sr. to negotiate with the Continental Congress. He returned with an implicit understanding: the

---

[41] Ibid., 14.
[42] Woody Holton, *Forced Founders: Indians, Debtors, Slaves, and the Making of the American Revolution in Virginia* (Chapel Hill, NC: University of North Carolina Press for the Omohundro Institute of Early American History and Culture, 1999), 117–118.
[43] Cullen, *St. George Tucker and Law in Virginia*, 12–13, 25.
[44] Ibid., 26.
[45] Ibid., 15–17.
[46] Hamilton, *Making and Unmaking of a Revolutionary Family*, 43.
[47] Cullen, *St. George Tucker and Law in Virginia*, 12.

FIGURE 2.1 St. George Tucker, by Asher Durand, *c.* 1785

Americans needed gunpowder, and a large amount of imperial gunpowder was stored on the island. If Bermudian ships could supply the gunpowder, the Continental Congress might exempt them from the embargo. During a night-time raid, the Tuckers and a few associates captured the colony's magazine while Bermuda's Governor James Bruere slept nearby. As one historian of the island has documented, the ships that Bruere sent in pursuit of the ammunitions "made deliberately slow progress," allowing the ships carrying gunpowder to escape. The Bermudian legislature created a joint committee to investigate the theft and to discover its instigators, but made no progress. Bermudian captains even declined to carry Bruere's news of the theft to General Thomas Gage in Boston.[48]

And there were further opportunities. Next, St. George learned from John Page back in Virginia that "several people in Maryland and the Northern states" were making "[i]mmense profit" by running goods past the Royal Navy. Soon the Tuckers turned their shipping expertise to smuggling. Bermuda's captains were already intimately familiar with the ports of the Chesapeake, and now they carried salt, sugar, guns, and munitions to the rebelling colonies and returned to the Caribbean with wheat, rice, tobacco, and indigo, largely from Virginia and South Carolina, in many ways a continuation of prewar maritime patterns.[49] Finally, thanks to war, it looked as if their fortunes might turn; they were finally prospering after, as St. George's brother Tommy put it, "having experienced so many bitter Disappointments and Difficulties."[50]

With these clandestine operations in full swing, in late 1776 St. George seized the opportunity to return to Virginia to run the mainland end of the new family business. He sailed on a family ship packed with salt and cotton and sold the supplies to the desperate Virginia government for an £1,800 profit. He also persuaded a few Virginia friends to join the operation as partners and received government contracts for much-needed supplies.[51] Between 1776 and 1779, St. George ran at least five family vessels in continuous operation between Williamsburg, Charlestown, Curacao, St. Eustatius, Demerara, Grand Turk, St. Christopher, Bordeaux, and London, carrying salt, Carolina rice, indigo, molasses, and tobacco.[52] His friend James Innes congratulated him on the "the Successes you have met with, in yr Mercantile Department – and may heaven grant, that, you may be soon enabled to amass a happy & independent Competency."[53]

He also renewed his contacts with his friends from William and Mary, and again found himself making inroads into Virginia society. Life was beginning to look hopeful again, and Tucker's excitement at his second chance to make it in Virginia was evident in the lighthearted poems he composed for his friend Thomas Nelson's wedding in 1777. In the first, "A Dream on Bridecake,"

[48] Ibid., 386–390.
[49] Cullen, *St. George Tucker and Law in Virginia*, 19; Jarvis, *In the Eye of All Trade*, 395–396.
[50] Hamilton, *Making and Unmaking of a Revolutionary Family*, 33.
[51] Ibid., 34.
[52] Jarvis, *In the Eye of All Trade*, 414.
[53] Jane Carson, *James Innes and his Brothers of the F.H.C.* (Williamsburg, VA: Colonial Williamsburg, 1965), 93.

Tucker told the story of his dreams the night before, and how, paralyzed by too much drink, he had been visited by his fictional love, Flora.

> Brimful of claret wine and perry,
> You know I went to bed quite merry,
> But, as I soon grew wondrous sick,
> I wished my carcass at Old Nick.
> At length I sunk into a nap,
> With head reclined in fancy's lap;
> She rubbed my temples, chaffed my brain,
> And then displayed this scene of pain.
>
> Methought, the claret I'd been drinking
> So far from giving aid to thinking,
> Had muddled my idea-box,
> And clapped my body in the stocks.
> ...
> Just then, my Flora passing by
> This pretty object chanced to spy;
> The wanton saw my hapless case,
> And clapped me in a warm embrace;
> Her balmy lips to mine she pressed,
> And leaned her bosom on my breast,
> Her fingers everywhere were gadding.
> And set my soul a madding;
> Whilst I, in vain, resistance made,
> Still on my back supinely laid.
> ...
> Then [she] cried, "Pray when will you be sober?"
> "My dear," said I, "not till October."[54]

In the second poem, evidently produced in response to popular demand for a sequel, Tucker again told about his "dreams" of the night before.

> Well – sure no mortal e'er was cursed
> With dreams like mine – for they're the worst
> That ever visited a sinner,
> E'en after a fat turtle dinner,
> And six good bottles to defend him
> From evils that might else attend him.

This time, he found himself on a desert island, turned by witches into a woman's silk stocking. ("And, in an instant – think how shocking! [The witches] Turned me into a white silk stocking.") Tucker's stocking-self passed through

---

[54] St. George Tucker, "A Dream on a Bridecake," in St. George Tucker, *The Poems of St. George Tucker of Williamsburg – 1752–1827*, ed. William S. Prince (New York, NY: Vantage Press, 1977), 42–43.

several shops, until his fictional love "Flora" unknowingly purchased him to wear to a wedding.

> She tried to draw me on her leg,
> I stuck, and would compassion beg,
> But as, alas, I could not speak,
> She forced me on without a squeak.
>
> Her polished knee I next embraced,
> And there I stuck until the last;
> For tho' she wished to draw me higher,
> Yet troth, I would not venture nigher.[55]

But Tucker's ease and playfulness were short-lived. By 1778, the family's financial situation again began to collapse. Commodity prices were fluctuating so rapidly that the Tuckers began to lose money between the purchase and sale of their cargo. To make matters worse, the Royal Navy had increased its presence in the Atlantic, making the entire venture riskier.[56] A few of the Tuckers' ships were lost or captured, and by the end of the decade, the Tucker family's newest attempt to make its fortune had also run aground. "Resignation," as St. George's brother Henry Tucker Jr. lamented, "is a Lesson we must all endeavor to learn."[57]

At that auspicious moment, Tucker slipped in late to a service at Williamsburg's Bruton Parish Church, during a day of celebration and prayer called by the governor in honor of the recent victory at Saratoga. As Tucker later recalled, "I happened unwittingly, to take my seat next to a pew in which all the Ladies were kneeling most devoutly." There, he "discovered a face I had seen some years before, with an infant in her Arms: she was now a Widow! And from that moment, had I been a Roman Catholic I should have applied to the Pope for absolution from my Vow."[58]

The widow had a name: Frances Bland Randolph, daughter of the wealthy Theodorick Bland, Sr., and niece of the pamphleteer and agitator Richard Bland, whose arguments against Parliament's recent overreaching had helped to shape colonial opposition. If St. George Tucker had struggled to break into Virginia's social world, Frances took it for granted. Her mother's Bolling family found its history and blood intertwined with those of Pocahontas, whose granddaughter Jane Rolfe had married Virginia's first Bolling, Robert.[59] Frances's late husband, John Randolph, had been a member of one of Virginia's wealthiest and most

[55] Tucker, "A Second Dream on Bridecake," in *Poems of St. George Tucker of Williamsburg*, 43–45.
[56] See Jarvis, *In the Eye of All Trade*, 421–427.
[57] Hamilton, *Making and Unmaking of a Revolutionary Family*, 38.
[58] Letter from St. George Tucker to Robert Walsh, October 2, 1812, quoted in Hamilton, *Making and Unmaking of a Revolutionary Family*, 40.
[59] Charles Campbell, ed. *Bland Papers, Being a Selection from the Manuscripts of Col. Theodorick Bland ...*, vol. 1, ed. (Petersburg, VA: Edmund & Julian C. Ruffi, 1840), xv.

dominant families, and in this era of tight kin connections between Virginia's elite, was also a close cousin of both of Frances's parents.[60] As one traveler to Virginia observed in 1782, "When travelling to Virginia, you must be prepared to hear the name of Randolph frequently mentioned," both because "it is among the first families of the country, since a Randolph was among the first settlers," and because "it is also one of the most numerous and wealthiest."[61]

Frances had been raised at Cawsons, her father's plantation in Prince George County, where he occupied some of the most important posts in county government. When she married John Randolph in 1771, her wealthy father had the means to grant her twenty slaves as a dowry.[62] And although her own father had not had much education, her brother, Theodorick, had trained in medicine at Edinburgh, like St. George's own brother, Tommy.[63] In 1775, young Theodorick had been one of the twenty-four men who removed arms from the Governor's Palace at Williamsburg, after Governor Dunmore fled to a man-of-war vessel.[64] In June 1776, he became the captain of the first troop of Virginia cavalry, and in 1777 he and his troops joined the main army.[65] By the time Frances and St. George met in 1778, the Bland family was a mainstay of Virginia's revolutionary effort as well as of its social network.

When she met St. George Tucker in Bruton Parish Church, Frances had been a widow for two years. John Randolph had died in 1775, leaving Frances with three sons, Richard, Theodorick, and John (later known as John Randolph of Roanoke). As a woman – first daughter, then wife – in colonial Virginia, Frances's life had been different from St. George's own Bermuda upbringing and his Virginia sojourn, or her own brother's multi-year stay abroad. She was not exactly sheltered, of course. She would have visited friends and relatives, attended balls, dances, and weddings, heard gossip concerning the affairs of the Virginia government, and possibly attended events surrounding the monthly county court session. In these sessions, each county's great landholders met in their capacities as justices of the peace, heard civil and criminal cases, and also made decisions about important county affairs.

As the Revolution approached, Frances would have listened to arguments around the dinner table or in the parlor about Virginians' rights and the way forward for the colony, and probably contributed her own thoughts. Known as a woman of "quick intelligence" who demanded to be treated accordingly,

[60] Hamilton, *Making and Unmaking of a Revolutionary Family*, 42; *Bland Papers*, 1:xiv.
[61] François-Jean, marquis de Chastellux, *Travels in North America in the Years 1780, 1781, and 1782*, ed. Howard C. Rice, Jr., vol. 2 (Chapel Hill, NC: University of North Carolina Press, 1963), 427. Quoted in Cynthia A. Kierner, *Scandal at Bizarre: Rumor and Reputation in Jefferson's America* (Charlottesville, VA: University of Virginia Press, 2006), 9.
[62] Hamilton, *Making and Unmaking of a Revolutionary Family*, 42.
[63] See *Bland Papers*, 1:xiv–xx, and Theodorick Bland, Jr. to Theodorick Bland, Sr., January 12, 1771, ibid., 30–32.
[64] See note, ibid., xxiii.
[65] Ibid., xxv.

FIGURE 2.2 Frances Bland Randolph Tucker, copy of portrait by Asher Durand, likely by William James Hubard, *c.* 1785

Frances seemed to possess many of the same gifts that would later characterize her son John Randolph, the fearsome and erudite US Representative. As one Virginian later remembered, "It was the joy of my boyhood to sit at [my tutor, Mr.] Robinson's knee and listen to his conversations with my father and John Randolph's mother, who lived at Matoax. The world thought that her son spake as never man spake; but *she* could charm a bird out of a tree by the music of her tongue."[66] And after her first husband's death, Frances found herself suddenly wealthy and independent, legally in charge of her late husband's considerable estate of three plantations, many slaves, and several thousand acres of land.[67]

Marriage to Frances cemented Tucker's social standing and rescued him from his financial woes. They moved with Frances's three sons to her plantation at Matoax, 1,300 acres on the Appomattox River, where they entertained friends and family even as they endured the ravages of war. "Mr. Tucker must be the best father-in-law [stepfather] in the world," one frequent visitor to Matoax commented during the 1780s, "or his stepchildren would not be so fond of him."[68] Over the next ten years, Frances and Tucker had six more children, five of whom survived: Frances (1779), Henry St. George (1780), Tudor (1782), Beverley (1784), and Elizabeth (1787).[69]

In 1781, their domestic harmony was interrupted by the British invasion of Virginia. The invasion chased St. George, Frances, and the children to estates further and further inland. As Tucker reported to his brother-in-law Theodorick Bland, Jr., "On the third inst., Patsy Bannister [Frances's sister] received a letter from her mother, acquainting her that the enemy were coming up the James River ... your sister [Frances] had then been but five days mother to her last child. I need not descant," Tucker continued, "on my own sensations on the occasion, but will only observe I was resolved to keep her utterly ignorant of the impending danger." Upon hearing the next day that the enemy approached, Tucker "came to a resolution, whatever might be the consequence, to remove your sister &c., out of the way of danger." They "abandoned Matoax, all of our effects, to their fate." Theodorick's and Frances's parents had also fled from their land. "As you may have heard," Tucker related, "the old gentleman has lost much by the absconding of his negroes," but "the most valuable fellows have returned." Tucker reported that: "I have lost none, but have not been without a small share at least in the calamities of war, by the loss of some rum at Richmond; but it was too trifling a quantity for a man to break his heart about."[70]

After the invasion, Tucker joined groups of volunteers raised for protecting the state. He fought and was wounded by friendly fire in 1781 at the Battle of Guilford Courthouse before being promoted to lieutenant colonel, a position in which he served until General Cornwallis's surrender at Yorktown.[71] He also wrote a poem entitled "Liberty: A Poem on the Independence of America,"

---

[66] Hamilton, *Making and Unmaking of a Revolutionary Family*, 50, 57.

[67] Ibid., 59–60.

[68] Hugh A. Garland, *The Life of John Randolph of Roanoke* (New York, NY: D. Appleton & Company, 1850), 13.

[69] Hamilton, *Making and Unmaking of a Revolutionary Family*, xii; Cullen, *St. George Tucker and Law in Virginia*, family tree (frontispiece) and 69.

[70] Letter from St. George Tucker to Theodorick Bland, Jr., January 21, 1781, in *Bland Papers*, 2:55.

[71] Cullen, *St. George Tucker and Law in Virginia*, 22–23.

which circulated widely in manuscript form during the war. A pleased Washington reportedly said that "Mr. St. George Tucker's poem on liberty was equal to the reinforcement of 10,000 disciplined troops."[72]

After the war, the family's life began to change as economic and political turmoil wracked the state, and the Tuckers watched as many of their friends and closest family members lost their financial battles. In 1787, Francis Tucker's brother-in-law, John Banister, became so financially distressed that he could not even pay state taxes; his "Chariot horses and several of [his] best Negroes" were taken in execution for his debts. In October 1787, while visiting her sister, Frances wrote to St. George, "from the most disturbed house I was ever in," relaying that Banister had been "a perfect Bedlamite ... these two days and nights." A year later the embarrassed Banister died, overcome by the weight of his financial collapse.[73] The Nelson and Page families, both of whom had been Tucker's closest companions and friends since his first introduction to Virginia, also fell on hard times. Like John Banister, in 1789 Tucker's friend Thomas Nelson, Virginia's former governor, whose father had opened the colony's social and professional doors for Tucker, died in the midst of his financial woes.[74]

In this new atmosphere, with old wealth crumbling and trade disrupted, Tucker concluded that Virginia had permanently changed. In the mid 1780s, he decided that surviving in the future would depend on professional income, not landed wealth. Although he had not "read a Page of Law" in six years he resumed his legal practice, first taking cases in county courts and then in the state superior courts.[75] Tucker complained about the transition to his friend Robert Innes; writing to him in 1783, Innes agreed with Tucker that the "fall of a gentleman of ease and pleasure to one Laborious occupation is disagreeable indeed."[76]

Soon the man who had once called the study of law "dry and tedious" had become one of Virginia's foremost lawyers. In 1782, a fellow member of the Bar asked him to offer arguments in the *Case of the Prisoners*, also called *Commonwealth v. Caton*, a critical case which tested the power and

---

[72] St. George Tucker, "Liberty: a Poem, on the Independence of America," in David Hill Radcliffe, comp., *Spenser and the Tradition: English Poetry 1579–1830*, accessed September 23, 2016, http://spenserians.cath.vt.edu/TextRecord.php?action=GET&textsid=37067. George Washington quotation originated from "St. George Tucker, Esq.," *The Gentleman's Magazine, and Historical Chronicle, Part 2*, ed. Sylvanus Urban (London: J. B. Nichols and Son, 1828), 472.

[73] Letter from Frances Bland Randolph Tucker to St. George Tucker, October 1787, Series 1 (Correspondence), Item 2158, Tucker-Coleman Papers. Hamilton, *Making and Unmaking of a Revolutionary Family*, 73.

[74] Hamilton, *Making and Unmaking of a Revolutionary Family*, 74–75.

[75] Hobson, "General Introduction," 1:20; see also Hamilton, *Making and Unmaking of a Revolutionary Family*, 71–97.

[76] Letter from Robert Innes to St. George Tucker March 25, 1783, Series 1 (Correspondence), Box 10, Item 1184, Tucker-Coleman Papers.

reach of the new state constitution.[77] In 1785, he wrote a pamphlet advocating greater power in the federal government to regulate commerce.[78] In 1786, the Virginia General Assembly appointed him to be a member of the commission that was to meet at Annapolis, to consider amendments to the Articles of Confederation. Tucker drafted resolutions to present at the convention, but the delegation opted to call another convention at Philadelphia, to revisit the Articles completely.[79]

Then, in 1787, just as the convention in Philadelphia neared the end of its work on a new federal Constitution, tragedy struck a double blow. First, Tucker's father died in Bermuda after a short illness, leaving the family inconsolable. Next, six months after the senior Tucker's death, St. George received a report from back home that his Bermuda family's grief had grown only more intense, "almost insupportable." Then, in December 1787, Frances gave birth to a baby girl after a difficult labor. It was her ninth birth, and this time she did not recover. She died on January 18, 1788.[80]

St. George had taken to his room for weeks – "Mr. Tucker's grief," the children's tutor, John Coulter, recorded, "will not permit him to say anything."[81] In his seclusion, he poured out his anguish onto paper.

> Come gentle Sleep and weigh my eyelids down
> And o'er my senses shed oblivion's balm,
> 'Tis thine alone corroding care to drown,
> 'Tis thine alone the troubled soul to calm
>
> ...
>
> Thy dreams past happiness can bring again,
> And to a dungeon give an Eden's charms;
> Pluck from my heart its agonizing pain,
> Restore my love – my Fanny to my arms –
>
> This bed the scene of all my joys and woes
> Awakes Remembrance with her busy train,
> Where Bliss unrivaled used to court repose,
> Unrivalled Sorrow wakes to endless pain.

---

[77] See St. George Tucker's Notes of Argument in Commonwealth v. Caton, Commonwealth v. Caton File, Series 3 (Legal Material), Box 17, Folder 1, Item 11, Tucker-Coleman Papers. For more on the *Case of the Prisoners/Caton*, see Chapter 7.

[78] Attributed to St. George Tucker, *Reflections on the Policy and Necessity of Encouraging the Commerce of the Citizens of the United States of America, and of Granting Them Exclusive Privileges of Trade* (New York, NY: Reprinted by Samuel and John Loudon, 1786).

[79] St. George Tucker, September 1786, Series 1 (Correspondence), Box 10, Item 1895, Tucker-Coleman Papers.

[80] Hamilton, *Making and Unmaking of a Revolutionary Family*, 68–69.

[81] Ibid., 69.

> Dear partner of my blissful hour and care
> Friend of my soul, and mistress of my heart
> With thee, e'en wretchedness could bliss appear,
> Without thee, even blessings yield a smart.
>
> Come then O Sleep, on downy pinions come
> By dreams attended, hover 'round my head,
> Convey my sorrows to the silent tomb
> And raise a sleeping angel from the dead.[82]

Tucker's life as Virginia gentry had, in many ways, been Frances's life. They had lived on her first husband's plantations, near her family, managing her inherited Randolph estates. Now that was over. The estates were still there, but belonged to her now-teenaged Randolph sons. Tucker opted for an emotional break from his previous life and moved back to Williamsburg. Both he and Virginia would, he grimly determined, require a new future.

Meanwhile, Virginia had ratified the new federal Constitution. It had been a hard fight and the wisdom of the new document had absorbed conversation and sparked debate across the state. As one visitor to southwest Virginia noted, "even in these remote wilds the people are deeply engaged in that science. The new constitution is the subject of universal discussion."[83] Tucker's support for the Constitution had vacillated. In October 1787, he had written to Frances that the "Topic of the day is the new Constitution – W. Nelson is the only one of our Acquaintance who is strenuously opposed to it." He added, "The Governor [Edmund Randolph] wishes it emended in some respects, but thinks it in it's [sic] present state the less of two Evils – I find myself wavering, but rather inclined to the latter opinion."[84] But only a month later, James Madison reported to Jefferson, who was in France, that Tucker was one of the influential opponents of the proposed government, along with his friends the Nelsons and a few others.[85] At the end of October 1787, Tucker confided to Frances that "Nelson and I begin to think that we gather strength."[86]

But the Virginia convention opted for ratification. Afterwards, Tucker wrote a long letter to his Randolph stepsons, warning them that British creditors could now enforce their debts on their father's estate – debts their father had contracted from endorsing a brother's notes to English creditors. "That event,

---

[82] St. George Tucker, "To Sleep," in *Poems of St. George Tucker of Williamsburg*, 48–49.

[83] Lorri Glover, *The Fate of the Revolution: Virginians Debate the Constitution* (Baltimore, MD: Johns Hopkins University Press, 2016), 27.

[84] Letter from St. George Tucker to Frances Bland Randolph Tucker, October 3, 1787, in *The Documentary History of the Ratification of the Constitution*, vol. 8: *Ratification of the Constitution by the States: Virginia, No. 1*, ed. John P. Kaminski, Gaspare J. Saladino, and Richard Leffler (Madison, WI: Wisconsin Historical Society Press, 1988), 35.

[85] Letter from James Madison to Thomas Jefferson, New York, October 24, 1798, ibid., 108.

[86] Letter from St. George Tucker to Frances Bland Tucker, Richmond, October 27, 1787 (excerpts), ibid., 125.

my dear children," he wrote, referring to the adoption of the Constitution, "affects your interest more nearly than those of most others. The recovery of British debts can no longer be postponed, and there now seems to be a moral certainty that your patrimony will all go to satisfy the just debts of your Papa to the Hanbury's." He reminded them that "the consequence, my dear boys, must be obvious to you – your sole dependence must be on your own personal Abilities & Exertions."[87]

From his boyhood, Tucker had learned how to adapt to financial adversities, and he now vigorously applied those lessons to his current life. In Williamsburg, he purchased three lots and a house from his friend Governor Edmund Randolph. He explained the move to the former capital as a desire to educate his children there "without parting from them under mine own eye," but there were also financial considerations at play.[88] Still convinced that Virginia's economy had been permanently altered, Tucker had sold the lands he had purchased since his marriage and began investing instead in banks and in companies promoting internal improvements.[89] In 1788, Tucker accepted an appointment to Virginia's General Court, and in 1790, he took over the professorship at William and Mary, glad for the steady income.[90] He also began to doubt the wisdom of continuing the slave system, and lectured to his law students about the impropriety and inhumanity of human bondage. "How frequently," he remarked after summarizing the laws regarding slaves, "the law of nature has been set aside in favor of institutions which are the pure result of prejudice, usurpation, and Tyranny."[91] Virginians, Tucker had decided (undoubtedly learning from his own family's long struggle in Bermuda), needed to embrace the changes that were coming their way.

By July 1791, as Tucker worked by candlelight in his Williamsburg study, the years of tragedy had left their mark. The formerly playful, optimistic young man found himself a middle-aged widower, driven by grim determination. In Williamsburg, Tucker drew up a set of rules for the household, which he called, "Garrison Articles to Be Observed By the Officers and Privates Stationed at Ft. St. George in Wmsbg." (Tucker appointed himself "fort commander.") On the one hand, the rules showed Tucker's characteristic humor, turning discipline into a game. For instance, rule number five stated, "No officer under the rank of Major or private shall run about in the parlour," while rule number ten advised, "Health and whole bones, being also Objects of the Government's

---

[87] Letter from St. George Tucker to John Randolph and Theodorick Randolph, June 29, 1788, Papers of John Randolph of Roanoke, Accession 3400, Series 1 (Letters and Documents), Box 1, Folder 5, UVA Special Collections. Hamilton, *Making and Unmaking of a Revolutionary Family*, 42.

[88] Hamilton, *Making and Unmaking of a Revolutionary Family*, 79.

[89] Hobson, "General Introduction," 1:8–9.

[90] Hamilton, *Making and Unmaking of a Revolutionary Family*, 42.

[91] Tucker, "Ten Notebooks of Law Lectures," Notebook 9, 45, Tucker-Coleman Papers.

attention, whoever does anything to endanger either will be considered guilty of a high misdemeanor."[92] On the other hand, the Garrison Articles were also evidence of Tucker's tendency towards sharp discipline and control – inclinations that had only become more pronounced in his grief.[93]

More tragedy loomed. His stepson Theodorick was ill, and had been wasting away for several years. He had traveled to Bermuda, Tucker's homeland, visiting with Tucker's mother and siblings in hopes that the climate would lead to improvement. But, as St. George confided to Theodorick's brother John that summer, "I have no hope of his recovery."[94]

Tucker had long mourned Frances. As he wrote on the second anniversary of her death, in 1790:

> O Death! Thy fatal triumph still I feel,
> Thy venom'd dart still rankles in my heart;
> My Wounds what human medicine can heal!
> What, less than pow'z divine, can ease their Smart?
>
> Relentless Tyrant! What Delights are thine!
> The tortur'd Victims' Groans enchant thine Ear,
> Pale Famine's Cries, Disease's sickly whine,
> The Shrieks of Agony, & mad despair.
>
> ....
>
> Insatiate Harpy! Rapine too is thine:
> You from my heart it's dearest treasure stole!
> More precious than the Gems of India's mine;
> Eternal Life scarce dearer to my soul!
>
> Detested Fiend! Still may'st thou be my Friend,
> And ten-fold Treasure to my soul restore;
> When this frail Life, thy fatal shafts shall end
> Bear me to her I love'd! I ask no more.[95]

His friend John Page, also widowed, had recently remarried. Page began writing to Tucker from Congress, enthusiastically relating the delights of his own bride. "I am truly happy my dear Tucker – Sanguine as my Expectations were,

[92] Available online from the Tucker-Coleman Papers. "Tucker, St. George (175201827)," *Earl Gregg Swem Library Special Collections Database*, accessed September 30, 2016, http://scdb. swem.wm.edu/?p=creators/creator&id=457.

[93] Hamilton, *Making and Unmaking of a Revolutionary Family*, 87–88.

[94] Letter from St. George Tucker to John Randolph, August 18, 1791, Papers of John Randolph of Roanoke, UVA Special Collections.

[95] St. George Tucker, "To Death, January 18, 1790," in "St. George Tucker Dated Poems, 1790–1799," Box 80, Tucker-Coleman Papers.

I do assure you I had no Idea of ever being so happy – Heaven seems to have found Miss Lowther to make me happy!"[96] A few weeks later, after noting that he had received Tucker's last letter while "in bed with my wife," he added, "Oh Tucker, how I wish you were blest with such a Wife as I am!"[97]

By the summer of 1791, St. George had a bright spot, too – an upcoming marriage to Lelia Carter, a twenty-four-year-old widow who had begun tutoring his daughter Frances in 1790.[98] Lelia was the daughter of Sir Peyton Skipwith, and the widow of George Carter. She was, as Frances had been, a wealthy widow with land and young children. The couple had become engaged in the spring of 1791, and although happy, Tucker now had many additional cares to weigh on him. But after almost four years as a widower, Tucker would finally have a companion of his own.[99]

By 1791, Tucker had – like Virginia – made his own transitions. Twenty years earlier, he had stepped onto Virginia soil for the first time, hoping to gain a cheap education before returning home. But Virginia society had opened new, exciting doors for him – even as the fight for independence had also fundamentally altered his new home. As the world around him changed, St. George Tucker's discernment, resourcefulness, good humor, and willingness to take risks had served him well. He had, amidst setbacks, managed to come out mostly on top. But the postrevolutionary world still presented many challenges. By 1791, Tucker had decided to use the law to meet those challenges, even as – again like his Virginia home – his old idealism had taken a more hard-headed turn.

Now, Tucker had things to do that would bring that contrast between past and present into stark relief. A wedding, but before that law classes, of course, and long meetings with the revisors of the law. And then a long trek west on the Winchester circuit, where John Crane waited.

---

[96] Letter from John Page to St. George Tucker, April 18, 1790, Series 1 (Correspondence), Box 10, Item 2558, Tucker-Coleman Papers.

[97] Letter from John Page to St. George Tucker, May 16, 1790, Series 1 (Correspondence), Box 10, Item 2569, Tucker-Coleman Papers.

[98] Hamilton, *Making and Unmaking of a Revolutionary Family*, 79.

[99] Ibid., 79.

3

Examination

Class, Procedure, and Local Courts in Crane's Virginia

As St. George Tucker worked in his Williamsburg study, on July 14, 1791, Isaac Merchant pushed past the crowds to make his way into the Berkeley County courtroom, ready to be called as a witness in the case against John Crane.[1] After all, he had been one of the men working alongside Abraham Vanhorn, harvesting wheat for Thomas Campbell, on the fateful day when someone – allegedly Crane – had stabbed Vanhorn. And far from observing as a mere bystander, Merchant had been deeply entangled in the day's events. Some Crane supporters even contended that he had provoked the fight.[2]

In July 1791 Isaac was a few days shy of thirty-one years old, and a man on the rise.[3] His life had not been easy. The Merchants had been early settlers in the area and had claimed respectable tracts of land, but strife had divided the family.[4] His grandparents were "of the people called Quakers," part of the

---

[1] "July 14, 1791," Berkeley County Minute Book, BCHS.

[2] "Deposition of Hugh McDonald, October 1, 1791," *Calendar of Virginia State Papers and Other Manuscripts*, vol. 5: *From July 2, 1789 to August 10, 1792*, ed. William P. Palmer and Sherwin McRae (Richmond, VA: Virginia State Library, 1885), 372.

[3] Isaac was born on July 17, 1760. See Register of Morgan's Chapel, Bunker Hill, WV, as copied by the Col. Morgan Morgan Chapter of the Daughters of the American Revolution, Fairmont, WV. There, the family name is listed as "Marchant," but the list is entitled "Sons and Daughters of William and Perasilla Merchant" and the children listed are the children listed in William Merchant's will (which refers to his wife Priscilla). Will of William Merchant, Berkeley County Will Book 1:5, BCHS. The name Isaac Merchant appears a number of times in Berkeley's records; because of the proximity of the William Merchant grants to Crane's land, and because of an Isaac Merchant buying land next to those grants, I have concluded that the Isaac Merchant in Crane's case was Isaac Merchant, son of William, who would have been the right age and in the right place.

[4] Will of Richard Merchant, Frederick County Will Books, 1743–1794, will dated March 25, 1752, probated September 1, 1752, Will Book 2, 62 (2:62), Reel 51, Local government records collection, Frederick County Court Records, The Library of Virginia; Virginia

old Hopewell Friends meeting on the west side of the Opequon, but younger generations had come into conflict with the meeting. The younger Merchants had been disciplined for dancing, and for marrying outside the faith.[5] Then Isaac's grandfather cut Isaac's father, William, out of the elder Merchant's 1752 will, pointedly bequeathing William only "one British shilling." Grandfather Merchant left his land to his son Richard instead, and had even curtly specified that if Richard had no heirs, the lands were to be sold and divided among Richard's sisters. Neither the land nor its proceeds, he implied, would go to William or his family.[6]

But William Merchant had land grants of his own, so his family got along fine until he fell sick in 1771 and died shortly thereafter. His will left land to some of his sons, but he promised Isaac only a horse, to be earned by "staying and assisting well till he comes of age."[7] The family must have struggled; that spring, Isaac's twenty-two-year-old brother appeared before the Berkeley County Court on the charge of "counterfeiting money of the coin of this

records list land grants of 81 acres, 358 acres, and 115 acres to William Merchant (May 1, 1760, May 2, 1760, and November 2, 1768), and 187½ acres to Richard Merchant (April 30, 1760), listed in Merchant Family File, BCHS, based on research carried out by the late Berkeley County historian and BCHS president Don Wood. For William, see "Land grant 1 May 1768," William Merchant, grantee, Northern Neck Grants K, 1757–1762, Frederick County, Reel 294, 119–120, Library of Virginia; "Land grant 2 May 1760," William Merchant, grantee, Northern Neck Grants K, 1757–1762, Frederick County, Reel 294, 119–120, Library of Virginia; "Land grant 2 November 1768," William Merchant grantee, Northern Neck Land Grants O, 1767–1770, Reel 296, 205, Library of Virginia. For Richard Merchant, see "Land grant 30 April 1760," Richard Merchant grantee, Northern Neck Land Grants K, 1757–1762, Reel 294, 18, Library of Virginia. Merchant family information on file at the Berkeley Historical Society indicates that the elder Richard Merchant's land was "surveyed but not patented," and that the younger Richard's 1760 grant was for the elder Richard's land, which the family already held. See notes in Merchant family file, BCHS.

5 Phrasing from Frederick County Court's description, upon probate, of the three witnesses to the will of Richard Merchant, Frederick County will Book 2:62–63, BCHS; disciplinary records from Joint Committee of Hopewell Friends, with John W. Wayland, *Hopewell Friends, A History* (Strasburg, VA: Shenandoah Publishing House, 1934), 497, 503 (see 496–521). Richard Merchant, Isaac's uncle, was disciplined for training with the militia in 1763; this, however, was after his father's death. See Wayland, *Hopewell Friends*, 497.

6 Will of Richard Merchant, probated September 1, 1752, Frederick County Will Book 2:62, BCHS. Presumably this was the result of Isaac's father and family being estranged from the Quaker meeting. Mary Bull Merchant, Isaac's first wife, was disowned by the meeting for marrying "contrary to discipline," suggesting that Isaac's family was already estranged from the meeting, although Isaac himself is not listed as disciplined or disowned. For Mary Bull as first wife of Isaac Merchant, son of William, see Merchant family file, BCHS (citing information from Isaac Merchant's family Bible); note, however, that Isaac's birthdate is there listed as 1756 instead of 1760. For Mary Bull's discipline in 1780, see Wayland, *Hopewell Friends*, 503.

7 Will of William Merchant, Berkeley County Will Book 1:5, BCHS.

colony," a capital offense.[8] Luckily, the Berkeley Justices had reduced the charge and found him and his co-defendant guilty only of a misdemeanor.[9] But Isaac probably remembered that brush with the law as he waited on yet another capital court hearing in July 1791, this one for John Crane.

It was not a regular court session. Instead, this county court had been called expressly for the purpose of examining Crane and a thief named Stirling Cooke, who had been charged with feloniously stealing "sundry goods" from Samuel Johnston.[10] While civil suits and other business took place during the monthly court sessions, the examining court convened specially when there had been a crime. For that reason, people sometimes referred to it as a "called court."[11] For many offenses, the county court had plenary power to adjudge guilt and mete out punishment, including by fines or lashes. But for felonies like Crane's, the county court functioned as a waystation, the place where the justices determined whether the offender should be sent on to the state court for trial, or set free.[12]

This was an old process, stretching deep into Virginia's past. When Virginia was still a colony there had been two types of courts, the county courts and the General Court in Williamsburg. The colonial General Court, made up of the members of the Governor's Council, had both exclusive jurisdiction over felonies and original and appellate jurisdiction in civil actions with over £10 in dispute.[13] When a felony arose, an examining court met locally in the county to consider the evidence against those charged; there, the justices would determine whether that evidence was sufficient to bind the accused over for trial at the capital. A "guilty" verdict from the county justices sent the offender on to Williamsburg to face the grand jury and perhaps trial and execution. The county court could also

---

[8] Counterfeiting became a more frequent crime in Virginia in the decades before the Revolutionary War, and in 1769 it was made a felony without benefit of clergy, although lawyers, courts, and juries sometimes attempted to find a way around this stiff sanction. See Hugh F. Rankin, *Criminal Trial Proceedings in the General Court of Colonial Virginia* (Williamsburg, VA: Colonial Williamsburg, 1965), 178.

[9] "November 20, 1772," Berkeley County Court Minute Book, BCHS.

[10] "July 14–15, 1791," Berkeley County Court Minute Book, BCHS.

[11] Rankin, *Criminal Trial Proceedings*, 78.

[12] Ibid., 78–79.

[13] For the General Court's history, see Hugh F. Rankin, "The General Court of Colonial Virginia," *Virginia Magazine of History and Biography* 70, no. 2 (1962): 142–153. For Virginia law reform, see Kathryn Preyer, "Crime, the Criminal Law and Reform," *Law and History Review* 1, no. 1 (1983): 53–85; Charles T. Cullen, *St. George Tucker and Law in Virginia, 1772–1804* (New York, NY: Garland Publishing, 1987); Markus D. Dubber, "An 'Extraordinarily Beautiful Document': Jefferson's Bill for Proportioning Crimes and Punishments and the Challenge of Republican Punishment," in *Modern Histories of Crime and Punishment*, ed. Markus Dirk Dubber and Lindsay Farmer (Palo Alto, CA: Stanford University Press, 2007): 115–150; Paul W. Keve, *History of Virginia Corrections* (Charlottesville, VA: University of Virginia, 1986), 7–27; A. G. Roeber, *Faithful Magistrates and Republican Lawyers: Creators of Virginia Legal Culture 1680–1810* (Chapel Hill, NC: University of North Carolina Press, 1981); and Arthur P. Scott, *Criminal Law in Colonial Virginia* (Chicago, IL: University of Chicago Press, 1930).

declare the offender "not guilty," insulating him or her from further prosecution. Sometimes, the justices found defendants guilty of lesser, non-felony charges, and punished them in the county instead of sending them on to the state. But the one thing that the examining court could not do was to distinguish between degrees of culpability; for instance, the justices could not find the prisoner guilty of mere manslaughter and take murder off the table at the state court.[14] So even if the justices considered manslaughter the more appropriate charge for Crane – which occasionally happened in Virginia's county courts – they had no power to limit the charges he would face at his state-level indictment or trial.

As Isaac Merchant waited to testify against John Crane in July 1791, the colonial process had changed only a little. The 1776 Virginia constitution had created separate courts of law and equity and a new Court of Appeals which heard appeals from both types of tribunals. The General Court had continued to hear both original cases at law and appeals from county courts, though it no longer had its old equity jurisdiction. In 1788, the legislature then took a further step: it divided up the General Court's responsibilities, and its judges, among new district courts. These new courts were circuit courts, each staffed by two General Court judges who traveled throughout the Commonwealth to hear cases within the General Court's jurisdiction. In 1791, there were five circuits, with two to five district courts within each circuit. District courts were held twice a year, once in the fall and once in the spring. If the two presiding district judges disagreed on a case, or found it otherwise troublesome, they could refer it "for difficulty" to the General Court, which was now essentially the district court judges assembled *en banc*.[15]

The Berkeley justices were still responsible for the first stage of the process. As in the colonial era, it was the justices' job to convene an examining court to determine whether Crane was, in their opinion, guilty of murder. If they decided that he was, he would be bound over to the Winchester District Court for indictment and trial during its next court session in September. If, on the other hand, they decided that he was innocent and declined to send him to Winchester, Crane would be discharged – for good.[16]

Back in 1772, when Berkeley's first justices of the peace met to set up the new county, they had focused much energy on designing their new courthouse. The exterior would be made of stone, to be provided by French and Indian War General Adam Stephen, on whose land the town would be located – that much

---

[14] Thomas Sorrel's Case (General Court 1786), in Charles F. Hobson, ed., *St. George Tucker's Law Reports and Selected Papers, 1782–1825*, vol. 1 (Chapel Hill, NC: University of North Carolina Press, 2013), 117–119.

[15] See the excellent description in Cullen, *St. George Tucker and Law in Virginia*, 71–82.

[16] The Virginia General Court mentioned this principle a few years later in *Commonwealth v. Samuel Myers*, 3 Va. 188 (1811), but it was in operation earlier. See Rankin, *Criminal Trial Proceedings*, 78–79.

was easy.[17] The interior was more complicated. The justices debated various designs for their bench, first opting for a "square" configuration before deciding in August 1773 that the "[p]lan of the Court House lodged in the Clerk's Office be altered [,] the seat for the Justices and the Walls to be Built in a Circular form instead of a square agreeable to the second plan."[18]

Back then, the justice's bench was of special significance, because during the colonial era Virginia's county courts had been the ruling bodies of the counties, in many ways virtually supreme over their subjects' lives.[19] In the words of historian A. G. Roeber, "No institution was more central to Tidewater Virginia culture than the county court, in both physical eminence and practical consequence."[20] Drawn by the governor from among a county's most important landowners, county courts were, as legal scholar and historian William Nelson has put it, "largely self-perpetuating bodies." Current justices sent names of new justices to the Governor for approval, and only rarely did the Governor vary from their recommendations.[21] When justices appeared in court they heard hundreds of legal cases, meted out discipline, administered the county, and generally reminded onlookers of their power. As the Anglican evangelist the Rev. Devereux Jarratt later recalled in relation to his boyhood in colonial Virginia, "when I saw a man riding the road, near our house, with a wig on … I would run off," from a mixture of fear and deference; such ideas "of the difference between *gentle* and *simple* were," Jarratt remembered, "universal among all of my rank and age."[22]

Berkeley County's first Commission of the Peace, issued in 1772, had included some of the wealthiest, most powerful men of the county. Berkeley itself was a social mix, made up of absentee Tidewater landlords who had received their land from Lord Fairfax's land agent, Robert "King" Carter, and local high-status settlers who had obtained their (competing) grants from colonial governors. The justices reflected both types of elites. Virginia planter Ralph Wormeley IV had been named first on Berkeley's first Commission of the Peace, a nod to his status in the state at large. Wormeley's wealthy, well-educated forebears had helped lead the colony since the seventeenth century.[23] But Wormeley

---

[17] For more on Adam Stephen, see Harry M. Ward, *Major General Adam Stephen and the Cause of American Liberty* (Charlottesville, VA: University of Virginia Press, 1989).

[18] "November 19, 1772," and "Aug 17, 1773," in Berkeley County Minute Book, BCHS.

[19] See, for instance, William E. Nelson, "Law and the Structure of Power in Colonial Virginia," *Valparaiso University Law Review* 48, no. 1 (2013): 757–883.

[20] A. G. Roeber, "Authority, Law, and Custom: The Rituals of Court Day in Tidewater Virginia, 1720–1750," *William and Mary Quarterly*, 3rd Series, 37, no. 1 (1980): 29–52, 30.

[21] See Nelson, "Law and the Structure of Power," 831–833 (n. 493 provides examples of governal refusals).

[22] Roeber, "Authority, Law, and Custom," 36, n. 12. Quoting Devereux Jarratt, *The Life of the Reverend Devereux, Rector of Bath Parish Jarratt* (Baltimore, MD: Warner and Hannah, 1806), 14 (emphasis in original).

[23] For a brief discussion of the Wormeley family, see "Wormeley Family," *Virginia Historical Society*, accessed August 23, 2016, www.vahistorical.org/collections-and-resources/virginia-history-explorer/virginias-colonial-dynasties/wormeley-family.

had obtained his Berkeley land somewhat by accident when, while intoxicated, he bid on a plot during a Williamsburg auction. After he won, friends teased him for "buying land in the moon"; Wormeley regretted his careless bid until George Washington, who had surveyed the area, congratulated him on his purchase.[24] Now Wormeley owned land in Berkeley but continued to live at his lavish family estate, Rosegill, in Middlesex County. According to his grandson, the home contained "a chapel, a picture-gallery, a noble library, and thirty guest-chambers."[25]

Other justices were men who actually lived in the Valley, whose families had emigrated from the northeast or overseas. Justice Jacob Hite's family had obtained one of the very first settlement grants. Justice Van Swearingen's father had in 1755 established the first ferry across the Potomac west of the Blue Ridge. Swearingen's son-in-law, Thomas Rutherford, was also a justice and his father had been on the first Commission of the Peace in Frederick County in 1743.[26] Hite, Swearingen, and Rutherford were some of the area's first grantees, well-to-do men with large land holdings.

Several of the other justices had connections to the Carter land or to Lord Fairfax more directly. Robert Carter Willis was a young man, but was the grandson of Robert Carter of Nomini Hall and "King" Carter's great-grandson.[27] George Washington's brother Samuel was also named a justice, as were Sheriff Adam Stephen and his brother Robert. The Washingtons had long been connected with the Fairfax family, and both Adam and Robert Stephen had been rent-collectors for Lord Fairfax.[28] Indeed, if there was a lesson to be

---

[24] *The Recollections of Ralph Randolph Wormeley, Written Down by His Three Daughters,* ed. Katharine Prescott Wormeley, Elizabeth Wormeley Latimer, and Ariana Wormeley Curtis (New York, NY: Privately Printed, 1879), 10, in UVA Special Collections.

[25] Alexander MacKay-Smith, "The Lower Shenandoah Valley as a Thoroughbred Breeding Center 1785–1842," *Proceedings of the Clarke County Historical Association* 7 (1947): 6–30, 6–7; *Recollections of Ralph Randolph Wormeley,* 10.

[26] Thomas Kemp Cartmell, *Shenandoah Valley Pioneers and Their Descendants* (Winchester, VA: The Eddy Press, 1909), 67, 181, 266. See A. D. Kenamond, *Prominent Men of Shepherdstown, 1762–1962* (Charles Town, WV: Jefferson County Historical Society, 1962), 110; William Kenneth Rutherford and Anna Clay (Zimmerman) Rutherford, *A Genealogical History of the Rutherford Family,* vol. 1 (Shawnee Mission, KS: Intercollegiate Press, 1969), 112. The elder Rutherford was of Scottish descent but had hailed more immediately from Essex County, Virginia, and had purchased over fifteen hundred acres of land in the Frederick/ Berkeley area beginning in 1736. The elder Thomas died in 1768, so the Thomas Rutherford on the Berkeley Court was his son. Rutherford and Rutherford, *A Genealogical History of the Rutherford Family,* 1:86.

[27] Stuart E. Brown, Jr. *Virginia Baron: The Story of Thomas, 6th Lord Fairfax* (Baltimore, MD: Clearfield Company, 2003), 158; Ward, *Adam Stephen,* 93, 97–98; Lyon G. Tyler, "Willis Family," *William and Mary Quarterly* 5, no. 3 (1897): 171–176, 172. On Carter see MacKay-Smith, "The Lower Shenandoah Valley," 7.

[28] Ward, *Adam Stephen,* 93.

learned from observing the identities of the justices, it was that association with Fairfax paid off.[29]

Being a justice was an honor reserved for the most important landowners in a county, but the position of justice was also one of great power and responsibility, particularly for those who resided locally and actually showed up to preside at court. In the colonial era, the county courts were the place for county business of all types, although most of their docket involved civil lawsuits. As historian Cynthia Kierner has noted, "as much as ninety percent of the [county] courts' business was in civil cases, the vast majority of which pertained to debt."[30] Berkeley followed this pattern. For instance, on a day like August 18, 1772, the Berkeley County clerk listed over one hundred cases in the court minutes: mainly actions on the case and in debt, but also petitions, suits in trespass, assault and battery, and assorted attachments and ejectments. The court also dealt with administrative duties, especially the maintenance of roads and tax lists.[31] March 1773 was another typical court; the justices addressed well over 200 pending lawsuits, in debt, in case, and in trespass. They ordered fourteen litigants to pay their witnesses in tobacco at a rate of twenty-five pounds per day. They also bound out seven orphans to the custody of various families, and gave licenses to Phillip Lower and Henry Bedinger to keep "ordinaries" (taverns) at their houses.[32]

Berkeley's men seemed to have had few qualms about suing each other. Names were allied for one case but at odds the next. This aligns with what scholars like William Nelson and Randolph Roth have demonstrated in this period – Virginians seemed not only willing but eager to go to law for solutions to their problems.[33] They also used lawyers to do so: at the first Berkeley County Court session in 1772, the justices quickly admitted six attorneys to practice, including Philip Pendleton, nephew of colonial leader Edmund Pendleton, and

---

[29] Other justices were James Nourse, William Little, John Neavill, Hugh Lyle, James Strode, Robert Stogdon, and James Seaton. Commission of the Peace dated November 6, 1772, but in undated minute book, sometime after January 1773, Berkeley County Minute Book, BCHS.

[30] Cynthia A. Kierner, *Scandal at Bizarre: Rumor and Reputation in Jefferson's America* (Charlottesville, VA: University of Virginia Press, 2006), 44–45.

[31] "August 18, 1772," in Berkeley County Minute Book, BCHS.

[32] "March 17, 18, 1773," in Berkeley County Minute Book, BCHS.

[33] William E. Nelson discusses the penchant for the rule of law in early Virginia in *The Common Law in Colonial America*, vol. 1: *The Chesapeake and New England, 1607–1660* (New York, NY: Oxford University Press, 2008); Randolph Roth explains that "In Virginia, once emerged from frontier conditions everyone – including the poor – began to turn to the county courts to resolve personal differences. They filed dozens of civil suits in every county every year for slander, trespass, assault (which included threats and verbal abuse), and assault and battery (which included physical violence). In long-established counties an average of one of every fifty white men were involved in any given year as complainants or defendants in a civil suit for assault or slander." Randolph Roth, *American Homicide* (Cambridge, MA: Harvard University Press, 2009), 88. See also William E. Nelson, *The Common Law in Colonial America*, vol. 3: *The Chesapeake and New England, 1660–1750* (New York, NY: Oxford University Press, 2016).

by June 1772 Magnus Tate was also appearing as counsel.[34] Alexander White, who had been educated in Edinburgh and studied law at London's prestigious Inner Temple and Gray's Inn, was appointed the county's first deputy attorney.[35] The court also directed William Jenkins to purchase "a sufficient number of law books for the use of this county."[36] "This day the parties came by their attorneys" was a common phrase in the county's minute book.[37]

The justices themselves may not have been legal professionals, but by the mid-eighteenth century proceedings in Virginia county courts paid great attention to legal niceties. As William Nelson has explained, legal knowledge in Virginia was always somewhat different from other colonies. Virginia "sent more of its sons to study law in the Inns of Court than did any other North American colony – over sixty in all," most of whom did not ultimately practice law. This meant that, instead of legal knowledge being consolidated in the colonial capital, it was often well dispersed throughout the colony, in county courts and among law-trained planters.[38] In some ways, Virginia's planter-judges did pay attention to general ideas of justice as well as legal niceties, but as Nelson points out, the "informality of Virginia's county courts" has been "overstate[d]."[39] By the mid eighteenth century, when Berkeley was founded, Virginia's legal system had become increasingly formalistic, though not always well supervised by the state courts. Attorneys used prewritten forms and paid attention to pleading, judicial discretion decreased, and conforming to "legal niceties" in criminal cases increasingly mattered.[40]

Berkeley's County Court heard few criminal cases, when compared to the hundreds of civil cases on its docket. But when a criminal case arose, the justices' power compared starkly with the powerlessness of many of the defendants put before them. For instance, in November 1772, enslaved workers belonging to Francis and Mathew Whiting (Catherine Whiting Crane's father) were charged with stealing hogs belonging to John Crane, Sr. (young John Crane's uncle). They may have been poorly provisioned by Whiting, who lived elsewhere.[41] They were brought before the county court for a hearing, and

---

[34] David J. Mays, *The Letters and Papers of Edmund Pendleton, 1734–1803*, 2 vols. (Charlottesville, VA: University of Virginia Press for the Virginia Historical Society, 1967), 2:44; "June 16, 1772," in Berkeley County Minute Book, BCHS.

[35] Hobson, *St. George Tucker's Law Reports*, 3:1850.

[36] "May 19, 1776," in Berkeley County Minute Book, BCHS.

[37] See "June 16, 1772," in Berkeley County Minute Book, BCHS.

[38] Nelson, "Law and the Structure of Power," 833–838.

[39] Nelson, *The Chesapeake and New England, 1660–1750*, 50.

[40] Nelson, "Law and the Structure of Power," 860–861; Nelson, *The Chesapeake and New England, 1660–1750*, 47–52.

[41] Frances Whiting may have been Catherine's uncle; the exact relationship is debated among Whiting descendants, and there are several Mathew Whitings, making it difficult to pinpoint his various land holdings elsewhere. See Dakota Best Brown, *Data on Some Virginia Families* (Berryville, VA: Virginia Book Company, 1979), 262. Two charges of hog-stealing by so many enslaved workers in so close proximity indicates malnutrition; a careful look at Whiting tax and estate records, and conversations with the late Don Wood of Berkeley County, the county's

there faced justices who were themselves mainly wealthy slaveholders. For their case, many justices – friends of their master – gathered to protect his property. Justice Samuel Washington even made one of his rare journeys to court.[42] Two months later, in January of 1773, twelve more of Whiting's "negroes" were back in front of the court, again charged with hog-stealing.[43]

As with hog-stealing, most criminal trials at the Berkeley Court were property crimes, and ranged from theft of personal property to horse-stealing to counterfeiting. Again, the gap between court and defendant was often obvious. On August 19, 1772, Richard Lewis was examined for horse-stealing and he bargained with the court for thirty-nine lashes instead of being sent to Williamsburg for a capital trial.[43] In what seems to have been another plea bargain, John Davis was examined on November 17, 1772 for a "felony"; the court considered the witnesses "and circumstances" and sentenced him to thirty lashes. November 20, 1772 was the day William Merchant's counterfeiting case was heard.[44] In September 1773, Adam Butler was examined for horse-stealing and determined to be guilty, and sent to the General Court.[45] Thomas Probate, "a convict servant," was examined for stealing "sundry goods and money" of Thomas Kennedy, and sent to the General Court, as was William White soon afterwards, on a charge of horse-stealing.[46] The justices also examined John Wright and John Bryan on horse-stealing charges, and sent them to the General Court for trial.[47] The justices found Nicholas Bond and Michael Kelly not guilty of "breaking and entering the house of Nicholas O'Bryan and stealing ... sundry goods," including cloth, shirts, patterns, and stockings.[48] Harry, a "negro man Slave of the property of Jno Kenwood," was tried for "feloniously breaking" into a house and "committing sundry violences."[49] The justices also examined Cornelius Conway, destined to be one of Berkeley's repeat offenders, for passing counterfeit money in July 1775.[50]

In early 1776, in the lead-up to the Revolution, the number of examining courts increased. First, the justices examined Hugh Gray for feloniously maiming James Nichols "and pulling out his eyes"; he was found guilty and bound to the next grand jury – another of those "rough and tumble" fights for which Virginia was becoming famous.[51] Three days later, they examined

---

knowledgeable local historian, indicate that Berkeley was not Mathew Whiting's primary residence.
[42] "November 1772," Berkeley County Minute Book, BCHS.
[43] "January 19, 1773," Berkeley County Minute Book, BCHS.
[44] "November 20, 1772," Berkeley County Minute Book, BCHS.
[45] "September 22, 1773," Berkeley County Minute Book, BCHS.
[46] "August 23, 1774," and "October 31, 1774," Berkeley County Minute Book, BCHS.
[47] "February 8, 1775," Berkeley County Minute Book, BCHS.
[48] "April 10, 1775," Berkeley County Minute Book, BCHS.
[49] "December 20, 1774," Berkeley County Minute Book, BCHS. This was a court of Oyer and Terminer, because slaves were tried locally, not by the General Court.
[50] "July 12, 1775," Berkeley County Minute Book, BCHS.
[51] "January 17, 1776," Berkeley County Minute Book, BCHS.

Daniel Newcomb and John Young and found them not guilty of stealing two mares; however, the justices admonished them that they were "persons who live disorderly lives" and ordered Newcomb and Young to give security for their good behavior.[52] Cornelius and Phebe Conway were in court the same day, this time on suspicion of concealing and "confederating with" yet a third horse thief. The justices found Phebe not guilty but bound Cornelius to the next grand jury.[53] And in April, the justices examined Mary Howell for allegedly murdering her bastard child, found her guilty, and sent her to the next General Court.[54] And in November they found a "negro man" guilty of theft, and sentenced him to hang.[55] The justices also accused four men of the murder of Henry Peyton.[56] By November 1776, Berkeley had had a handful of serious criminal cases in the four years since the county's establishment, compared to many hundreds of civil cases.

After the Revolution, criminal cases continued to be few, compared to the civil docket. There was a case of breaking into a barn and stealing wheat, an alleged watch-stealing, and a charge that four defendants broke into a smith's shop and stole "tools and sundry articles." One presentment did allege felonious wounding and robbing, but the charge was reduced to larceny.[57] Two other defendants faced allegations of counterfeiting.[58] There were also some nonspecific charges for "felony," a case where a magistrate was assaulted in the course of his duties (bystanders refused to intervene), and a murder. However, Jan Logan, who was charged with the murder, was found not guilty in the examining court and ordered discharged, while co-defendant Arthur Gordon was sent to the district court for trial.[59]

But if criminal prosecutions remained sporadic after the war, other things had changed. As historian Rhys Isaac has demonstrated, the deference of the old society had been replaced by the rumblings of Virginians eager to have their own voices heard in their new government.[60] There had always, of course, been evidence of dissention in the county courts, like a bystander who neglected to remove his hat or who appeared in court intoxicated, or a planter who told

---

[52] "January 20, 1776," Berkeley County Minute Book, BCHS.

[53] Ibid.

[54] "April 27, 1776," Berkeley County Minute Book, BCHS.

[55] "November 20, 1776," Berkeley County Minute Book, BCHS.

[56] "November 19, 1776 Berkeley County Minute Book, BCHS. (The court determined that they were guilty.)

[57] See entries for "October 3, 1789," "February 8, 1790," "June 22, 1790," and "April 15, 1789," in Berkeley County Minute Book, BCHS.

[58] See entry for "Jan 7, 1790," in Berkeley County Minute Book, BCHS.

[59] See entries for "Jan. 2, 1790," "May 18 and 19, 1790," and "June 22, 1790," in Berkeley County Minute Book, BCHS.

[60] Rhys Isaac, *The Transformation of Virginia: 1740–1790* (Chapel Hill, NC: University of North Carolina Press for the Omohundro Institute of Early American History and Culture, 1982), 319–322, esp. 321.

one county undersheriff to "Kiss his Arse" in front of the court (for which he received a fine).[61] But the economic pressures of war and the social and political space it opened exploded any latent discontent into plain view. As Virginian Thomas Mann Randolph lamented, thanks to the Revolution, "the spirit of independency was converted into equality, and everyone who bore arms esteemed himself on [equal] footing with his neighbor."[62]

When it came to the county courts, the rumbling dissatisfaction was partly about money and partly about class – the two frequently mixed together. On the money side, the county courts held the unenviable position of collecting debts and taxes, in an era when the postwar recession and deflation made specie scarce and taxes high. States needed to collect specie to send to Congress in order to pay on the nation's debts to foreign nations incurred during the war and to pay the sizable domestic debt, now mainly in the hands of speculators.[63] Indeed, Judge Tucker's brother, Thomas Tudor Tucker, now a member of the South Carolina House of Representatives, observed in 1786 that without the bondholders, the assembly of that state could have gotten by with only a "very light tax."[64] And Edmund Pendleton complained that gold and silver seemed to "circulate only in the Vortex of Phila. or what other place Congress may set in."[65]

But without specie in circulation, prices plummeted, making it even harder to pay taxes. Farmers could sell their livestock to obtain cash to pay their taxes or their debts, but with so very little specie on hand the sale brought in an artificially depressed return. Even James Madison, who attributed money problems more to an unfavorable balance of trade, admitted: "Our situation is truly embarrassing. It can not perhaps be affirmed that there is gold & silver eno' in the country to pay the next tax."[66]

Citizens from Brunswick County, VA summed up their view of the situation in 1786, when they complained to the General Assembly that "the honest laborer who tills the ground by the sweat of his brow Seams hithertoo [sic] be the only sufferors by a revolution ... by which the undeserving only reap the benefit off [sic]."[67] Some wanted paper money to ease the pain.[68] As a report from Baltimore, reprinted in the *Virginia Journal,* explained, "Before the

---

[61] Roeber, "Authority, Law, and Custom," 39.

[62] Kierner, *Scandal at Bizarre,* 17.

[63] Letter from James Madison to Ambrose Madison, August 7, 1786, in *The Papers of James Madison,* vol. 9: *9 April 1786–24 May 1787 and Supplement 1781–1784,* ed. Robert A. Rutland and William M. E. Rachal (Chicago, IL: University of Chicago Press, 1975), 89.

[64] Woody Holton, *Unruly Americans and the Origins of the Constitution* (New York, NY: Hill and Wang, 2007), 32.

[65] Letter from James Madison to Thomas Jefferson, May 12, 1786, in *Papers of James Madison,* 9:54, n. 5.

[66] Letter from James Madison to James Monroe, June 4, 1786, ibid., 74.

[67] Holton, *Unruly Americans,* 131.

[68] For an excellent account of the debate over the role and character of money in this period, see Andrew Edwards, "A Period of Distress and Madness" (working paper, Modern America Workshop, Princeton University Department of History, Princeton University, March 31, 2015).

Revolution we could not do without paper," the article reminded readers, "why do we torment ourselves now?"[69] The newspapers spoke for many Virginians who felt that they experienced unnecessary hardship.

But others objected that paper money hurt the value of property. In 1780, St. George Tucker summed up Virginia's disastrous war-time experiment with paper money for his friend John Page. "Last May or rather last July," he observed, "a silver dollar was worth forty paper ones by act of the Assembly. We have since found the Philosopher's Stone, and by a mere breath of Hocus Pocus, a paper dollar is now worth," legally, he meant, "as much as a silver one, for the man who is or has been in debt for their twenty years. But," he continued, "stranger to tell, no sooner is the bill transferred from debtor to creditor but it becomes paper again, and worth but the eighteenth part of what he received it for."[70] Tucker's dry humor reflected the consensus of the men who had to accept this worthless paper as creditors and felt that these currency measures effectively redistributed property. As Virginia attorney William Grayson wryly observed, "The Antients were surely men of more candor than We are … They contended openly for an abolition of debts, while we strive as hard for the same thing under the decent & specious pretense of a circulating medium."[71]

After the Revolution, desperate debtors closed courts around the country. In 1787, in Greenbrier County, farmers complained that they paid "greater Taxes than any people under the Sun," and burned down the county jail. They bound themselves not to pay the "certificate tax," a new tax aimed at calling in war bonds, and pledged to stand by each other, in "preventing the Sheriff from taking their property for debt or taxes." They sent copies of their new Association to other backcountry counties.[72]

The economic crisis hit counties like Berkeley in the Shenandoah Valley especially hard, with insolvency rates that rose steadily after the Revolution.[73] And Berkeley's mobile, west-moving population made collecting debt particularly hard. As one of Berkeley County's deputy sheriffs complained in 1783, "he hath not received any part of the above sums and that many of the People is removed out of the County and others not able to pay."[74] Adding to their frustration, sheriffs could themselves be personally liable for the taxes they were

---

[69] "Baltimore," *Virginia Journal and Alexandria Advertiser* (Alexandria, VA), June 14, 1785.

[70] Letter from St. George Tucker to John Page, December 13, 1780, papers of St. George Tucker, 1780–1801, UVA Special Collections.

[71] Holton, *Unruly Americans*, 58.

[72] Ibid., 11.

[73] Frank Garmon, "Mapping Distress: The Geography of Tax Insolvency in Virginia, 1783–1787" (Master's thesis, University of Virginia, 2010).

[74] "Delinquent and Insolvent Taxpayers: 1781–1830, returns," Box 1216, Berkeley County 1783 Folder, APA 427, Library of Virginia.

bound to collect.[75] James Crane, John Crane's father, knew these problems at first hand – he had been Berkeley's deputy sheriff during the mid 1780s.[76]

Maybe that is why, in 1792, James Crane would sign on to a petition protesting the inefficiency of Berkeley's County Court. Along with a number of other citizens, including two Berkeley Justices of the Peace, Crane reminded the General Assembly, "The great objects of civil government are to protect individuals in the enjoyment of their civil rights & property, to punish wrongdoing and to redress the injured." But the justices had made it hard to collect a "just debt."[77] "In vain," the petitioners explained, "are constitutions formed and laws made for these valuable purposes, unless the laws are executed and justice regularly administered." County courts, they complained, so delayed their suits that a creditor suffered "a greater loss from the delay of justice, than he would have suffered by giving up the debt or submitting to the injury." Moreover, the "delay produces a want of punctuality in the payment of debts and in the compliance with contracts and is destructive of that confidence which ought to exist among men," and was an "encouragement to the ill-disposed to do wrong." They recommended paying magistrates for their duties, to ease the burdens of attending court, or allowing a single magistrate to dispose of low-level suits.[78]

But frustration with the justices was not just about problems with debt. It was also about the waning eminence of the justices themselves and declining respect for authority in general. Since the Revolution, common Virginians had seemed less inclined to defer to their social "betters." During the recent fight over the Constitution's ratification, Virginia's voters, in choosing their representatives to the state's ratifying convention, had sometimes opposed the document even in the face of George Washington's known endorsement. As one author had encouraged, "every freeman in Virginia" should "nobly dare to think for himself, and will not be lulled, perhaps into a fatal stupor, by the whistling of any names whatsoever."[79] (Berkeley's own citizens had enthusiastically supported ratification.[80])

At the same time, in the near-decade since the end of the Revolutionary War, the identities of Virginia's justices had changed. In the colonial period, the

---

75 See Garmon, "Mapping Distress." See also William Waller Hening, *The Statutes at Large ...*, vol. 12 (Richmond, VA: George Cochran, 1823), 93–96.

76 James Crane is mentioned as deputy sheriff to Henry Whiting "October 16, 1785," Berkeley County Court Minute Book, BCHS.

77 "Freeholders & Inhabitants: Petition," Berkeley County, October 6, 1792, Legislative Petitions Digital Collection, Library of Virginia (online).

78 Ibid.

79 Lorri Glover, *The Fate of the Revolution: Virginians Debate the Constitution* (Baltimore, MD: Johns Hopkins University Press, 2016), 69.

80 *The Documentary History of the Ratification of the Constitution*, vol. 8: *Ratification of the Constitution by the States: Virginia, No. 1*, ed. John P. Kaminski, Gaspare J. Saladino, and Richard Leffler (Madison, WI: Wisconsin Historical Society Press, 1988), 22.

Commission of the Peace had been made up of each county's greatest landowners, and the House of Burgesses had been the province of the colony's elite. But by the 1780s, many of those who had traditionally held county power now preoccupied themselves with other offices. This took many elite Virginians out of the House of Delegates and relocated them to other roles, and left openings for a broader base of men to serve in the Virginia House, where they bucked demands for taxes and began to manifest an independence of spirit that left Virginia's older gentry worried. Now, the Virginians who used to run the county courts were governors, served on the Council of State and the new Senate, or in federal offices. Sometimes newer names filled the resulting void.[81] Illustrating this shift, one historian reports that by the 1780s, "the overwhelming majority of the members of Virginia's bicameral legislature had not been lawmakers during the colonial period."[82] And, as the prestige of the county court fell, both Virginia justices from "old" families and "new men" were often absent from the bench, or refusing commissions entirely.[83]

In Berkeley, some of the old families continued to have power. For instance, Robert Stephen, brother of Revolutionary War general Adam Stephen, had signed the minutes of almost every county court since 1772, and continued to do so. But at most courts many justices were not those who had appeared so often in the 1770s. The county's representatives in the General Assembly were different, too.[84] The lines of Virginia's political participation had shifted to a different place on the social scale.

Amid these changes and the rising dissatisfaction, Virginia's grand juries began to turn on their own magistrates. They presented their justices for dereliction of duty or complained to the central government about the justices' absence, drunkenness, or other failings.[85] Berkeley was not exempt. In the spring of 1790, for instance, the Berkeley County Court minutes reported that justice James Maxwell had been attacked "while in the execution of his office as magistrate." Not only did the justices haul the assailant before the County

---

[81] Kierner makes a similar observation in *Scandal at Bizarre*, 16–17.

[82] Ibid., 17.

[83] Roeber, *Faithful Magistrates and Republican Lawyers*, 173–175. As Roeber has concluded, after the Revolution there was a subtle shift: it is difficult to pinpoint exactly when the makeup of the county courts began to change.

[84] For instance, one newer Berkeley justice was Andrew Waggoner. In the 1750s, a Waggoner had served under George Washington on General Braddock's ill-fated expedition to expel the French from the Ohio territory, while George Washington was also Berkeley's representative (as part of Frederick County) to the Virginia House of Burgesses. By 1791, it was Andrew Waggoner who was a Berkeley justice of the peace and the county's representative to the General Assembly, and Washington who was now the new President of the United States. For Waggoner as Berkeley's representative to the General Assembly, see Earl G. Swem and John W. Williams, *A Register of the General Assembly of Virginia and of the Constitutional Conventions* (Richmond, VA: Davis Bottom, Superintendent of Public Printing, 1918), 32.

[85] Isaac, *Transformation of Virginia*, 317–322.

Court, but also two others for refusing to help (Maxwell had apparently been assaulted while others looked on).[86]

By 1791, Berkeley's County Court was not what it used to be. But what would these changes mean for John Crane? As he waited, Isaac Merchant probably wondered the same thing.

Crane's was not the first case. Instead, the justices first heard charges against Stirling Cooke.[87] Cooke was a swindler; newspapers reported that he had gone to the springs at Bath (also called Berkeley Springs), famed for their healing potential, "under the pretense of being dumb," and after being there for some time, had "pretended to come to the use of his tongue." He had been treated well by his victim, Johnston, "whom he rewarded by stealing from his benefactor some wearing apparel and some money."[88]

As they examined Cooke, Berkeley County's justices would have peered down from their imposing circular bench. Now the courthouse was almost twenty years old and worn, just as the justices themselves were a less august, more embattled version of their predecessors. There was also the new Winchester district court, which sometimes reversed their decisions.[89] This may have felt like a come-down for the justices.

But although some things had changed, examining courts followed largely the same procedures as they had before the Revolution. The justices heard the case against Cooke, and found him guilty. As in colonial times, they decided to reduce the charge. Instead of sending him to Winchester for further trial, they sentenced him to "twenty-five lashes ... well laid on."[90] Next, they turned to Crane.

As Crane's case began, Isaac Merchant probably went back over the events of July 4 in his head, planning what he would say to the justices when he testified. And as he did, the anger he had felt that day may have come roaring back. After all, in reports of the case, Isaac's fury in the fields on July 4 would be clear, along with Crane's own violence.

---

[86] "May 18, 1790," Berkeley County Minute Book, BCHS.
[87] "Examination of Stirling Cooke," July 14, 1791, Berkeley County Court Minute Book, BCHS.
[88] "Shepherds-Town, July 18," *The Pennsylvania Mercury* (Philadelphia, PA), August 2, 1791.
[89] See, e.g., John Baker v. John Briscoe, April 23, 1790 (Berkeley) (agreed by parties); Samuel Rudd, David Kennedy, and George Riley v. Beard's executors, Alexander Henderson, April 23, 1790 (Berkeley); Robert Throckmorton and John Crane v. William Carr, April 23, 1790 (Berkeley); George Rootes v. William Hammond, April 23, 1790 (Berkeley); Ephraim Worthington executor of Robert Worthington v. Cornelius Conway, April 25, 1791 (Berkeley); Benjamin Beeler and Walter Clark v. George Hite, administrator of Isaac Hite, April 25, 1791 (Berkeley); Jacob Hackney et al. v. Overton Cosby and James Ross, executors of James Mills, April 25, 1791 (Berkeley); Jackob Hackney et al. v. Overton Cosby and James Gregory, surviving partners of James Mills & Co., April 25, 1791 (same) (Berkeley); Amos Nichols v. John Light, April 23, 1791 (Berkeley); Robert Wilson v. John Carrick, April 16, 1791 (Berkeley); Morgan v. Seakin Dorsey, April 16,1791 (Berkeley), all in Winchester District Court Order Book.
[90] "July 14, 1791," Berkeley County Court Minute Book, BCHS.

What had made Isaac so angry? There were two possible reasons, reasons beyond Crane's alleged treatment of Vanhorn and his horses. First, for Isaac, there had been a personal background to the events of July 4: some of Campbell's land had once belonged to Isaac's own family. When Isaac's grandfather had disinherited Isaac's father, he had instead left his lands to his younger son, Richard Merchant. But Uncle Richard had not kept the land; instead, in 1771 he sold the Merchant family's homeplace to Thomas Campbell.[91] Perhaps this is why Isaac's father had insisted that year in his own will that "these heirs are not to sell any of this land"; instead, they were to leave it to the "the next heir lawfull begotten of their body." Isaac's father had repeated the phrase to stress his point: "No one of these heirs are not to sell any of this land."[92]

Isaac had been raised to know that land mattered. Although he had inherited no land himself, as soon as he was able, Isaac began buying parcels, especially around his family's original holdings. By 1791, thanks to his careful purchases, Isaac owned over 300 acres of land – more than John Crane's Berkeley lands.[93] And he worked hard; despite owning 300 acres, Isaac did not currently own slaves (although he had owned a slave the year before and would again in 1793).[94] He was also careful with his money: in 1793 Berkeley's deputy sheriff made a special, unusual note in his ledger that Isaac had paid his taxes "in cash."[95]

So Isaac may have felt territorial on July 4, as he worked in Thomas Campbell's fields, on land that his own family had once owned. But there was more, a second reason for his anger: an explosive slur spoken by Catherine Crane. As the men squared off at the fence, already angry, Catherine Crane had come out into the fields to intervene, calling out to her husband: "Mr. Crane, I am surprised that you would demean yourself to fight with such a set of negrofied puppies!"[96] In the eighteenth century, "puppies" was the type of insult that almost always provoked a fight. As historian Joanne Freeman has explained, "Rascal, scoundrel, liar, coward, and puppy: these were fighting words, and anyone who hurled them at an opponent was risking his life." Freeman continues: "The hushed anticipation at their mention is almost palpable in accounts of honor disputes. Faces

---

[91] See "History of the Merchant, Merchant, and Marchant Family of Frederick County, Va.," Merchant Family File, BCHS.

[92] Will of William Merchant, Berkeley County Will Book 1:5, BCHS. Although entail was abolished by the General Assembly's postrevolutionary reforms, Isaac and his brothers seem to have mostly obeyed their father's wishes, sometimes shuttling land back and forth between family members as they moved in and out of the county. See September 18, 1792 Indenture, John Merchant to Isaac Merchant for land on the "waters of Opeccon and drains of Mill Creek," Merchant Family File, BCHS.

[93] Berkeley County Land Tax, East 1790 (Crane, 200 acres), BCHS. In 1784, Isaac Merchant had purchased 300 acres "on the western side of the Opeccon Creek," Berkeley County Deed Book, 6:316.

[94] Berkeley County Personal Property Tax, West 1790 and 1793, BCHS.

[95] Adrian Davenport, *Berkeley County list of Taxpayers*, 1790, West Virginia State Archives, Charleston, WV.

[96] This fact would later appear in the district court jury's verdict. *Crane*, 3 Va. at 12.

blanch. People go still. Background noise stops. And all eyes turn to the accuser and his victim, waiting to see how the moment will play out."[97]

And Catherine – this genteel woman from one of Virginia's richest families – had not only called Isaac and Campbell's other workers "puppies," but "negrofied puppies." Adding in the "negrofied" undoubtedly only made a snide insult all the more biting. Here was Isaac, who owned more land than Catherine's own husband, working with his hands in his neighbor's field, and this elite woman – this Whiting – had called him "negrofied." Especially in light of pre-existing tensions in the area between new families from the Tidewater and old families who had long farmed with their own hands, Catherine's words must have exploded onto the already tense field. A later report would relay that, with this, Isaac stripped off his shirt, ready to fight.[98]

It was an insult that a hard-working white man like Isaac would not soon forget. Isaac may have owned more land than this haughty, well-bred woman's husband, but Catherine Crane still considered him "negrofied."

Although Cooke's proceeding had been quick, John Crane's examination lasted for two full days, the longest recorded in Berkeley's history. It involved many familiar faces. Justice Cato Moore was a neighbor of the Cranes who assessed their taxes each year and who also served as a Charles Town trustee with James Crane.[99] George Cunningham's family had been early settlers in the area of the Opequon Creek. James Campbell's family had come to Berkeley from Scotland via Pennsylvania, and a James Campbell, probably the same one, had served in the Virginia legislature for two terms, and as Berkeley's sheriff. Others present were William Little, John Turner, James Maxwell, Nicholas Arrick, John Briscoe (another Crane neighbor), and John Kearsley, who had served in the Revolutionary War.[100] Kearsley and More would soon sign, with James Crane, the petition complaining about the Berkeley County Court.[101]

---

[97] Joanne B. Freeman, *Affairs of Honor* (New Haven, CT: Yale University Press, 2001), xvi.

[98] *Crane*, 3 Va. at 13.

[99] Millard Kessler Bushong, *A History of Jefferson County, West Virginia* (Charles Town, WV: Jefferson Publishing Company, 1941): 17.

[100] For Robert Stephen, see Ward, *Adam Stephen*, 93. For George Cunningham, see Betty Cunningham Newman, *Adam and 500 More Cunninghams of the Valley of Virginia c. 1734–c. 1800* (Westminster, MD: Heritage Books, 2000), 235, and passim for more information on the Cunningham family. See also Berkeley County, Virginia Land Tax Records, West 1791, BCHS, which names "George Cunningham, Esq.," owning 186 acres. For James Campbell, see Willis F. Evans, *History of Berkeley County, West Virginia* (Westminster, MD: Heritage Books, 1928), 273; Berkeley County Land Tax Records, West 1791, BCHS, names "James Cunningham, Esq." as owning 310 acres. For Cato Moore, see Berkeley County Personal Property Tax Records, East 1784, BCHS, collecting taxes from John Crane the elder and other nearby landowners. For Kearsley, see Bushong, *A History of Jefferson County*, 353. For Maxwell, see Berkeley County Minute Book, May 18, 1790, BCHS.

[101] "Freeholders & Inhabitants: Petition," Berkeley County, October 6, 1792, Legislative Petitions Digital Collection, Library of Virginia (online).

Crane's examination began on July 14. Moses Hunter, the County Clerk, recorded in his minutes that Crane was "brought to the bar"; the justices "demanded of him whether he is Guilty of the Offence wherewith he stands charged or not Guilty."[102] Crane answered, the clerk using the form language of the time, "he is in no wise thereof Guilty."[103] After Crane's plea, Isaac Merchant and the other witnesses finally had their chance to speak. The record of what they said does not survive, but Hunter recorded in the court minutes that "Sundry witnesses were sworn & Examined as well on behalf of the Prisoner at the bar or the Commonwealth."[104] Whatever they said, it took a long time. The proceeding dragged on and at the end of the day the justices determined that "there not being time sufficient to go thro the Business of this day" the court would be adjourned until tomorrow.[105] This was unheard of in Berkeley – the justices typically concluded their examinations within a single day, sometimes even conducting multiple examinations on the same day.

The justices reassembled on July 15, but not all returned. Cato Moore, the Cranes' neighbor, did not appear at court on this second day.[106] Did he sense that the proceeding would go against John Crane, and stay away? But Crane's case continued, and now the attorneys took over. Newspaper reports of the hearing stressed the role that attorneys had played: the arguments "of the attorney's employed on the occasion," the *Pennsylvania Mercury* reported, "took up the greater part of the two days."[107] County Clerk Moses Hunter recorded in the minutes that "the court proceeded to hear Counsel as well as on behalf of the Prisoner at the bar or the Commonwealth."[108] After those arguments, the court found Crane guilty, and decided that he should be "sent to the District Court for farther trial."[109] The court, the *Mercury* also informed its readers, had made its decision after a "full hearing" of the evidence.[110] This had been no cursory proceeding, but if John thought that name and connections would be lead to his release, he now knew better.

Isaac Merchant must have been pleased – Crane would not get off easily. But Merchant still had more responsibilities. After the justices made their decision, he posted a £100 bond – a high one – to assure the Commonwealth that he would appear at Crane's Winchester trial.[111] The other witnesses, including

[102] "July 14, 1791," Berkeley County Minute Book, BCHS.
[103] Ibid.
[104] Ibid.
[105] Ibid.
[106] "July 15, 1791," Berkeley County Minute Book, BCHS.
[107] "Shepherds-Town, July 18," *The Pennsylvania Mercury* (Philadelphia, PA), August 2, 1791.
[108] "July 15, 1791," Berkeley County Minute Book, BCHS.
[109] Ibid.
[110] "Shepherds-Town, July 18," *The Pennsylvania Mercury* (Philadelphia, PA), August 2, 1791.
[111] "Winchester, July 16," *New Hampshire Gazette, and General Advertiser* (Portsmouth, NH), August 11, 1791; "July 14, 1791," Berkeley County Court Minute Book, BCHS.

Joseph Vanhorn, John Dawkins, and Thomas Campbell, did the same thing.[112] Newspapers reported that a "strong guard" escorted Crane to the Winchester jail to await trial during the district court's September session.[113] This meant that John Crane – son of James Crane, gentleman, and husband of Catherine Whiting Crane – would spend the next two months in the Winchester jail. In the meantime, "the passions and prejudices of the people ran very high against" young John.[114]

[112] "Winchester, July 16," *New Hampshire Gazette, and General Advertiser* (Portsmouth, NH), August 11, 1791; "July 14, 1791," Berkeley County Court Minute Book, BCHS.

[113] "Winchester, July 16," *New Hampshire Gazette, and General Advertiser* (Portsmouth, NH), August 11, 1791; "July 14, 1791," Berkeley County Court Minute Book, BCHS.

[114] "J. Peyton to the Governor, April 30, 1792," *Calendar of Virginia State Papers and Other Manuscripts*, vol. 5: *From July 2, 1789 to August 10, 1792*, ed. William P. Palmer and Sherwin McRae (Richmond, VA: Virginia State Library, 1885), 519.

4

The Bloody Code and the Logic of Legal Reform

Back in Williamsburg, St. George Tucker paused on August 18, 1791, to sum up his summer for his stepson John Randolph. "When at home," he advised the Columbia College student, "I have been completely absorbed by duties of one kind or another. Though very unwell, I have for these six weeks been engaged in the business of a revisal of our laws – besides my duty as a professor with the college. Add to these a thousand private concerns ..."[1]

As he wrote, the judge was preparing to set out on his 600-mile, multi-month circuit to the west. Tucker had been assigned the Winchester/Monongalia circuit, which would take him into Virginia's outer reaches towards the Ohio River.[2] "I will probably not have it in my power to write again until I am home," he cautioned. "Do not attribute my silence to any inattention to or forgetfulness of you – when abroad I am seldom in a situation to write letters."[3] The fact that John's brother, Theodorick, was quite ill made the inability to communicate even more difficult. Theodorick was currently in Bermuda with Tucker's family, in the hopes that the island climate would help his constitution. "I lament," Tucker told John, "that I have no hope of hearing from him before I leave on my circuit, and I go tomorrow."[4]

Tucker's first stop would be Winchester; afterwards he would travel on to the Monongalia District Court, in Morgantown (today West Virginia), which served counties even further west – Monongalia, Harrison, Ohio, and

---

[1] Letter from St. George Tucker to John Randolph, August 18, 1791, in Papers of John Randolph of Roanoke, UVA Special Collections.
[2] For a discussion of Virginia's roads, see Alan Taylor, *The Internal Enemy: Slavery and War in Virginia 1772–1832* (New York, NY: W. W. Norton, 2013), 19.
[3] Letter from St. George Tucker to John Randolph, August 18, 1791.
[4] Ibid.

Randolph – before returning back home to Williamsburg.[5] It was one of five circuits scattered throughout the state; the judges held district courts twice a year, once in the fall and once in the spring. After a previous trek on the same route, back in the spring of 1790, Tucker's friend William Nelson had congratulated him on "returning unscathed from the west."[6]

Tucker had quickly wearied of all the travel. Not only did his circuit riding keep him on the road all fall and spring, but in November and June, after each circuit, he then attended a session of the General Court in Richmond. In Richmond, he lodged at the Swan tavern; during one stay, he composed some short doggerel about his professional plight:

> There was a sorry judge who lived at the Swan by himself.
> He got but little honor, and he got but little pelf [wealth],
> He drudged and judged from morn to night, no ass drudged more than he,
> And the more he drudged, and the more he judged, the sorrier judge
> was he.[7]

At least this fall would be different. Because he planned to marry Lelia Skipwith Carter in October, Tucker would miss the General Court's November session.[8]

Tucker may have been especially weary in August 1791 because the revisors' meeting had not been cordial. The various committee members had different ideas as to what their aims should be. James Monroe, William Nelson, and Judge Joseph Prentis thought they should confine themselves to simply compiling existing laws in one place, but Judge Henry Tazewell, Arthur Lee, and Tucker had more ambitious designs.[9] A frustrated Monroe reported to his friend Thomas Jefferson that the question had arisen whether the revisors should "prepare a bill conformable to the law as it now stands," or whether they could, as he sarcastically described it, "propose on it any new project they thought fit." The committee compromised by deciding that any member who thought an existing "policy defective might prepare a bill for the purpose of amending it," which would, with the approval of the committee, be sent to the legislature along with the bill merely reenacting existing law. Monroe was

---

[5] St. George Tucker, Monongalia District Court, September 1791 term, in *Notes on Cases*, Tucker-Coleman Papers. See also Charles T. Cullen, *St. George Tucker and Law in Virginia, 1772–1804* (New York, NY: Garland Publishing, 1987), appendix C.

[6] Letter from William Nelson, Jr. to St. George Tucker, May 28, 1790, in Tucker-Coleman Papers.

[7] "St. George Tucker," *Colonial Williamsburg Foundation*, accessed October 11, 2016, www.history.org/almanack/people/bios/biotuck.cfm. Tucker's poems are on file at the Tucker-Coleman Papers at William and Mary.

[8] Phillip Hamilton relates that they began courting in fall 1790, and became engaged in the spring of 1791. Phillip Hamilton, *The Making and Unmaking of a Revolutionary Family: The Tuckers of Virginia, 1752–1830* (Charlottesville, VA: University of Virginia Press, 2003), 79.

[9] Charles T. Cullen, "Completing the Revisal of the Laws in Post-Revolutionary Virginia," *Virginia Magazine of History and Biography* 82, no. 1 (1974): 84–99, 92.

still not sure, however, how the revisors who disagreed with him, "particularly Tucker and Lee," would "execute their part."[10]

Tucker was apparently, from Monroe's perspective, making trouble. Perhaps Tucker's experience on the bench and as a professor had made him aware of the ways in which Virginia's law could be improved; maybe his innovative temperament made compiling old, flawed laws distasteful. But it was also, perhaps, because he seems to have been assigned at least some provisions related to Virginia's criminal law.[11]

In the summer of 1791, everyone knew that criminal law – the law that John Crane would soon face – needed to be reformed. Virginia still mostly followed the English common law of crimes, what commentators often referred to disparagingly as the "bloody code." It had earned the name. In his treatise, the great English legal commentator Sir William Blackstone had counted "no less than an hundred and sixty" capital crimes declared by Act of Parliament "to be felonies without benefit of clergy; or, in other words, to be worthy of instant death," inflicted "perhaps inattentively" by "a multitude of successive independent statutes upon crimes very different in their nature."[12] At the same time, the use of the benefit of clergy also created stark disparities. That ancient doctrine had originally allowed clerics of the medieval church to escape the authority of the state in capital cases; it had evolved into a kind of safety valve of leniency which gave a free pass on many crimes to first offenders.[13]

Many people criticized this harsh but inconsistent practice. Some had recommended getting rid of the death penalty altogether, and all – even Blackstone, who tended to think of English law as the very best already – agreed that punishments needed to be more carefully tailored to the crime.[14] Plus, some theorists felt that the old criminal law presupposed a monarch, who both dealt out punishment and offered mercy to the criminal as a subject. But in a republic, the criminal was a fellow citizen, and the law, as Paine put it, was "king." This suggested that criminal law should look different in a republic – but what did that mean in practice?

---

[10] Letter from James Monroe to Thomas Jefferson, July 25, 1791, in *The Papers of James Monroe*, vol. 2: *Selected Correspondence and Papers, 1776–1794*, ed. Daniel Preston and Marlena C. Delong (Westport, CT: Greenwood Press, 2003), 507–508; Cullen, "Completing the Revisal of the Laws," 93–94.

[11] Letter from James Monroe to St. George Tucker, August 18, 1791, in *Papers of James Monroe*, 2:508–509. Monroe referenced a criminal provision that was included in his assignment, which he thought was more appropriately included with Tucker's portion, suggesting that Tucker may have been, at least in part, assigned the criminal portion of the revisal.

[12] St. George Tucker, *Blackstone's Commentaries with Notes of Reference to the Constitution and Laws of the Federal Government of the United States; and of the Commonwealth of Virginia*, vol. 5 (Philadelphia: William Young Birch and Abraham Small, 1803), 13–18.

[13] For more on the benefit of clergy, see George W. Dalzell, *Benefit of Clergy in America & Related Matters* (Winston-Salem, NC: John F. Blair, 1955).

[14] Tucker, *Blackstone's Commentaries*, 5:2–4.

In 1776, Virginia's revisors of the law – particularly Thomas Jefferson – had tackled this question. Jefferson's draft bill had recommended extensive reform, but the effort failed by a single vote in the Virginia legislature.[15] Now, in the summer of 1791, the new committee of revisors took yet another look at Virginia's laws. In the meantime, the state's criminal cases, like Crane's, lumbered along, embarrassingly still governed by old laws in a new world.

In the late eighteenth century, every well-educated American knew that criminal law and punishment – that site where the power of the state met the individual most intimately – was about more than protecting victims and punishing vice. Instead, it was about the nature of the state itself.[16] John Locke had, for instance, begun his important *Second Treatise on Government* by asserting that criminal punishment was the defining aspect of political power. He explained that political power was the "right of making laws with penalties of death" and "consequently all less penalties."[17] Moreover, Locke argued, the law of nature prescribed limits on criminal punishment. Society could punish the law-breaker only to secure his repentance, to deter him from further actions, and deter others from committing the same offense. Or it could punish to repair the injury of whoever was harmed by the act. It could not punish for mere vengeance.[18]

A country's criminal law, theorists also argued, could tell you that nation's character: if it was despotic or free, whether it had a monarch, or was a republic. In his *Spirit of the Laws*, Montesquieu had argued that harsh punishments reflected despotic regimes, and were unnecessary in more moderate governments. "Despotic governments," he explained, needed to use severe punishments that afflicted the body, making death very painful, because in those societies "people are so unhappy as to have a greater dread of death than regret for the loss of life."[19] This was because "experience shows that in countries remarkable for the lenity of their laws the spirit of the inhabitants is as much affected by slight penalties as in other countries by severer punishments." Instead, "the love of one's country, shame, and fear of blame are restraining motives."[20]

[15] See Kathryn Preyer, "Crime, the Criminal Law and Reform in Post-Revolutionary Virginia," *Law and History Review* 1, no. 1 (1983): 53–85, 62; Arthur Scott, *Criminal Law in Colonial Virginia* (Chicago, IL: University of Chicago, 1930), 69.

[16] For a good discussion of criminal law in the eighteenth century, see Holly Brewer, *By Birth or Consent: Children, Law, and the Anglo-American Revolution in Authority* (Chapel Hill, NC: University of North Carolina Press for the Omohundro Institute of Early American History and Culture, 2005), 216–220.

[17] John Locke, *Second Treatise on Government* (Devon, UK: Dover Publications, 2002), 1–2.

[18] Ibid., 5.

[19] M. de Secondat, baron de Montesquieu, *The Spirit of Laws*, vol. 1 (New York, NY: George Bell & Sons, 1897), 88.

[20] Ibid., 88, 90.

Punishments, Montesquieu argued, should be proportionate and certain. First, they should be proportioned to the seriousness of the crime, protecting that "which is more precious to society rather than that which is less." It was a "great abuse," he contended, "to condemn to the same punishment a person that only robs on the highway and another who robs and murders."[21] Second, in republics, the law ruled. In despotic governments, Montesquieu reminded his reader, "the judge himself is his own rule." In monarchies, laws guided judges – "where these are explicit, the judge conforms to them; where they are otherwise, he endeavors to investigate their spirit."

But in republics, the laws were dominant and explicit: "the very nature of the constitution requires the judges to follow the letter of the law."[22] This was because the law proceeded from the people, and if the judges could extrapolate away from the law itself, it could be applied with bias. So in republics, judges had little discretion. "The nearer a government approaches a republic," Montesquieu explained, "the more the manner of judging becomes settled and fixed."[23]

Italian theorist Cesare Beccaria picked up on Montesquieu's work and liberally cited *Spirit of the Laws* in his 1764 treatise *On Crimes and Punishments*, which elaborated on ideas of proportionality and the rule of law. But Beccaria took an additional step beyond the French philosopher and condemned the death penalty altogether. Execution, he explained, was a "war of the nation against the citizen," and not within the power of the state.[24] The sovereign's ability to punish, he argued, stemmed from the social contract, and was confined to "the necessity of defending the depository of the public welfare against the usurpations of private individuals."[25] All punishments that exceeded what was necessary to preserve the bond "necessary to hold private interests together" – what men had deposited by virtue of the social contract – were for Beccaria "unjust by their very nature." Men had not, he insisted, trusted their very lives to the state.[26] Even worse, the death penalty incited compassion for the criminal: it became "an entertainment for the majority and, for a few people," made the criminal "the object of pity mixed with scorn." Rather than operating to deter crime, "these sentiments alike fill the hearts of the spectators to a greater extent than does the salutary fear that the law claims to inspire."[27]

Beccaria argued for a more lenient, but also more certain, criminal law. First, like Montesquieu, he argued that the legislature should focus on preventing the most serious crimes. Punishments should be tailored for maximum impressions

---

[21] Ibid., 97–98.

[22] Ibid., 81.

[23] Ibid.

[24] Cesare Beccaria, *On Crimes and Punishments*, trans. David Young (Indianapolis, IN: Hackett Publishing Company, 1986), 48.

[25] Ibid., 8.

[26] Ibid., 9.

[27] Ibid., 49.

on the minds of others – maximum deterrence – with least pain and harm done to the criminal.[28] Punishment should not aim to "torment and afflict a sentient being," nor could "the cries of a poor wretch turn back time and undo a crime which has already been done."[29] Instead, punishment should be "to dissuade the criminal from doing fresh harm to his compatriots and to keep other people from doing the same."[30] Beccaria argued that punishments that were definite and certain did a better job of preventing crime than severe ones did: "The certainty of chastisement, even if it be moderate, will always make a greater impression than the [uncertain] fear of a more terrible punishment."[31]

Second, Beccaria also agreed with Montesquieu that punishments should be clearly delineated and imposed according to law. After all, how could a criminal be deterred if the punishment for his crime varied widely? As with Montesquieu, reform was for Beccaria about restricting the power of the judge. Judges, Beccaria reasoned, received their laws not from ancestors but from a "living society"; it was their job to apply the law, not interpret it.[32] That interpretation belonged to the legislature; judges should "only to examine whether or not a certain man has committed an action contrary to the laws." For Beccaria, this meant that judicial reasoning was simple. "A fixed legal code that must be observed to the letter," Beccaria reasoned, "leaves the judge no other task than to examine a citizen's actions and to determine whether or not they conform to the written law."[33]

Finally, after the judge made his simple determination of whether or not the defendant had transgressed the clear, written laws of the legislature, punishment would come quickly to the guilty. Beccaria opposed pardons, believing them unnecessary – even "dangerous" – in a state with appropriately mild laws. Pardons undermined the certainly he felt necessary in order for the laws to exercise their proper deterrence. Instead, they tended to show "men that crimes may be pardoned and that punishment is not their inevitable consequence," arousing "the enticing hope of impunity," and "making people believe that, since remission is possible, sentences which go unremitted are violent acts of force rather than emanations of justice."[34] Punishment, Beccaria advised, should be "inexorable." When summarizing his theory, he posited that punishment "should be public, prompt, necessary, the minimum possible under the given circumstances, proportionate to the crimes, and established by law." He continued, "Let the laws … be inexorable … but let the lawgiver be gentle, indulgent, and humane."[35]

[28] Ibid., 23.
[29] Ibid.
[30] Ibid.
[31] Ibid., 46.
[32] Ibid., 10–11.
[33] Ibid., 11–12.
[34] Ibid., 80.
[35] Ibid., 80–81.

These ideas all seemed to push against the English legal tradition, with its extensive use of the death penalty and emphasis on the common law, judicial reasoning, and pardons. But in 1769, even Blackstone, in his *Commentaries on the Laws of England*, referenced Montesquieu and Beccaria and acknowledged the too-sanguinary nature of England's criminal punishment.[36] Although affirming that "in England ... our crown law is with justice supposed to be nearly advanced to perfection," Blackstone advised that offenses against "social" instead of "natural" rights – offenses like forgery or theft – should not be capital because the right to property owed its existence "merely to civil society." Blackstone disagreed with Beccaria that death should never be used as a penalty, but he conceded that "the enormity, or dangerous tendency, of the crime ... alone can warrant any earthly legislature in putting him to death that commits it." And like Beccaria, Blackstone agreed that the proper end of punishment was not "atonement or expiation," which must be left to the "Supreme Being," but concerned whether the punishment provided "precaution against future offenses of the same kind." This deterrence operated both on the offender himself and on those who observed his example. But he also affirmed that the amount of punishment should be proportioned to the end it was to serve and the more severe punishments "have less effect in preventing crimes than such as are more merciful in general."[37]

The contemporary situation, of course, was significantly different. In England, the long list of capital crimes – "so dreadful a list," Blackstone called it – meant that, in practice, laws went unenforced. After all, with such severe penalties, it was no wonder that "the injured, through compassion, will often forbear to prosecute: juries, through compassion, will sometimes forget their oaths, and either acquit the guilty or mitigate the nature of the offense: and judges, through compassion, will respite one-half of the convicts, and recommend them to the royal mercy." As a remedy, Blackstone cited Beccaria's "ingenious" proposal and recommended that in "every state a scale of crimes should be formed, with a corresponding scale of punishments, descending from the greatest to the least." Or, at a minimum, "not assign penalties of the first degree to offences of an inferior rank."[38]

Only seven years after Blackstone's recommendations, Virginia's revisors sat down to reconsider the Commonwealth's laws in light of American independence. For years, changes in law and government had been subject to royal review, with varying degrees of attention. Now, as the new states drafted constitutions, and created new legislatures and new courts, it seemed to many Americans that the Revolution had provided them with the kind of blank slate of which thinkers like Locke and Montesquieu and Beccaria had only dreamed.

[36] Tucker, *Blackstone's Commentaries*, 5:17–18.
[37] Ibid., 5–18.
[38] Ibid., 17–18.

Writing to George Wythe, John Adams exulted that, "You and I, dear friend, have been sent into life at a time when the greatest lawgivers of antiquity would have wished to live. How few of the human race have ever enjoyed an opportunity of making an election of government, more than of air, soil, or climate, for themselves or for their children!"[39]

Wythe was, indeed, about to become a lawgiver – he had been appointed, with Jefferson and several others, including Virginia senior statesman Edmund Pendleton, to Virginia's new committee to revise the laws.[40] Jefferson and Pendleton had been thinking about criminal law reform since almost immediately after independence. As early as August 1776, Pendleton cautiously shared his thoughts with the much-younger Jefferson:

I don't know how far you may extend your reformation as to Our Criminal System of Laws. That it has hitherto been too Sanguinary, punishing too many crimes with death, I confess, and could wish to se [sic] that changed for some other mode of Punishment in most cases, but if you mean to relax all Punishments and rely on Virtue and the Public good as Sufficient to promote Obedience to the Laws, You must find a new race of Men to be the Subjects of it.[41]

Jefferson quickly assured Pendleton that he meant no such thing, and outlined his goals for the revisal:

The fantastical idea of virtue and the public good being a sufficient security to the state against the commission of crimes, which you say you have heard insisted on by some,

---

[39] Letter from John Adams to George Wythe, printed in pamphlet form as *Thoughts on Government: Applicable to the Present State of the American Colonies* ... (Philadelphia, PA: John Dunlap, 1776), 27.

[40] The political importance of the members of the committee reflects the seriousness with which the new Virginia legislature approached the task of revising the laws. Wythe was a well-respected Williamsburg legal scholar, educator, and recent signer of the Declaration of Independence; Edmund Pendleton was a prominent lawyer, the Speaker of the Virginia House of Delegates, and would soon become Virginia's first chief justice. George Mason was a longtime public servant and author of the Virginia Declaration of Rights. Thomas Ludwell Lee was a member of the Committee of Safety (which had governed the colony after Lord Dunmore's departure), co-author of the state's initial resolution supporting a declaration of independence, and a member of the Virginia Senate. And Jefferson, the final member of the committee, had, of course, recently become the draftsman for American independence, in both his *Summary View of the Rights of British America* and the Declaration of Independence. For brief biographical sketches of Wythe and Pendleton, see Charles F. Hobson, ed., *St. George Tucker's Law Reports and Selected Papers, 1782–1825*, vol. 3 (Chapel Hill, NC: University of Nortch Carolina Press, 2013), 1839–1840, 1853–1854; for Lee, see "Thomas Ludwell Lee," *Stratford Hall*, accessed September 27, 2016, www.stratfordhall.org/meet-the-lee-family/thomas-ludwell-lee/; for Mason see Jeff Broadwater, *George Mason: Forgotten Founder* (Chapel Hill, NC: University of North Carolina Press, 2006). For Jefferson's participation in Virginia state politics during the revolutionary period, see Dumas Malone, *Jefferson and His Time: Jefferson the Virginian* (Boston, MA: Little, Brown & Co., 1948), 169–403.

[41] Letter from Edmund Pendleton to Thomas Jefferson, August 10, 1776, in *The Papers of Thomas Jefferson*, vol. 1: *1760–1776*, ed. Julian P. Boyd (Princeton, NJ: Princeton University Press, 1950), 489–490.

I assure you was never mine. It is only the sanguinary hue of our penal laws which I meant to object to. Punishments I know are necessary, and I would provide them, strict and inflexible, but proportioned to the crime ... Laws thus proportionate and mild should never be dispensed with. Let mercy be the character of the law-giver, but let the judge be a mere machine. The mercies of the law will be dispensed equally and impartially to every description of men; those of the judge, or of the executive power, will be the eccentric impulses of whimsical, capricious designing man.[42]

Jefferson clearly had been reading Beccaria. This was not a surprise; Beccaria's views had become increasingly popular across Europe, and Jefferson would continue to cite him favorably – including the principle, "Let the legislators be merciful but the executors of the law inexorable."[43] Throughout his life, Jefferson would include Beccaria on lists of necessary reading for aspiring young lawyers and students.[44]

Not only were Beccaria's ideas popular across the "enlightened" western world, but his concerns also dovetailed with the colonists' own problems with colonial justice, particularly suspicion of judicial discretion. As historian Gordon Wood has explained, at the Revolution, the colonists had a "profound fear of judicial independence and discretion." This stemmed from the experiences of the colonial period, when lay judges, irregular recording of colonial court decisions, and the intricacies and uncertainties of colonial legal systems meant that judges frequently innovated in their judicial role.[45] Legal historian Morton Horwitz has also described the revolutionary generation as suspicious of judges, arguing that their concerns fixed particularly on judicial constructions of statutes.[46] At the same time, as Wood observes, the patchwork of rules and statutes also created a strong emphasis on law's authority as derived from its reasonableness and justice, "being found in the nature and fitness of things,"

---

[42] Letter from Thomas Jefferson to Edmund Pendleton, August 26, 1776, ibid., 505.

[43] For Jefferson's comments, see "Jefferson's Observations on Dèmeunier's Manuscript," in *The Papers of Thomas Jefferson*, vol. 10: *22 June to 31 December 1786*, ed. Julian P. Boyd (Princeton, NJ: Princeton University Press, 1954), 47. Several French jurists took public stands supporting Beccaria's ideas and a German translation made his ideas popular in Germany. However, philosopher Immanuel Kant was predictably more critical, particularly of Beccaria's call to abolish the death penalty. Marcello Maestro, *Cesare Beccaria and the Origins of Penal Reform* (Philadelphia, PA: Temple University Press, 1973), 126–130.

[44] Letter from Thomas Jefferson to John Garland Jefferson, June 11, 1790, in *The Papers of Thomas Jefferson*, vol. 16: *30 November 1789 to 4 July 1790*, ed. Julian P. Boyd (Princeton, NJ: Princeton University Press, 1961), 480–482; see also "Course of Reading for Joseph C. Cabell," in *The Papers of Thomas Jefferson*, vol. 32: *June 1800 to February 1801*, ed. Barbara Oberg (Princeton, NJ: Princeton University Press, 2005), 32:179; "Course of Reading for William G. Munford," in *The Papers of Thomas Jefferson*, vol. 30: *1 January 1798 to 31 January 1799*, ed. Barbara Oberg (Princeton, NJ: Princeton University Press, 2003), 595.

[45] Gordon Wood, *The Creation of the American Republic, 1776–1787* (Chapel Hill, NC: University of North Carolina Press, 1998), 296–298.

[46] Morton Horwitz, *The Transformation of American Law, 1780–1860* (Cambridge, MA: Harvard University Press, 1977), 5.

instead of tradition.[47] In the immediate aftermath of the Revolution, this desire for reasonableness and fitness led to movement for law reform: for simple and clear statutes that could be easily put into practice, while discarding perceived relics of the English past. Adding, of course, to this turn to law reform was the fact that, in this era, the legislature – the voice of the people – tended to be the "republican" branch of government. The Revolution and formal separation from Britain offered the opportunity to make significant reforms.

What would Virginia's new law – their "republican" law – be? In January 1777, the new state's revisors of the law met to lay out parameters for their work. They listed areas in need of reform, especially land law and criminal law, and they had sweeping goals.[48] As Jefferson would later explain, they planned for the whole legal system to be "reviewed, adapted, to our republican form of government, and ... corrected in all it's [sic] parts, with a single eye to reason, and the good of those for whose government it was formed."[49]

On the criminal law bill, the revisors agreed on a few guidelines. First, as the committee had recommended, the death penalty would apply only to treason and murder, and certain types of murder – murders involving one's own household – would receive the additional, dreaded sanction of dissection of the condemned after death.[50] The new laws would treat suicide as a disease, not a crime, which also kept the deceased's goods and chattels from forfeiture.[51] The new laws would punish rape, sodomy, and bestiality with castration. Beyond that, the default punishment for most crimes would be forfeiture, fine, and labor in the public works.[52] Their reforms would abolish the benefit of clergy, and some other relics of the common law, like "corruption of blood," which prevented those convicted passing on their titles (in England) or property to their heirs.[53]

The reformers' proposals represented a real change. In general, English law had been in force in the colony. Virginia's General Assembly also made laws for the colony, which were transmitted to the Privy Council for approval but considered to be in force by default unless later disallowed. Because of the many legal sources at play, however, the details of what was in force and what was not were often, as one commenter wryly put it, "in the judge's breast" – meaning

---

[47] See Wood, *Creation of the American Republic*, 298–300.

[48] "Plan Agreed upon by the Committee of Revisors at Fredericksburg," January 13, 1777, in *The Papers of Thomas Jefferson*, vol. 2: *2 January 1777 to 18 June 1779 including the Revisal of the Laws*, ed. Julian P. Boyd (Princeton, NJ: Princeton University Press, 1950), 325–328.

[49] Quoted in Wood, *Creation of the American Republic*, 300–301.

[50] Steven Wilf, *Law's Imagined Republic: Popular Politics and Criminal Justice in Revolutionary America* (New York, NY: Cambridge University Press, 2010), 165–192.

[51] For former treatment, see Hugh F. Rankin, *Criminal Trial Proceedings in the General Court of Colonial Virginia* (Williamsburg, VA: Colonial Williamsburg, 1965), 69–70.

[52] "Plan Agreed upon by the Committee of Revisors at Fredericksburg."

[53] Ibid.

that judges got to pick and choose what would be applied.[54] In general, however, the corpus of English criminal law, including benefit of clergy and the importance of judicial and executive discretion, was in force in Virginia.[55] The revisors proposed instead a new system, more like that recommended by Beccaria and, to a lesser extent, by Blackstone.

Jefferson ultimately drafted the bill himself, and called it a Bill for Proportioning Crimes and Punishments in Cases Heretofore Capital (Table 4.1).[56] In his preamble, he gave three rationales for the bill. First, it would proportion punishments to the crime. Citizens, Jefferson wrote, echoing Locke, did not "forfiet" [sic] all of their rights upon committing a crime. Instead, the legislature's duty, he affirmed, channeling Beccaria, was to arrange crimes and punishments in a "proper scale."[57] Second, the bill aimed to reform as many convicted offenders as possible, instead of sentencing them to death, while making them useful during the term of their punishment. "[T]he reformation of offenders," Jefferson complained, "tho' an object worthy of the attention of the laws, is not effected at all by capital punishments, which exterminate instead of reforming." The death penalty could have only one justification: "the last melancholy recourse against those whose existence is become inconsistent with the safety of their fellow citizens." Instead of execution, most crimes would be punished by public labor, which offered an opportunity for reform, and made offenders useful.[58] Finally, with more moderate punishments in place, the bill aimed to secure enforcement of the law, since "cruel and sanguinary laws defeat their own purpose by engaging the benevolence of mankind to withhold prosecutions, to smother testimony, or to listen to it with bias" – and, in other cases "by producing in many instances a total dispensation and impunity under the names of pardon and privilege of clergy."[59]

Jefferson's bill laid out a long list of crimes and defined punishments, as Beccaria had recommended. Now, only murder and treason would be capital. As the committee had recommended, murder of one's own master, husband, wife, parents, or children would be punished by hanging and then anatomization. Murder by poison would be punished with death by poison. Duelers who killed their foe would be executed then, if the challenger, gibbeted. Gibbeting in Virginia seems to have previously been reserved primarily for lawbreaking slaves, so decreeing that a challenging member of the gentry should be gibbeted

---

[54] Quotation in Scott, *Criminal Law in Colonial Virginia*, 29. A popular medieval saying was that the King carried the laws "in his breast." See Ernst H. Kantorowicz, *The King's Two Bodies: A Study of Mediaeval Political Theology* (Princeton, NJ: Princeton University Press, 1957), 28.

[55] Preyer, "Crime, the Criminal Law and Reform," 14–17. See also Brewer, *By Birth or Consent*, 204–205.

[56] "A Bill for Proportioning Crimes and Punishments in Cases Heretofore Capital," in *Papers of Thomas Jefferson*, 2:492–504.

[57] Ibid., 492.

[58] Ibid., 493.

[59] Ibid., n. 3 (for expanded preamble text from alternate draft).

TABLE 4.1 *Selected Punishments from the Bill for Proportioning Crimes and Punishments*

CRIME	PUNISHMENT
Treason (limited to: levying war against the Commonwealth, being adherent to the enemies of the Commonwealth, giving aid or comfort to the enemies of the Commonwealth. Must be convicted of open deed by evidence of two sufficient witnesses or own voluntary confession)	Hanging Forfeiture of land and goods to Commonwealth
Murders of the Household (servant murdering master, husband murdering wife, wife murdering husband, parent murdering child, child murdering parent)	Hanging Forfeiture of one half land and goods to the victim's next of kin; other half to go to defendant's heirs. Body to be delivered to anatomists
Murder by Duel	Hanging Forfeiture of one half land and goods to the victim's next of kin, unless the victim was the challenger, in which case land and goods go to the Commonwealth. If defendant was the challenger, body is gibbeted.
Murder, other	Hanging Forfeiture of one half land and goods to the victim's next of kin; other half to go to defendant's heirs.
Murder by Poison	Death by poisoning Forfeiture of one half land and goods to the victim's next of kin; other half to go to defendant's heirs.
Rape, Polygamy, Sodomy	If man, castration. If woman, hole to be bored in her nose of ½ inch diameter.
Maiming and Disfiguring ("whoever on purpose shall disfigure another, by cutting out or disabling the tongue, slitting or cutting off a nose, lip, or ear, branding, or otherwise …")	Defendant to be maimed in same way as victim was, or a near as possible in estimation of the jury. Forfeiture of one half land and goods to the victim.
Manslaughter	First offense: seven years' hard labor in the public works.

(continued)

TABLE 4.1 (*cont.*)

CRIME	PUNISHMENT
	Forfeiture of one half land and goods to the victim's next of kin; other half be sequestered during defendant's labor sentence, with reasonable part of the profits to the support of his family.
	Second offense: to be treated as murder.
Involuntary homicide arising from trespass or larceny or other "unlawful deed"	No transferred intent: not manslaughter unless manslaughter was intended, or murder unless murder was intended.
Robbery and Burglary	Four years' hard labor in the public works. Restitution to victim of two times the amount taken.
Housebreaking	Three years' hard labor in the public works. Restitution to victim of amount taken.
Horse-stealing	Three years' hard labor in public works. Restitution to victim of amount taken.
Grand Larceny (Goods stolen are greater than or equal to $5)	One half hour in pillory. Two years' hard labor in public works. Restitution of amount taken.
Petty Larceny (Goods stolen are less than $5)	One quarter hour in pillory. One years' hard labor in public works. Restitution of amount taken.
Counterfeiting (Included counterfeiting or knowingly passing counterfeited goods or paper)	Six years' hard labor in public works. Forfeiture of all land and goods to Commonwealth.
Arson	Five years' hard labor in public works. Restitution to victim of three times amount of damage.

made a strong statement.[60] Crimes that had formerly qualified for the benefit of clergy, like manslaughter, would receive actual punishment. Indeed, under the proposed bill, manslaughter would be punished more severely than property crimes like horse-stealing which, under current law, were capital crimes: manslaughter would bring seven years' hard labor, but horse-stealing only three. Other formerly capital crimes would now be punished with hard labor.[61]

The bill also guaranteed that execution would happen shortly after conviction – the "next day but one," as the bill put it – and there would be no

---

[60] See Scott, *Criminal Law in Colonial Virginia*, 196–197; Taylor, *The Internal Enemy*, 25.
[61] "A Bill for Proportioning Crimes and Punishments," 493–502.

pardons.[62] Beccaria had argued that punishment should be carried out swiftly, shortly after conviction, in order to create maximum certainty that the law would be enforced. Jefferson's bill followed suit. But Beccaria had wanted to eliminate the death penalty, which meant that Jefferson effectively upped the ante, decreeing that *execution* would be carried out swiftly, two days after the court pronounced sentence, unless that day was Sunday.[63] This was a far cry from the colonial practice, which set execution not less than ten days after conviction, and sometimes included long waits requesting pardon.[64]

In many ways, the bill was the masterpiece of Jefferson's revisal.[65] Beautifully and carefully drafted, it drew from Beccaria, but it also put the full range of Jefferson's learning on display. In his annotations, Jefferson explained how the bill also set out to reinstate ancient punishments, from an earlier, Anglo-Saxon time, which he and others saw as friendlier to freedom and self-government. Jefferson covered his notes with citations in Anglo Saxon; those currents appeared in the bill's text itself, particularly in the forfeiture and restitution provisions. In these, the bill redirected the remedy towards compensating the victim, instead of enriching the state. It also endeavored to provide for the convict's family and to preserve his property, even as it punished. At the same time, in the bill's simple format Jefferson sought to demonstrate what statutes could (and should) look like. As he told George Wythe, "In its style I have aimed at accuracy, brevity and simplicity ... Indeed I wished to exhibit a sample of reformation in the barbarous style into which modern statutes have degenerated from their antient [sic] simplicity."[66]

The bill also made an explicit statement about the values that would govern the new republic: law and reason, not extralegal violence. Not only did the bill brand dueling as especially odious, but it also sought to address maiming and disfiguring fights like the "rough and tumble" brawls of the Virginia backcountry. These would be punished by the convicted losing, as near as possible, the same body part he had caused to be mutilated in the victim: literally, an eye for an eye. This was known as the *lex talionis* (law of retaliation), and Blackstone had described this principle as problematic.[67] In his November 1, 1778, introductory letter to George Wythe, enclosed with a draft copy of the bill, Jefferson noted, "I have strictly observed the scale of punishments set by the committee without being entirely satisfied with it." Particularly concerning, he thought, was the "Lex Talionis, although a restitution of the Common

[62] Ibid., 503.

[63] Ibid., 497. If the day was on Sunday, the execution would be moved to the next day, Monday.

[64] See Rankin, *Criminal Trial Proceedings*, 114.

[65] For more discussion, see the editorial note to the bill, in "A Bill for Proportioning Crimes and Punishments," 492–504.

[66] Letter from Thomas Jefferson to George Wythe, November 1, 1778, in *Papers of Thomas Jefferson*, 2:229–230.

[67] Tucker, *Blackstone's Commentaries*, 5:12–13.

law ... [which] will be revolting to the humanized feelings of modern times." He added, "this needs reconsideration."[68] Recalling the bill in his autobiography, he wrote, "How this ... revolting principle came to obtain our approbation, I do not remember."[69]

Ultimately the bill met a narrow defeat. First, the General Assembly tabled the revisal package until after the war. Then, in 1785, Jefferson's friend James Madison took up the effort but quickly discovered that not all members of the General Assembly eagerly embraced Jefferson's proposed system. The bill had been, he wrote to James Monroe in December 1785, "assaile[d] on all sides. Mr. Mercer has proclaim'd unceasing hostility against it." But Madison remained optimistic. He reported to Monroe that "some alterations have been made, and others probably will be made, but I think the main principle of it will finally triumph over all opposition."[70] In particular, the provisions of the bill related to maiming – the part that Jefferson had already considered problematic – had been removed, and replaced with hard labor in the public works.[71] But by January 1786, progress had again stalled. Madison wrote to Jefferson, then in Paris serving as Minister to France, that the session had proceeded "slowly but successfully," until it hit the "bill concerning crimes and punishments." Here "the adversaries of the code exerted their whole force," and the "work was postponed till the next Session."[72]

In that next session, the bill again faced steep opposition. The "bill proportioning crimes and punishments, on which we were wrecked last year," Madison reported to Jefferson in December 1786, "has after undergoing a number of alterations got thro' a Committee of the Whole," but he expected a "vigorous attack" on the floor of the House.[73] On November 30, 1786, Madison reported to Edmund Pendleton that, "the Criminal bill on which we were wrecked formerly has been shunned till yesterday. It will receive its doom tomorrow, in a

[68] Letter from Thomas Jefferson to George Wythe, November 1, 1778, in *Papers of Thomas Jefferson*, 2:229–230.

[69] Thomas Jefferson, "The Autobiography," in *Thomas Jefferson: Writings*, ed. Merrill D. Peterson (New York, NY: Library of America, 1984), 39.

[70] Letter from James Madison to James Monroe, December 9, 1785, in *The Papers of James Madison*, vol. 8: *10 March 1784–28 March 1786*, ed. Robert A. Rutland, William Munford, and Ellis Rachal (Chicago, IL: University of Chicago Press, 1973), 437.

[71] "Amendments to a Bill for Proportioning Crimes and Punishments" [*c.* 10 December 1785], in *The Papers of James Madison*, vol. 17: *31 March 1797–3 March 1801*, ed. David B. Mattern, J. C. A. Stagg, Jeanne K. Cross, and Susan Holbrook Perdue (Charlottesville, VA: University of Virginia Press, 1991), 510–511.

[72] Letter from James Madison to Thomas Jefferson, January 22, 1786, in *The Papers of Thomas Jefferson*, vol. 9: *1 November 1785 to 22 June 1786*, ed. Julian P. Boyd (Princeton, NJ: Princeton University Press, 1954), 195.

[73] Letter from James Madison to Thomas Jefferson, December 4, 1786 in *The Papers of Thomas Jefferson*, vol. 10: *22 June to 31 December 1786*, ed. Julian P. Boyd (Princeton, NJ: Princeton University Press, 1954), 575.

form somewhat different from that in which it stands in the Code."[74] Part of the negotiations on the bill had involved amending the bill's contents, what Madison referred to as its "objectionable peculiarities." But even after it had been "purged" of those, Madison reported to George Washington that the bill had been "thrown out on the third reading by a single vote."[75]

What had been the problem? In trying to explain the defeat to Jefferson, Madison confided his suspicion that the "rage against Horse stealers had a great influence on the fate of the Bill."[76] The bill prescribed merely three years' hard labor, but current Virginia law punished horse-stealing with the death penalty – a big reduction. And not only had the bill been defeated, but the legislature had also declined to reauthorize the conditional pardon. Since 1776, Virginia's governors had been using conditional pardons to commute some death sentences to hard labor, but the Act authorizing them had expired and the General Assembly had declined to reauthorize them. This led Jefferson to interpret the General Assembly's rejection of the Bill for Proportioning Crimes and Punishments broadly, as reflecting a much deeper opposition; "the general idea of our country had not yet advanced," he later explained in his autobiography, to the point of accepting Beccaria's rejection of the death penalty.[77] Madison himself would later have mixed feelings about the bill, recalling that "the Revisors were unfortunately misled into some of the specious errors of Beccaria, then in the Zenith of his form as a philosophical Legislator."[78]

In any case, with the Bill for Proportioning Crimes and Punishments defeated and the conditional pardon gone, reform stalled. As Madison lamented to Jefferson in 1787, "our old bloody code is by this event fully restored." But he confided, "I am not without hope that the rejected bill will find a more favorable disposition in the next General Assembly."[79]

By 1791, however, as St. George Tucker contemplated the next stage of the revisal, the bill's failure did not seem like such a bad thing. It was, Tucker told his students, good that the bill had failed to pass – not because the judge loved the bloody code, but because the bill had sought to eliminate pardons. The revisors had, he explained to his students, "proposed to abolish the power of pardoning, in all Cases, and generally, to mitigate & apportion punishments according

---

74 Letter from James Madison to Edmund Pendleton, November 30, 1786, in *The Papers of James Madison*, vol. 9: *9 April 1786–24 May 1787 and supplement 1781–1784*, ed. Robert A. Rutland and William M. E. Rachal (Chicago, IL: University of Chicago Press, 1975), 185–187.
75 Letter from James Madison to George Washington, Richmond, December 24, 1786, in *Papers of James Madison*, 9:225.
76 Letter from James Madison to Thomas Jefferson, February 15, 1787, *The Papers of Thomas Jefferson*, vol. 11: *1 January to 6 August 1787*, ed. Robert A. Rutland and William M. E. Rachal (Princeton, NJ: Princeton University Press, 1955), 152.
77 Jefferson, "Autobiography," 40–41.
78 Editorial Note in "Bills for a Revised State Code of Laws," in *Papers of James Madison*, 8:391–399.
79 Letter from James Madison to Thomas Jefferson, February 15, 1787, 152–155.

to the nature of the Crime." Tucker admitted that he himself did not know "on what principle the bill was rejected, but I have presumed that the Legislature thought it safer to entrust the power of pardon in a single magistrate, than to transfer it, in effect, to Juries."[80]

The bill, of course, had not explicitly given juries the power to pardon. But Tucker meant that it would have worked out that way in practice. After all, he explained, if a jury knew that their verdict against a criminal would be final – that there would be no appeal for a pardon based on factors that might not be taken account of in the law, but which would have moved for clemency – then the jury itself would be likely to take those factors into account. Juries' "lenity might too often interest them in Cases," he explained, "where their Verdict against a Criminal must be final, & endure inevitable punishment, whatever circumstances in mitigation of the guilt of the offender should appear."[81] In this case, jurors would step outside the law to consider other factors – the type of factors which would have previously been considered by the executive when granting pardon. In other words, the jurors would have been "transformed into a kind of criminal Court of Equity; they would no longer have been triers of fact," but would have rendered a decision based on what they thought the outcome should be. In that case, acquittals would also lose their meaning. They would no longer be evidence of innocence or even afforded a "presumption of innocence of the person accused," but would have merely indicated what the jury thought the outcome should be, not what they thought of the actual facts of the case that were relevant to the defendant's conviction.[82] Tucker concluded that in a regime like this only guilty defendants would have benefited by the law, "which in time would have totally corrupted the Foundations of Justice."[83] "I am therefore inclined to believe it was a happiness for the State," he concluded, "that the Bill not take effect."[84]

But Tucker also found a further lesson in the bill's demise. "The power of pardon," he told his students, "seems, then to be necessary, to be entrusted somewhere, so long as the frailties of human nature continue to subject us to the influence of momentary passion, of misguided zeal, or other causes impelling us to Error."[85] So long as there were flawed people who could be overwhelmed by their passions, there would be a need for pardon – a need for taking into account factors that did not accord strictly with the law.

This was, indeed, different from the view which had undergirded Jefferson's bill. Jefferson (and Beccaria) had desired strict penalties, which were guaranteed to be enforced, in hopes that such certainty of punishment would deter potential criminals. They had wanted those extraneous factors previously considered

---

[80] St. George Tucker, "Ten Notebooks of Law Lectures," Notebook 5:179, Tucker-Coleman Papers.
[81] Ibid.
[82] Ibid., 179–180.
[83] Ibid.
[84] Ibid.
[85] Ibid., 180.

in pardons to be eliminated, in favor of uniformity. The first Virginia revisors had also worried that harsh laws tended to make people not want to see the laws enforced.

But Tucker concluded that their proposals were naive, and too rigid. Perceived harshness, Tucker suggested, was not just about the punishment itself, but also about the particular offender; about how well the punishment fit the person as well as the crime. And, the judge pragmatically concluded, mitigating factors would always be considered somewhere, whether or not they were officially allowed.

Tucker's opinion on pardons embodied the shift in ideas that embroiled Virginia law in the late eighteenth century. The revolutionary moment – the moment of Jefferson's Bill for Proportioning Crimes and Punishments – had been a moment of broad statements and big principles. But, as Virginians were discovering, sometimes things that looked or sounded good did not work out so well in real life. For instance, Jefferson's bills abolishing primogeniture and entail had been enacted despite the General Assembly rejecting his changes to the criminal code. But they had, in the views of some, caused a mess.[86] These two doctrines had structured land law in colonial Virginia and had been a chief target of Jefferson's work on the 1776 revisal.[87] He proposed abolishing entail and his measure passed the General Assembly on October 14, 1776; three years later, Jefferson drafted another bill replacing primogeniture with partible inheritance in equal shares to children of a decedent, which passed in 1785.[88] The idea behind Jefferson's land reforms was, as he put it, to "prevent the accumulation and perpetuation of wealth in select families," thus eradicating "every fibre" of "antient [sic] or future aristocracy" so that a "foundation" would be laid for "government truly republican."[89]

But over ensuing years, Virginia's lawyers and judges complained that Virginia's new land law was poorly drafted and caused more problems than it fixed. As Edmund Randolph – recent Virginia Governor, a representative to the Constitutional Convention, and the new US Attorney General – remarked to James Madison in 1789, "the law of descents is in practice often found to be most unrighteous and difficult of execution. Nay I might say, that it is almost

---

[86] Just as theorists and Virginia reformers linked the bloody criminal law with outdated, monarchical government, they also linked primogeniture and entail with feudalism, which was also detested in republican Virginia. These two doctrines functioned as restraints on land alienation, meaning that future generations would not be free to dispose of the land as they wished. The details of land law could be complicated and entails could sometimes be altered by the General Assembly. See Holly Brewer, "Entailing Aristocracy in Colonial Virginia: 'Ancient Feudal Restraints' and Revolutionary Reform," *William and Mary Quarterly*, 3rd Series, 44 no. 2 (1997): 307–346, 313–315.

[87] Ibid.

[88] See Stanley N. Katz, "Republicanism and the Law of Inheritance in the American Revolutionary Era," *Michigan Law Review* 76, no. 1 (1977): 1–29, 12–13.

[89] Ibid., 15.

contradictory sometimes."[90] Part of the problem was that many centuries of doctrine had grown up around English land law, but Jefferson's reform statutes were new so there was no case law interpreting their words or explicating their meaning.[91] "To tell the truth," Randolph confided to Madison, "I absolutely fear, that the new language, which these laws contain, is far, very far, from being fixed by adjudications. This is acknowledged by some of the revisors themselves, that the law of descents must be considerably changed." And, Randolph continued, the concerns did not stop there. "None of them," he added, again referring to the revisors, "can explain the Act, intended to determine who shall be mulattos" – another of Jefferson's creations –"which makes a man more of a mulatto, in proportion as he is more a negro."[92] Indeed, Randolph admitted, some of the new laws were, he felt, "productive of very little benefit, if not of real harm in many instances."[93] But the 1776 revisors had refused his requests to help on these new changes. Finally, the General Assembly had appointed the new, 1791 committee, the one which included Judge Tucker.[94]

By 1791, ideas about what law should look like under the new, independent, "republican" government – the "Govt of the People" as Tucker put it – were changing. Montesquieu had written that republics were governed by the rule of law, and their judges followed the letter of the law, not ancient precedents or its spirit.[95] In many ways, Jefferson's first revisal proposals had been along those lines. But fifteen years of experience now suggested the need for other options.

So in 1791, John Crane found himself caught up in a criminal law about which people hotly disagreed. Over the next few months, that maze of law would itself come to symbolize for Crane, in the best enlightenment sense, the turmoil of postrevolutionary Virginia.

[90] Letter from Edmund Randolph to James Madison, May 19, 1789, *The Papers of James Madison*, vol. 12: *2 March 1789–20 January 1790 and Supplement 24 October 1775–24 January 1789*, ed. Charles F. Hobson and Robert A. Rutland (Charlottesville, VA: University Press of Virginia, 1979), 168.
[91] See Cullen, "Completing the Revisal of the Laws," 86.
[92] Letter from Edmund Randolph to James Madison, March 27, 1789, in *Papers of James Madison*, 12:32.
[93] Letter from Edmund Randolph to James Madison, May 19, 1789, 168.
[94] See Cullen, "Completing the Revisal of the Laws," 86–88.
[95] Montesquieu, *The Spirit of Laws*, 81, 90.

5

Indictment

Power Shifts and Power Continuities in Virginia's Courts

Tucker arrived in Winchester in time for the first day of court on September 1, 1791. Normally he would have been accompanied by a second judge – two General Court judges typically presided at Virginia's district courts and Judge Henry Tazewell had also been assigned to the circuit. But Tazewell was "sick & unable to attend," so Tucker presided alone.[1]

As he settled in for court, Tucker had been on the road for weeks and still had much travel ahead of him. But despite the difficulty of the journey, he thought highly of Winchester. Tucker had presided over three of the new Winchester Court's seven sessions, more than any other judge, and had become familiar with the area.[2] Only ten years later, in 1801, he would advise his son, newly minted lawyer Henry St. George Tucker, to set up his practice there. The senior Tucker was especially impressed with some of the Winchester lawyers, including Robert White, who would be appointed a General Court judge in 1793. Additionally, Winchester offered growing trade and commercial activity, unlike the stagnant Tidewater. Tucker thought that Winchester would be Virginia's future, particularly for a hard-working young lawyer.[3]

---

[1] See Tucker's notes for September 1, 1791, in Charles F. Hobson, ed., *St. George Tucker's Law Reports and Selected Papers, 1782–1825*, vol. 1 (Chapel Hill, NC: University of North Carolina Press, 2013), 247.

[2] The district courts' first sessions were in the spring of 1789. The first surviving records for the Winchester District Court are from the fall 1789 session. For more on court reform, see Charles T. Cullen, *St. George Tucker and Law in Virginia, 1772–1804* (New York, NY: Garland Publishing, 1987), 71–95.

[3] On White, see Hobson, *St. George Tucker's Law Reports*, 3:1851; for Tucker's advice to Henry St. George Tucker, see Phillip Hamilton, *The Making and Unmaking of a Revolutionary Family: The Tuckers of Virginia, 1752–1830* (Charlottesville, VA: University of Virginia Press, 2003), 108–113.

Though there were plenty of civil cases waiting, Tucker first assembled the grand jury, which always gathered on the first day of court. This session, the grand jury only had one item of business to attend to: *Commonwealth v. John Crane*.

It was hardly the first time that the Winchester District Court had faced a capital case. In fact, since its first session in 1789, Winchester grand juries had not only heard various charges of horse-stealing (a common capital crime), but had also considered at least two other murder cases.[4] In the April 1790 term, Berkeley laborer Arthur Gordon had been charged with murder, but had not been indicted.[5] The county court had exonerated his co-defendant, so likely the evidence against Gordon was weak, too.[6] Then, the following fall, in the September 1790 term, Dr. James Medlicott, a "doctor of medicine or practitioner of Physick," was indicted for and found guilty of the murder of William Hefferman.[7]

Medlicott's case was, in many ways, like Crane's: a sensational case that filled the national papers and began with a fight. Newspapers reported that Hefferman was "a man of a troublesome character, and had made frequent attempts to murder his wife."[8] On a previous occasion, she had fled to Medlicott for refuge; an angry Hefferman had broken into Medlicott's home. Medlicott admitted that he told Hefferman, in the presence of witnesses, that "if he came to my house again, I would kill him."[9] On the night of Hefferman's death, Mrs. Hefferman had again fled to Medlicott's home seeking protection. Medlicott refused her and she went elsewhere, but Hefferman still sought her there. "In endeavoring to drive him off," Medlicott later admitted, "I unhappily gave the blow productive of such melancholy circumstances," although he insisted he bore no malice towards his victim.[10] A petition signed by a "large number of the inhabitants of Frederick and adjoining areas" seeking Medlicott's pardon had explained that he was "exceedingly provoked with abusive epithets, and struck with a heavy cudgel" by Hefferman. But despite the outstanding circumstances, Medlicott had been hanged.[11] If a Winchester jury would convict Medlicott of murder, things did not bode well for Crane, either.

---

[4] Others had been indicted for crimes ranging from horse-stealing to forgery to grand larceny to assault. Records for the first Winchester court session no longer exist.

[5] "April 16, 1790," Winchester District Court Order Book, Library of Virginia.

[6] "January 2, 1790," Berkeley County Court Minute Book, BCHS.

[7] "September 2" and "September 3, 1790," Winchester District Court Order Book.

[8] "Winchester, July 28." *New York Packet* (New York City, NY), August 12, 1790.

[9] "A Brief Account of the Life of Doctor James Medlicot ... To which is added A Declaration, published at his own particular request," *Salem Gazette* (Salem, MA), January 25, 1791.

[10] Ibid.

[11] Medlicott, of course, had interfered with the relationship between a man and his wife, which made his crime in some ways a little less sympathetic than it might appear to modern eyes. On the other hand, he had also been defending his home. Crane, however, had pulled out a knife during a fight. Both, it would emerge during Crane's case, had made prior threats. For more on Medlicott, see "September 20, 1790," *Calendar of Virginia State Papers and Other Manuscripts*, vol. 5: *From July 2, 1789 to August 10, 1792*, ed. William P. Palmer and Sherwin

Plus, Winchester's grand juries tended to indict. Of the seventeen cases presented since the spring 1790 term, with crimes including murder, horse-stealing, forgery, grand larceny, assault, and buggery, Winchester's grand juries had indicted all but four.[12] So as John Crane prepared for court, he knew that, most likely, he would stand trial.

In 1791, the Winchester District Court was still a new court. Before 1789, all felonies had been tried at the General Court in the capital.[13] But for the past ten years, the General Court – which had exclusive jurisdiction over felonies, and functioned as the primary court for many suits at law – had been getting slower, less efficient, and behind in its docket. In 1789, the General Assembly acted to change this by establishing district courts throughout the state, staffed by the General Court judges riding circuit.[14] These new courts were supposed to make justice swifter, more efficient, and more convenient. They also had their critics – some claimed that they took power from the local justices of the peace, and put it into state hands, centralizing Virginia's legal system and squashing local power.[15]

McRae (Richmond, VA: Virginia State Library, 1885), 209; *Journals of the Council of the State of Virginia*, vol. 5, ed. Sandra Gioia Treadway (Richmond, VA: The Virginia State Library, 1982), 212.

[12] The buggery charge was among the four. The records for the first days of the fall 1789 session are missing. In the April 1790 term: Solomon Watson and James Ridley were indicted for horse-stealing; James McIlhaney was indicted for forgery, as was John Brown; Benjamin Bussell was accused of grand larceny but not indicted; and Arthur Gordon, accused of murder, was also not indicted. In September 1790: John Manning, labourer, was indicted for grand larceny, James Medlicott was indicted for murder, John Alfin and Matt Wright were indicted for burglary and felony, John Brown was indicted for perjury, James McIlhaney was indicted for a misdemeanor, James Blue was indicted for assault and battery committed upon Alexander Rogers, and John Laches was indicted for an assault committed upon Dennis Deerfield. During the April 1791 court, James Price was accused of grand larceny but not indicted; Pumrick George was accused of buggery but not indicted. All records from the Winchester District Court Order Book. The grand jury records for the spring and fall 1789 terms do not survive.

[13] In name, the General Court was Virginia's oldest court: during the colonial era, when the Governor's Council had assembled to hear cases (including felonies), they had been called the General Court, and had been the sole state court; all other business had been handled in Virginia's county courts by lay justices of the peace. The Virginia constitution of 1776 had eliminated the old General Court and instead created state courts of both law and equity, all with professional judges. It named one of these new courts the "General Court," although the new General Court no longer heard equity cases, only felonies and cases on the law side, including appeals from the county courts. William Waller Hening, *The Statutes at Large* ..., vol. 9 (Richmond, VA: George Cochran, 1823), 474. On court reform, see Cullen, *St. George Tucker and Law in Virginia*, 71–94.

[14] This was a revised version of an earlier proposal, made after the previous proposal encountered a number of objections. See Cullen, *St. George Tucker and Law in Virginia*, 72–82.

[15] A. G. Roeber, *Faithful Magistrates and Republican Lawyers: Creators of Virginia Legal Culture, 1680–1810* (Chapel Hill, NC: University of North Carolina Press, 1981), 192–202.

But for defendants like Crane, the new courts had the opposite effect. In the old days, the grand jury would have been drawn from wealthy men gathered at the state capital for the General Court's session – maybe local, maybe there on business.[16] Now, Crane's grand jury would be filled with local, prominent men drawn from the district, especially from Winchester and Berkeley. This meant that as the grand jury gathered on September 1, they looked, in many ways, like a combined panel of the old justices of the peace who had ruled those counties in the years before the Revolution – powerful, well-connected, wealthy landowners. The district court may have taken the focus away from the county courts, but it had also put much power right back into the hands of the very families and types of elites who dominated the county courts – including those who had held sway before the Revolution.

Would this new, more local venue be to Crane's advantage, or not? In September 1791, the Crane family probably wondered the same thing.

After Tucker called the court to order, he summoned the grand jury. To many bystanders, this would have reminded them of the assembling of the justices of the peace – in fact, the grand jurors were many of the same powerful men, this time in a different role.[17] And together, they reflected and embodied the messy, conflicted history of the Valley.

First there was the grand jury foreman, General Daniel Morgan. Morgan, aged about fifty-six in 1791, would have also been the grand jury's most imposing member. Like many Valley men, Morgan had moved to western Virginia via Pennsylvania and the Great Wagon Road, arriving in the area during the winter of 1752/3. He first worked as a farm hand, then switched to wagon-driving; within a year, Morgan had purchased his own team and gone into business for himself.[18] Soon afterward, the British government dispatched Major General Edward Braddock to lead an assault on the French Fort Duquesne; in 1755, Braddock arrived with British Regulars and also drew heavily from Virginia's men to fill out his ranks.[19] In addition, the army recruited wagon-drivers to haul supplies to the main force at Fort Cumberland, on treacherous roads to the north; Morgan and other drivers hauled supplies to the fort, where Braddock impressed them into further service. As discontent grew, the Valley's impressed wagon-drivers became, in the words of Morgan's biographer, a "troublesome group."[20] Amid this frustration, Morgan got into a fight with a British officer, and a court martial ordered Morgan to receive hundreds of lashes. According

[16] Rankin, *Criminal Trial Proceedings*, 81.
[17] "September 1, 1791," Winchester District Court Order Book.
[18] Don Higginbotham, *Daniel Morgan: Revolutionary Rifleman* (Chapel Hill, NC: University of North Carolina Press, 1961), 1–15. Higginbotham estimates Morgan's birth year as 1735.
[19] Harry M. Ward, *Major General Adam Stephen and the Cause of Liberty* (Charlottesville, VA: University of Virginia Press, 1988), 15–16.
[20] Higginbotham, *Daniel Morgan: Revolutionary Rifleman*, 4.

to his biographer, "before the ordeal ended, his back was bathed in blood and his flesh hung down in ribbons."[21]

But Morgan's experience did not alienate him from military life entirely, only from the British. Back home after Braddock's disastrous expedition, he joined the county militia, eventually serving as an officer. When the American Revolution came, Morgan led one of the two companies of Valley sharp-shooters sent by Virginia to Cambridge, Massachusetts to reinforce the new Continental Army.[22] He rose through the ranks, and by the end of the war, Morgan was a national hero.[23] Morgan returned to the Valley after the war, but was not fully retired. Only a few months after *Commonwealth v. Crane*, Washington would appoint him a commander in the army sent to confront the Whiskey Rebellion. In fact, the same Berkeley County newspaper that con-tained the news of Vanhorn's death also contained a long description of the new excise tax on liquor.[24] And Morgan had not given up his fighting ways. When, during the Whiskey Rebellion, a tavern keeper overcharged his men, Morgan personally "broke his mouth."[25]

But if Morgan rose to military, political, and social prominence, and became (in his own way) a conservative, perhaps due to his "habit of command," he never forgot his first encounter with British power.[26] For the rest of his life he would tell the tale of his whipping on Braddock's expedition, and boast that the soldier who administered the beating had miscounted – the British still owed him one lash.[27] What had begun as punishment became, in Morgan's tell-ing, yet another story of British incompetence and American victory.

Morgan was the grand jury's foreman, but his fellow grand jurymen were – like the lower Valley itself – a conglomeration of opposites. As he sat on Crane's grand jury in 1791, Morgan carried the thirty-year-old scars of British lashes, but another member of the grand jury, John Wormeley, was a former British officer and from a family of "unrepentant Tories."[28] Wormeley was the young-est son of Ralph Wormeley IV, the wealthy Middlesex planter who had been named one of Berkeley's first justices of the peace.[29] With ancestors who had been early members of the colonial Virginia Council, the Wormeleys had deep

[21] Ibid., 4–5.

[22] Ibid., 16–26.

[23] Ibid., 135–155.

[24] "Shepherd's-Town July 11," *The Potowmac Guardian and Berkeley Advertiser*, July 11, 1791.

[25] David Hackett Fischer, *The Revolution in American Conservatism: The Federalist Party in the Era of Jeffersonian Democracy* (New York, NY: Harper and Row, 1965), 375–376.

[26] The "habit of command" explanation is from ibid., 376.

[27] Higginbotham, *Daniel Morgan: Revolutionary Rifleman*, 4–5.

[28] Roeber, *Faithful Magistrates*, 199.

[29] *The Recollections of Ralph Randolph Wormeley, Written Down by His Three Daughters*, ed. Katharine Prescott Wormeley, Elizabeth Wormeley Latimer, and Ariana Wormeley Curtis (New York, NY: Privately Printed, 1879), 11–12. The senior Wormeley's relationship to the Berkeley County Court is discussed in Chapter 3, supra.

FIGURE 5.1 Daniel Morgan, by Charles Wilson Peale, *c.* 1794–1797

British connections and loyalties. Ralph Wormeley V, the eldest of John's brothers, had – like all the eldest Wormeley sons before him – attended Eton and
Oxford, where he became close friends with leading members of the English
upper class; John himself had been sent to Scotland at the age of eight to

learn the mercantile trade.[30] When the Revolution came, Ralph, John, and their middle brother James all became prominent Loyalists. Ralph offered aid to Virginia's exiled royal governor, and the Virginia Committee of Safety banished him to the family's Berkeley lands. James fled to England with other Loyalist Virginians, serving in the "King's Body-Guard," as his grandson recalled.[31] And John, then sixteen, returned from Scotland to New York, and joined the British Army, serving primarily as a captain.

Thanks to his service in the British Army, John Wormeley became a Virginia pariah. Virginia's military authorities forbade him to travel in the state even to visit his family, though enforcement of this order was spotty. In 1783, after much controversy, the Virginia legislature finally readmitted Wormeley to citizenship, but banned him from holding office for four years. By then the family's fortunes had been ravished by war, and John Wormeley retreated to his family's Frederick County lands.[32] It gives a sense of the family's outlook that, when John's brother James moved to England permanently, he met with financial distress but refused offers of employment; according to a descendant, he insisted that he "had never had anything to do with commerce," and "did not think such employment becoming a member of his family."[33]

But, at the Winchester District Court, British officer John Wormeley, a Loyalist whose patrician family had been brought low by the war, and the rough, backwoods Daniel Morgan, made a hero by his service for the Continental Army, sat side by side. It was a fitting illustration of the changes that the Revolution had wrought in Virginia. As historian Alan Taylor has described, many of "Virginia's leading Patriots" – like Jefferson, Madison, and others – "owned large plantations, but they did not belong to the oldest, richest and most prestigious families who had dominated Virginia during the colonial era" – families like the Wormeleys and Catherine Crane's Robinsons. With a few exceptions, "the leading Patriots held relatively recent fortunes" thanks to "their own commercial exertions and favorable marriages or to inheritance from their fathers rather than their grandfathers."[34] Moreover, patriots like Daniel Morgan marked even another rung on this new, revolutionary power ladder – men who had truly come from nothing, but risen to power thanks to courageous and successful military service.

---

[30] Ibid.; also Gregory Harkcom Stover, "Politics and Personal Life in the Era of Revolution: The Treatment an Reintegration of Elite Loyalists in Post-Revolutionary Virginia" (Master's thesis, Virginia Commonwealth University, 2006), 42–50. According to Ralph Randolph Wormeley, while at Oxford Ralph Wormeley V even sat for a portrait by Sir Joshua Reynolds with Eton friends Charles James Fox, future Foreign Secretary, and Frederick Howard, Fifth Earl of Carlisle.

[31] Stover, "Politics and Personal Life," 43; *Recollections of Ralph Randolph Wormeley*, 15.

[32] Stover, "Politics and Personal Life," 43–48.

[33] *Recollections of Ralph Randolph Wormeley*, 10–15.

[34] Alan Taylor, *The Internal Enemy: Slavery and War in Virginia 1772–1832* (New York, NY: W. W. Norton, 2013), 29.

But despite all their differences, Wormeley and Morgan also had something in common. They had both served on at least one Frederick County Court jury together and with the victim, Abraham Vanhorn. In the November 1789 court, all three men had sat together in judgment on a civil case involving George Washington's cousin, Warner Washington.[35] So, at least two members of this grand jury actually knew Vanhorn, and had spent time with him in a civic duty that had crossed social boundaries, even if it had not leveled hierarchy.

Two other men on the grand jury panel were somewhere in between the extremes of backwoods Morgan and patrician Wormeley. John and Matthew Page came from a family with deep, patriotic Virginia roots. The Page brothers – cousins to Tucker's friend John Page of Rosewell – each owned nearly 2,300 acres and retained dynastic ties to their families in eastern Virginia. They were part of the group of old Virginia families who had inherited or purchased Carter land in eastern Frederick County and had relocated to their western holdings to enjoy a healthier climate and the fertility of Valley lands. Once out west, as historian Warren Hofstra has explained, these new residents "began to recreate the life into which they had been born." They "erected imposing manor houses," and "in many subtle ways altered the tenor of economic and social life."[36] John Page had married Maria Byrd, daughter of William Byrd III of Westover; the couple moved to Page's father's Valley lands, "drove off the squatters," and built a large house called "Page Brook," complete with an entrance hall, library, sitting room, and six bedrooms.[37]

There was also a fourth type of Valley elite on Crane's grand jury – the men whose families had founded the Valley's first towns and settlements. For instance, grand juror Robert Wood was the son of James Wood, the founder of Winchester, who had also served as a justice of the peace and as the first Frederick County Court clerk.[38] Robert Wood himself now served as a Frederick County justice, and his brother, General James Wood (so named after his Continental Army service), currently served as Virginia's lieutenant governor and the head of its Council of State, the body established to advise and limit the governor's exercise of executive authority.[39] The Woods did not have

[35] "November 1789," Frederick County Court Order Book 1789–1791, Reel 76, Library of Virginia (hereafter Frederick County Court Order Book). *William McPherson v. Warner Washington.* Vanhorn had also served on several other juries that term, including criminal ones.

[36] Warren R. Hofstra, *A Separate Place: The Formation of Clarke County, Virginia* (Lanham, MD: Rowman and Littlefield, 1999), 11–12.

[37] See Everard Kidder Meade, "Notes on the History of the Lower Shenandoah Valley: Great Houses of the Millwood Area," *Clark County Historical Association Proceedings* 14 (1956–1957): 144–156, 152; Alexander MacKay-Smith, "The Lower Shenandoah Valley as a Thoroughbred Breeding Center, Clarke County," *Clark County Historical Association Proceedings* 7 (1947): 6–30, 10–11.

[38] See Thomas Kemp Cartmell, *Shenandoah Valley Pioneers and Their Descendants* (Winchester, VA: The Eddy Press Corporation, 1909), 19.

[39] "James Wood," in *Journals of the Council of the State of Virginia*, 5:409.

the Tidewater roots of the Wormeleys or Pages, but they held significant local and state power. Similarly, former Berkeley County justice of the peace Thomas Rutherford, Wood's cousin, often served on the Winchester grand jury, and he did so again this term. Years earlier, George Washington had recommended Thomas Rutherford for a position in the militia, citing his "modesty and good behavior" and his "very good reputation." In 1777, Washington had offered Rutherford another position – wagon master in the Continental Army – but Rutherford declined it because of poor health. Rutherford was also the brother of Robert Rutherford, current member of the Virginia General Assembly and later a United States Congressman.[40]

Critics of Virginia's district courts had claimed that the new courts would take power away from the county courts and local justices of the peace, but the faces on this grand jury, at least, were awfully familiar. Many had even served as justices of the peace in the counties, including those that comprised the Winchester district. Grand juror Charles Yates, for instance, was a Fredericksburg merchant (although he owned land in Berkeley) and was also the current caretaker for Thomas Rutherford's son, who was apprenticing with him in Fredericksburg.[41] More significantly, Yates had served as a Spotsylvania County justice of the peace with John Scanland Crane, defendant John Crane's grandfather.[42] Grand juror John Woodcock was a Frederick County justice who had been Frederick's delegate to the Virginia convention that had ratified the new federal Constitution.[43] John Page had been recommended as someone to be added to the Frederick County Commission of the Peace.[44] Thomas Rutherford had formerly been a Berkeley justice; John Wormeley's father had also been a justice.[45] Grand jurors Charles Smith and John Page had both served as foremen on Frederick County's grand juries.[46]

One grand juror, Moses Hunter, had even heard the case already. Hunter, who was also the son-in-law of Martinsburg's founder General Adam Stephen,

---

[40] The elder Thomas Rutherford was the brother-in-law of Colonel James Wood, founder of Winchester; this second generation would have been first cousins. William Kenneth Rutherford and Anna Clay (Zimmerman) Rutherford, *A Genealogical History of the Rutherford Family*, vol. 1 (Shawnee Mission, KS: Intercollegiate Press, 1969), 86, 110–113.

[41] Thomas Rutherford letters, in John Briscoe Papers, Charles Town Public Library, Charles Town, WV. According to surviving letters, the young Rutherford ran up large bills that vexed his father.

[42] H. R. McIlwaine, ed., "Justices of the Peace of Colonial Virginia, 1757–1775," *Bulletin of the Virginia State Library* 14, nos. 2 and 3 (1921): 67–68.

[43] See May 1790 session of the Frederick County Court, in Frederick County Court Order Book; Earl G. Swem and John W. Williams, *A Register of the General Assembly of Virginia, 1776–1918, and of the Constitutional Conventions* (Richmond, VA: Davis Bottom, Superintendent of Public Print, 1919), 243–244 (hereafter Frederick County Court Order Book).

[44] May 1790 session of the Frederick County Court, in Frederick County Court Order Book.

[45] See Chapter 3, supra.

[46] For Smith, see April 20, 1790, Frederick County Court Order Book. For Page, see March 1790, Frederick County Court Order Book.

had been the county court clerk for Berkeley County since 1785.[47] He had heard and recorded the case against Crane – the two days of testimony and argument – in the county court. Now, he would decide whether Crane should be indicted in the district court.[48]

The overlap between district and county stretched far beyond the grand jury members. Indeed, in many ways, the Winchester District Court as a whole looked like the courts of the counties from which it drew its cases. Its first sessions were packed with the names of longstanding Berkeley elites, men like Adam Stephen, Ralph Wormeley, Jr., and Robert and Thomas Rutherford.[49] Even the lawyers were often those who had previously practiced in the county court, Alexander White, Philip Pendleton (nephew of Edmund Pendleton), and others.[50] Men who were justices or former justices in their counties frequently served as members of juries and grand juries in the Winchester District Court, sometimes repeatedly. Thomas Rutherford had been on Berkeley's first Commission of the Peace in 1772, and served on virtually every grand jury in the Winchester District Court.[51] Robert Throckmorton, Berkeley sheriff and a sometime Berkeley justice of the peace, served on the September 1790 grand jury.[52] Berkeley justice Nicholas Orrick was made an arbitrator by the district court in a suit in the April 1790 term.[53] Berkeley sheriff Smith Slaughter served on multiple juries in the fall 1789 term, while also answering suits in his official

---

[47] Hunter was appointed county court clerk on December 20, 1785, after the death of Berkeley's previous clerk. See Berkeley County Court Minute Book, BCHS.

[48] "September 1, 1791," Winchester District Court Order Book.

[49] "September 1789," Winchester District Court Order Book.

[50] See Thomas Bryan Martin and Gabriel Jones, executors of Thomas Lord Fairfax v. Adam Stephen, September 3, 1789 (Philip Pendleton, attorney for Stephen); "September 1, 1790" (Alexander White admitted to practice), Winchester District Court Order Book. For these attorneys in Berkeley, see "August 20, 1776," Berkeley County Court Minute Book, BCHS. White was appointed Berkeley's deputy attorney for the Commonwealth on May 19, 1772. See "May 19, 1772," Berkeley County Court Minute Book, BCHS.

[51] See grand jury list for April 15, 1791, including, among others, John Briscoe and Thomas Rutherford. Grand jury list for April 15, 1790, including Thomas Rutherford, Winchester District Court Order Book.

[52] "September 1790," Winchester District Court Order Book. Throckmorton was appointed in 1789, see "June 16, 1789," Berkeley County Court Minute Book, BCHS, and was still listed as Berkeley sheriff on a July 9, 1790 bond from John Cook and Colonel William Darke to Robert Throckmorton, sheriff of Berkeley County. Legal Papers, Box 1 Folder 30, 1789–1791, Virginia Misc. Papers 1656–1850, UVA Special Collections. Throckmorton is also still listed as the Berkeley sheriff on papers for the September 1791 court, where he or his representatives execute the summons for Berkeley County. See "Commonwealth of Virginia to Sheriff of Berkeley County," *Daniels v. Blue*, April 18, 1791, Box Barcode 1117433, Frederick County Ended Causes, Frederick County District Court Records, September 1791, Folder 2, Library of Virginia.

[53] Amos Nichols v. Peter Light, April 15, 1790, Winchester District Court Order Book. For Orrick as a Berkeley justice of the peace, see "February 20, 1788," and "January 1789," Berkeley County Court Minute Book, BCHS.

capacity.[54] Of course, when acting as justices in the county, these men would have held full sway; when they served on juries or grand juries, they were summoned by the court to serve in those capacities and faced sanctions when they failed to appear. For instance, the court found Berkeley County justice John Briscoe in contempt in 1790 when he failed to appear at court in time to serve on a grand jury.[55] Once present at court, Briscoe then served on a petit jury in a misdemeanor case and when the court called him for grand jury service the next April he appeared on time.[56] The district court could compel these men who sat as county justices, but the flip side of that reality was also true: it also chose to give them tremendous power in the new court – not to exclude them from court duties.

Plus, judging from their court activities, many of these men eagerly embraced the new district courts. Men serving in county positions even themselves appealed county decisions to the district court.[57] Justices or other county officers instituted their own, original suits in the district court instead of the county.[58] Sometimes, they were defendants, particularly in debt cases, when Berkeley's leading men often found themselves in front of the district court having to account for their arrears.[59] But the same person frequently appeared

[54] Slaughter was identified as Berkeley's sheriff in September 1789 court records, and seems to have been sheriff before Throckmorton. See Thomas Bryan Martin and Gabriel Jones, Executors of Thomas Lord Fairfax v. Adam Stephen, Sept. 3, 1789, Winchester District Court Records. In the same court session, Slaughter served as a juror in Thomas Shepherd v. Jasper Ball and Sigumund Stribling, a suit in trespass, assault, and battery. See "September 4, 1789," Winchester District Court Order Book. He was also a juror the next day, in William Glascock v. James Gumiel Dowdall, a suit in case, see "Sept. 5, 1789," Winchester District Court Order Book. Also named in a suit in his official capacity on the same day. See William Allason v. James Crane, in debt, and again the next day, on September 7, in George Hite v. William Brady and Alexander White, a debt case. See "September 7, 1789," Winchester District Court Order Book.

[55] Briscoe appeared three days later and offered reasons for his absence and was excused. "September 1, 1790"; "September 4, 1790," Winchester District Court Order Book.

[56] Commonwealth v. James McIlhaney, September 7, 1790, Winchester District Court Order Book. "April 15, 1791," Grand jury list, Winchester District Court Order Book.

[57] See James Wilson, Philip Pendleton, Moses Hunter, Andrew Wagginer v. John Smith, on appeal from Berkeley County, April 23, 1790 (two suits), and September 10, 1790; Morgan, Sheriff of Berkeley County, v. Larkin Dorsey, on appeal from Berkeley County Court, April 16, 1791; Robert Throckmorton and John Crane, appellants v. William Carr, April 23, 1790; Robert Throckmorton v. Richard Gray, April 23, 1790, in Winchester District Court Order Book.

[58] See Adam Stephen v. John Rheinfield, debt, April 16, 1791; Adam Stephen v. David Mitchell, September 3, 1791, abated because of Stephen's death; Thomas Rutherford v. Lewis Stephens, September 5, 1789; Adam Stephen v. John Hollenbeck, April 14, 1790; Thomas Rutherford v. Lewis Stephen, April 22, 1790; David Hunter v. Joseph Thompson, April 14, 1790; John Cooke v. Morgan, late Sheriff of Berkeley, September 2, 1790 (two suits); James McAlister v. John Vanmeter, April 25, 1790; James Wilson and Son v. Humphrey Keyes, April 22, 1790; Andrew Waggener v. William Baylis, September 7, 1789. All in Winchester District Court Order Book. For list of Berkeley justices of the peace as of 1789, see list at the beginning of the 1789 term, Berkeley County Court Minute Book, BCHS.

[59] John Bull v. William Little, September 2, 1789; John Cook v. Morgan Morgan, September 3, 1789; Joseph Cockrall v. Moses Hunter et al., April 14, 1790; Preeson Bowdoin v. Robert

in several different capacities in the same session, on several different juries, for instance, and prosecuting a suit while defending another. In the April 1790 session, Berkeley's Thomas Rutherford had served on the grand jury, as a defendant in a lawsuit, a juror in four civil cases, and a plaintiff in another.[60] The legal reality was shifting, but was, in many ways, still made up of the same basic parts. When it came to the Winchester District Court, county and state authority overlapped in important ways.

In fact, to the extent there was a shift at all, it was slightly regressive. The identities of the grand jury who considered Crane's case suggest that when it came to court reform the local elites had regained a bit of their power in the new district court. They tended to no longer preside at the county court, even if they were still sometimes technically justices – that duty had mostly gone to less important men. But they now held sway at the district, aided by the workings of the state machinery, made more accessible and convenient by reforms. Perhaps this is why, as historian A. G. Roeber has suggested, the loudest opposition to the new district courts came from justices of lower status who had only recently gained their positions.[61] At the same time in Winchester, current county figures were also in and out of the district court. As Roeber has suggested, more commercial areas of Virginia, like Winchester, tended to

Rutherford, Thomas Rutherford, and William Little, April 20, 1790; John Bull v. William Little, April 22, 1790; Executors of Thomas Lord Fairfax v. Adam Stephen, Edward Beeson, and James Strode, April 22, 1790; George Rootes, William Brady, James Crane v. John Augustine Washington, Charles Washington, James Nourse, executors of Samuel Washington, appeal from Berkeley, April 23, 1790; Thomas Stewart, John McCormick, George Rootes v. John Augustine Washington, Charles Washington, James Nourse, executors of Samuel Washington, appeal from Berkeley, April 23, 1790; Thomas Bryan Martin and Gabriel Jones, executors of Thomas Lord Fairfax v. Robert Stephen, Edward Beeson and James Strode, April 24, 1790; Charles Tomkies Jr. v. William Little and will Brady, September 2, 1790; John Cooke v. Morgan, late Sheriff of Berkeley, September 2, 1790; John O. Farrel & Co. v. Adam Stephen, September 4, 1790; David Mitchell v. Josiah Swearingen, Hezekiah Sweringen, and Thomas Rutherford, executors of Van Swearingen, September 4, 1790; Governor, for the use of Moses Hunter v. Morgan Morgan, Philip Pendleton, George Rootes, Smith Slaughter, Ephriam Worthington, Abraham Shepherd, Ephriam Gaither, and Robert Cockburn, September 8, 1790; Commonwealth on behalf of John Hough v. Adam Stephen, Samuel Oldham, William Hanaker, George Cunningham, Archibald Shearer, George Stockton, George Briscoe, Daniel Morgan, and Henry Newkirk, September 9, 1790; John Brown v. Morgan Morgan, late Sheriff of Berkeley, April 23, 1791. All in Winchester District Court Order Book.

60 Grand jury listed on April 15, 1790; Preeson Bowdoin v. Robert Rutherford, Thomas Rutherford, and William Little, April 20, 1790; Edmund Pendleton and Peter Lyons, Trustees v. William Throckmorton, April 22, 1790 (juror); John Bull v. William Little, April 22, 1790 (juror); Thomas Rutherford v. Lewis Stephens, April 22, 1790 (juror); John Murray et al. v. William Jennings, April 22, 1790 (juror); Edward Snickers v. Joseph Butler, April 22, 1790 (juror). All in Winchester District Court Order Book.

61 Roeber notes that "the real opposition" to the new courts "was in the Piedmont and Southside counties. It may well have been that the justices and lawyers of those areas, who had only recently acceded to prestigious posts, were more jealous of independence or fearful of interference in local affairs." Roeber, *Faithful Magistrates*, 198.

favor the new courts because of their need for efficient debt-collection.[62] At least Rutherford, as Berkeley's representative to the General Assembly, had supported court reform, as had James Campbell, Berkeley's other delegate.[63] They surely preferred traveling to Winchester for court to a long journey to Richmond.

These similarities and overlap between state and county did not mean, of course, that the creation of the Winchester court had meant nothing for the balance of power. After all, the Winchester District Court heard appeals from county courts and often reversed them. Most appeals were from Berkeley County and the majority of appeals from the Berkeley County Court were reversed – the most of any county in the district.[64] Apparently James Crane and the other Berkeley men who complained to the General Assembly about the county court were not alone in their disapproval. At the same time, however, the high reversal rate is misleading. Although the General Court's records have not survived, the limited surviving evidence suggests that – in the years

[62] Ibid.

[63] "December 18, 1786," *Journal of the Virginia House of Delegates of the Commonwealth of Virginia ...* (Richmond, VA: Thomas W. White, Opposite the Belltavern, 1828), 106–107; Swem and Williams, *Register of the General Assembly*, 259. Support for reform tended to track support for the new federal Constitution, which was also strong in the Berkeley area. See Roeber, *Faithful Magistrates*, at 198, n. 85. (These were the votes on the first, more controversial assize bill.) Frederick's Charles Mynn Thurston had voted against it, and its second representative, John Smith, does not seem to have voted. The delegates from the other three counties in the district, Hardy's Isaac Vanmeter, Hampshire's Elias Poston, and Shenandoah's Abraham Bird and Isaac Zane, had also supported it. See Swem and Williams, *Register of the General Assembly*, 284 (Hampshire), 285–286 (Hardy), 327–328 (Shenandoah), and "December 18, 1786," *Journal of the Virginia House of Delegates*, 106–107.

[64] What follows is a rough breakdown of Berkeley County appeals. **Affirmed:** William Dark and John Dark v. Ignatius Simms, April 23, 1790 (Berkeley); William Brudy, Benjamin Beeler and Magnus Tate v. Francis Willis Jr., April 23, 1790 (Berkeley); William Brady, Magnus Tate, and John Smith v. Warner Washington Jr., April 23, 1790 (Berkeley); George Rootes v. Thomas Nelson, Thomas Nelson Jr., and Hugh Nelson, executors of William Nelson, April 23, 1790 (Berkeley); William Askew v. Francis Willis, April 23, 1790 (Berkeley); George Rootes, William Brady, and James Crane v. John Augustine Washington, Charles Washington, and James Nourse, executors of Samuel Washington, April 23, 1790 (Berkeley); Thomas Steward, John McCormick, and George Rootes v. John A. Washington, Charles Washington, and James Nourse, executors of Samuel Washington, April 23, 1790 (Berkeley); **Reversed:** John Baker v. John Briscoe, April 15, 1790 (Berkeley) (agreed by parties); David Kennedy, Samuel Read, and George Riley v. Beard's executors, April 23, 1790 (Berkeley); Robert Throckmorton and John Crane v. William Carr, April 23, 1790 (Berkeley); George Rootes v. William Hammond, April 23, 1790 (Berkeley); George Rootes v. Henry Baker, April 23, 1790 (Berkeley); Ephraim Worthington, executor of Robert Worthington v. Cornelius Conway, April 25, 1791 (Berkeley); Benjamin Beeles v. George Hite, co-administrator of Isaac Hite, April 25, 1791 (Berkeley); Jacob Hackney et al. v. Overton Cosby and James Ross, executors of James Mills, April 25, 1791 (Berkeley); Jackob Hackney et al. v. Overton Cosby and James Gregory, surviving partners of James Mills & Co., April 25, 1791 (Berkeley); Amos Nichols v. John Light, April 25, 1791 (Berkeley); Robert Wilson v. John Carrick, April 16, 1791 (Berkeley); Morgan v. Seakin Dorsey, April 16,1791 (Berkeley). All in Winchester District Court Order Book.

after the Revolution and before the establishment of the district courts – it too had reversed the vast majority of cases appealed to it from the counties, both in colonial Virginia and after the Revolution.[65] Given the fee structure in Virginia's courts, this should not be a surprise. Because appeal was arduous and the losing party often bore both parties' costs of appeal, the General Court and then district courts were likely to draw only strong appeals in the first place.[66] And in some appeals from the counties, cases were reversed because *both* parties agreed that the county court's ruling was incorrect.[67] Focusing on reversal statistics alone thus has the potential to overstate a rise in antagonism between county justice and state courts.

So, although some Virginians complained that the district courts took power from the county courts, the reality was more complicated. Although the new district courts boasted professional judges, they also, in some significant ways, made justice more local, not less. The reforms meant that grand juries were drawn from locals and made the state court system more accessible to local litigants, jurors, and witnesses. The greater accessibility made county appeals and original suits easier. Some saw the new district courts as trying to make local justice more professional, but it also made state justice more local. In Winchester, local citizens had eagerly embraced the opportunity.

But what would this mean for John Crane? As the grand jury prepared to consider whether to indict Crane for murder, Judge Tucker had a few words for them – not just about their job, but about what it meant to be a grand jury in a republic. "Grand-Juries" were, he told them, "one of the wisest provisions which our Ancestors have introduced into the Jurisprudence of that Country," England, "from whose Constitution and Laws we have selected many of the most important regulations." (Americans had also, he added quickly, avoided English defects and learned from experience.) He continued:

The Object of the Institution of Grand-juries is, that a regular Inquiry, at stated, and these not distant, periods, may be made into all Offenses against the common happiness; and an impartial punishment, where such offences are discovered, be inflicted without regard to the Circumstances of the Offender. In a republic where there is no sovereign but the laws; – where no discrimination of interests prevails; where all are equally bound to afford, & entitled to receive that protection which the laws only

---

[65] For colonial decisions, see *Virginia Colonial Decisions: The Reports by Sir. John Randolph and by Edward Barradall of Decision of the General Court of Colonial Virginia, 1728–1741*, vols. 1 and 2, ed. R. T. Barton (Boston, MA: Boston Book Co., 1909). For the postrevolutionary General Court, St. George Tucker's notes provide the best record, and suggest that the General Court reversed most appeals from county courts. See Hobson, *St. George Tucker's Law Reports*, 1:117–232.

[66] See, for instance, William Brady, Benjamin Beeles, and Magnus Tate v. Frances Willis Jr., April 23, 1790, in Winchester District Court Order Book, calculating costs.

[67] John Baker v. John Briscoe, April 23, 1790 (Berkeley) (agreed by parties), in Winchester District Court Order Book.

can afford to the Individual, such Enquiries; such Vigilance; and such Impartiality are indispensably necessary to the preservation of the Government, & to the security & happiness of the Citizens.

Here, Tucker laid out a few key principles. First, punishments should be inflicted "without regard for the Circumstances of the Offender." Second, a republic had "no sovereign but the laws." Furthermore:

This important trust by the happy Constitution & laws of our Country you are this day called upon to perform, & enjoined by the solemn obligation of an oath to perform it, with diligence, and with Impartiality: – You are the accusers of the Commonwealth, on the one hand, and the Guardians of the lives & fortunes of your fellow Citizens on the other; – As accusers you are bound to present all offences that have, or shall come to your knowledge, whilst you are impanell'd on the present Occasions ... Hence arises that protection to your fellow Citizens, which entitles you to the Appellation of the Guardians of their lives & fortunes: for no man can have his Live, his Limbs, or his Estate put in hazard by any Accusation, unless that accusation first receives the solemn sanction of your Oaths.[68]

An accusation against a citizen could only come from his fellow citizens. This was again both ancient and modern, the Anglo-American legal tradition combined with republican principles.

After consideration, the grand jury indicted Crane for the murder of Abraham Vanhorn. They used formulaic language but to John Crane it must have still been striking. On July 4, 1791, they charged, Crane "feloniously, willfully, and of his malice aforethought did made an Assault" on Vanhorn. The indictment went on to allege that Crane had used a "certain knife made of Iron and Steel of the Value of three shillings" to stab Vanhorn, and that the "said Abraham Vanhorne ... of the said mortal wound did die." The indictment listed the witnesses the grand jury had relied upon, including Isaac Merchant, Henry Church, John Dawkins, Joseph Vanhorne, Maryland Hale, Thomas Campbell, Jacob Beals, James Ducker, and David Beales. Both Merchant's and Dawkins's names were crossed off the witness list, then rewritten later – had they been late to court?[69] Delayed, or for some reason reluctant to testify?

But there was one important issue on which the jury hesitated: Crane's class. In the eighteenth century, Virginia indictments customarily listed the defendant's class after his name – "John Smith, laborer," for instance.[70] Crane's "circumstances" were, as Tucker had charged the jury, irrelevant to his guilt. However, they still needed to determine his situation to complete the indictment. And although indictments, especially in big cases like Crane's, were

[68] St. George Tucker, Grand Jury Charge, filed with General Court Docket 1793, Tucker-Coleman Papers.
[69] Indictment, Commonwealth v. John Crane, Frederick County, Misc. Court Records, 1744–1835, District Court, Criminal Cases, Box 1 (Barcode 1150972), Folder – 1791, September, Commonwealth v. Crane, Library of Virginia.
[70] Ibid.

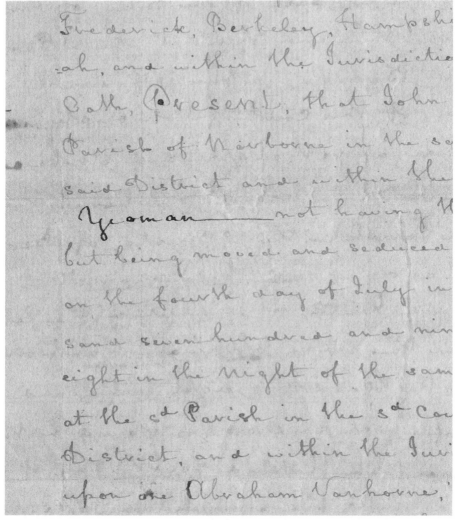

FIGURE 5.2 Indictment of John Crane for Murder, 1791
The grand jury left a blank for Crane's class. It was later filled in with "Yeoman."

sometimes written ahead of time and handed to the grand jury with blanks left for items that were in question, Crane's indictment left only one blank – his class.[71]

The grand jury returned the indictment, with the blank still unfilled. The Winchester district court clerk wrote the indictment into the court minutes, and

[71] Ibid.

left room to fill in the designation.[72] Would Crane be a gentleman? A yeoman? Something else? Someone – the court, the grand jury – then had to decide: where did John Crane fit in the jumble of the Valley's elites? To be sure, Crane owned not thousands of acres, like the Page brothers, but a mere 200. But gentility was more complicated than that. His father, James Crane "gentleman," did not own much more – only 204 acres along with nine slaves.[73] And other Berkeley gentlemen also seemed to own about the same amount of land, although some owned much more, and others, like some of the Catherine Crane's Whiting relatives, were vast slaveholders. Additionally, John had married Catherine Whiting, joining a family that had long been one of the most important families in the state. His own grandfather had even been Spotsylvania's high sheriff and the highest-ranking member of the county's militia during the colonial era, positions doled out at that time according to the highest social standing.[74] John Crane may not have owned vast acreage, but that did not prevent him from being genteel like his father (whatever being genteel entailed).

But in the end, heritage was not enough. The court designated John a "yeoman," a decision that likely shocked the Crane and Whiting families. As historian Turk McCleskey has observed, in eighteenth-century Virginia yeomen were men "on the make," at the same time "independent like landed gentlemen but sweaty, sunburned, and callused like untutored farmhands."[75] Over time, yeomen typically worked to turn themselves into gentry, but the grand jury had demoted John Crane. He fit this description on paper but his family background was quite different.

But the decision had been made. Judge Tucker dismissed the grand jury, and the clerk, or maybe foreman Daniel Morgan, wrote John's new class into indictment in awkward, extra-large script (though still not large enough to fill the space).[76]

The results of John Crane's first appearance before the Winchester District Court had not gone well. It had taken some debate, but John Crane had become a "yeoman" in the Commonwealth's records. He thus moved on to trial reduced to the status of some of the men who worked for him in his fields on the day of Vanhorn's death – the very men whom his wife, Catherine Whiting Crane, had derided as "negrofied puppies."

---

[72] "September 1, 1791," Winchester District Court Order Book.
[73] Berkeley Land Tax Records, East 1791, BCHS; Berkeley County Personal Property Tax Records, East 1791, BCHS. James, John, and Joseph Crane, however, had all obtained large land grants for farther west.
[74] For John Scanland Crane's service as a justice, see Virginia State Library, *Justices of the Peace of Colonial Virginia 1757–1775* (Richmond, VA: State of Virginia, 1922), 91; for his appointment as high sheriff, see "November 19, 1772," Spotsylvania County Order Book, 1768–1774, Reel 45, Library of Virginia.
[75] Turk McCleskey, *The Road to Black Ned's Forge: A Story of Race, Sex, and Trade on the Colonial American Frontier* (Charlottesville, VA: University of Virginia Press, 2014), 13.
[76] Indictment, Commonwealth v. John Crane.

6

Crane's Trial and Its "Imperfect" Verdict

After the grand jury returned its indictment on September 1, 1791, John Crane had a choice. Two judges were supposed to preside at each of Virginia's district courts, and since Judge Henry Tazewell was ill, there was not a full court to conduct Crane's trial. As a result, John could delay his trial and instead stay in the Winchester jail until the next term of court in April. Then, if two judges were still not available, he could post bail and have his trial delayed again. Finally, if there was still only one judge at that third term, he would be discharged.[1]

By September, Crane was probably a little worse for wear. He had been confined in the Winchester jail for two months since his examining court date in July, and the facility left much to be desired. A committee appointed by the court to look into the jail's condition had concluded that it was poorly suited for its purpose. The roof was "open in various parts and the Shingles in general decayed" with only "very small rooms without passage or entry." One room housed debtors and another single room provided for "the confinement of Criminals of every description and Sex." The whole building also had "but one fire place, by which means the confined are deprived of that necessary comfort." In fact, the building was so dilapidated that, the committee concluded, the expenses necessary for its repair "would not be very unequal to a new building."[2]

---

[1] See, Charles F. Hobson, ed., *St. George Tucker's Law Reports and Selected Papers, 1782–1825,* vol. 1 (Chapel Hill, NC: University of North Carolina Press, 2013), 35; St. George Tucker, ed., *Blackstone's Commentaries with Notes of Reference to the Constitution and Laws of the Federal Government of the United States; and of the Commonwealth of Virginia,* vol. 4 (Philadelphia, PA: William Young Birch and Abraham Small, 1803), appendix A, 17.

[2] "September 8, 1789," Winchester District Court Order Book, 1789–1793, Library of Virginia. Although this report was made two years earlier, subsequent records do not indicate the construction of a new jail or the renovation of the old one.

So Crane could delay his trial, but there was a big cost: spending the winter in the Winchester jail. Since Virginia's judges had to travel long distances on circuit to preside at the district courts, the chance of later release was real; indeed, Judge Tucker observed that, because of this rule, "some of the most atrocious offenders that were ever brought to the bar of a court" had "escaped the punishment due to their crimes."[3] But winter fast approached, and the open, inadequately heated Winchester jail seemed an uninviting, dangerous place to pass the coldest months. As a petition later filed on Crane's behalf noted, he had already "suffered much indeed from a long and painful confinement in a wretched and loathsome prison."[4]

Crane waived his right to two judges, and petitioned Judge Tucker to be tried immediately.[5] To ask for immediate trial, Crane and his family must have been optimistic that John would either be acquitted or convicted of manslaughter only. This optimism may have been due in part to John's claim that there had been a big fight and that Vanhorn was stabbed in the fight, but not necessarily by him. Although records are sparse, two pieces of surviving evidence indicate that this was one of John's arguments. First, in a deposition introduced later into the record, Hugh McDonald, who had been working for Crane, put the responsibility for the fight on Isaac Merchant and Crane's neighbor and reaper, John Dawkins. McDonald described the fight, then made the oblique statement that "in the fight Vanhorn was stabbed" without attributing the stabbing to Crane.[6] But for some reason, the court did not call McDonald to testify at the trial, and he did not give his deposition until after the trial's end. Crane's supporters later reported that Crane was "deprived of some of his material evidences, particularly a certain Hugh McDonald," a "very sober, industrious, & honest young man."[7] There is no record of why McDonald did not testify. In any event, there is no record of a summons for him (although some records may be missing) and he did not appear at the county court, either. His deposition would enter the record a month later, on October 1, 1791.[8]

[3] Tucker, *Blackstone's Commentaries*, appendix A, 17. Tucker suggested fixing this problem by using the procedure he used in *Crane* – presiding alone, and then certifying the case to the General Court.

[4] "Petition of Citizens for the Pardon of John Crane, Jr.," April 28, 1792, *Calendar of Virginia State Papers and Other Manuscripts*, vol. 5: *From July 2, 1789 to August 10, 1792*, ed. William P. Palmer and Sherwin McRae (Richmond, VA: Virginia State Library, 1885), 511.

[5] See "Petition of John Crane," in Frederick County, District Court, Criminal Cases, 1791–1799, Box 1 (barcode 1150972), folder – 1791, September, Commonwealth v. Crane, Library of Virginia (hereafter Commonwealth v. Crane District Court File).

[6] "Deposition of Hugh McDonald, October 1, 1791," *Calendar of Virginia State Papers*, 5:372.

[7] Ibid.; "Berkeley County," May 29, 1792, *Calendar of Virginia State Papers* 5:598–599.

[8] "Deposition of Hugh McDonald," October 1, 1791, *Calendar of Virginia State Papers*, 5:372.

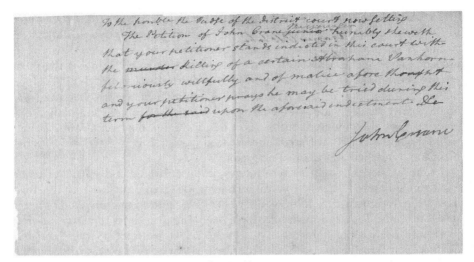

FIGURE 6.1 John Crane's Petition to be Tried, 1791

The second piece of evidence indicating that Crane claimed to be actually innocent related to the knife that had killed Vanhorn – the one the indictment described as a "certain knife made of Iron and Steel of the Value of three shillings."[9] After Vanhorn was stabbed, it had been found not on Crane but, according to a later letter of Judge Tucker, "on the negro."[10] What "negro"? Had the knife perhaps been found on the "negro man of Mr. Crane's" who Hugh McDonald said had carried the original challenge from Campbell's men? As McDonald put it in his deposition, "a negro man of Mr. Crane's informed John Dawkins and the rest of us that Campbell's men had sent us a challenge."[11] This evidence, though scant, provides context to Crane's claim that he was innocent. Whether he was, or whether he had planted his knife on his enslaved worker to attempt to avoid detection (likely), is unclear.

But there was also another potential outcome: that the jury would find him guilty only of manslaughter, not murder. Since the stabbing had occurred during a fight, it was a distinct possibility. Murder required preformed malice. It arose, as Blackstone put it, "from the wickedness of the heart." Manslaughter, on the other hand, came from the "sudden heat of the passions," without premeditation.[12]

[9] Indictment, Commonwealth v. Crane, District Court File, Library of Virginia.

[10] Letter from St. George Tucker to Charles Lee, September 4, 1791, Series 1, Item 2757, Tucker-Coleman Papers.

[11] "Deposition of Hugh McDonald," October 1, 1791, *Calendar of Virginia State Papers*, 5:372.

[12] Tucker, *Blackstone's Commentaries*, 5:190.

In the context of a fight, there were a few key ingredients which required special attention. First, if one person assailed another, he might of course kill his attacker in self-defense, but such a claim was unlikely to be available to Crane. As Blackstone put it, "a man may protect himself from an assault, or the like, in the course of a sudden brawl or quarrel, by killing him who assaults him," but it needed to appear that "the slayer had no other possible (or, at least, probable) means of escaping from his assailant."[13] And if it was a consensual fight, things changed. Blackstone acknowledged that in this situation it could be difficult to distinguish self-defense from manslaughter, but suggested that the key difference was whether they were already fighting at the time of the fatal blow. If "the slayer hath not yet begun to fight, or (having begun) endeavours to decline any farther struggle, and afterwards being closely pressed by his antagonist, kills him to avoid his own destruction, this is homicide excusable by self-defence."[14] The slayer could not, however, invoke self-defense after a duel or similar context – after all, previous malice had led to the duel in the first place.[15]

Manslaughter, on the other hand, happened when someone killed during the course of a fight, but not out of bare self-preservation. If, Blackstone explained, "upon a sudden quarrel two persons fight, and one of them kills the other, this is manslaughter." It was also still manslaughter if the parties "upon such an occasion go out and fight in a field; for this is one continued act of passion." It was also manslaughter if "a man were to be greatly provoked, by pulling his nose, or other great indignity" and killed the aggressor.[16]

The key was the heat of passion. Without that, the same kind of interpersonal conflict could be murder. If, for instance, after the provocation, "there be a sufficient cooling-time for passion to subside and reason to interpose, and the person so provoked kills the other, this is deliberate revenge and not heat of blood, and accordingly amounts to murder."[17]

John Crane thus had at least two potential defenses. First, that someone else had stabbed Vanhorn, not him; and second, that his actions – stabbing in the heat of a fight – amounted to manslaughter, not murder. For this second, Crane would have to emphasize that the stabbing arose from a fight, that he had no previous malice, and had not had time to "cool off."

Whatever the exact scope of his defense, Crane petitioned to be tried immediately, and Judge Tucker obliged. The district court clerk scheduled the trial for the very next day, September 2, 1791. Some witnesses were already at court, men such as Isaac Merchant and John Dawkins, who postponed his move

[13] Ibid., 183–184.
[14] Ibid., 184.
[15] Ibid., 185.
[16] Ibid., 190–191.
[17] Ibid., 191.

to Kentucky to be at Crane's trial.[18] But the clerk also summoned additional witnesses to appear for both the Commonwealth and Crane. Most of the new witnesses were for the Commonwealth, new names to the case, perhaps additional men who had been in Crane's and Campbell's fields.[19] The court also summoned four additional witnesses for Crane. Robert Worthington (a Crane in-law) testified, as did Andrew McCormick, son of one of the area's earliest settlers, who lived near Charles Town and had run a tavern there since 1768.[20] But the clerk also summoned two unexpected witnesses, "John Vanhorn and his wife," probably Abraham Vanhorn's parents. And not only were they summoned, they were summoned to "speak on behalf of John Crane jun."[21] Why were Vanhorn's parents summoned to speak for Crane? Were they hostile witnesses, summoned to impeach accounts of Abraham's death, to suggest an intervening cause, or to elicit other information that might help Crane's case? Had Vanhorn made a dying statement that had exculpated Crane?

Now, Crane had a top lawyer, too: attorney Charles Lee, future US Attorney General. It may have been good for Crane and for Lee that Judge Tazewell was ill and not at court because Tazewell did not think highly of Lee. A few years later, when Lee was Washington's Attorney General, Tazewell would privately comment that with a "confidential Council" of Timothy Pickering, Oliver Wolcott, James McHenry, and Charles Lee, Washington had surrounded himself with "a council not more remarkable for their Talents, than they will prove to be for their attachment to the principles of Republicanism."[22]

Next, Judge Tucker called and appointed a jury. If it was like other Virginia criminal cases Lee, on behalf of Crane, would have had an opportunity to challenge jurors for cause, including for "partiality," which included malice, favor, or relationship to a party or other member of the court. Defendants also had preemptory challenges, which would have allowed Crane to challenge prospective jury members without having to show a cause. Those removed would have been replaced by bystanders or others from the community.[23]

---

[18] See Lela Wolfe Prewitt, *The Dawkins and Stewart Families of Virginia and Kentucky* (N.p.: 1968), 5.

[19] Summons for Cornelius Baldwin, John Fleming, Edward Violet, Jr., Jacob [illegible] and Michael Hinton, Commonwealth v. Crane District Court File, Library of Virginia.

[20] "Welcome!! To White House Farm," *White House Farm*, accessed October 12, 2016, http://whitehousefarmwv.org/.

[21] Summons for "Robert Worthington, Andrew McCormick, John Vanhorn and Wife ... to speak on behalf of John Crane jun.," Commonwealth v. Crane District Court File, Library of Virginia.

[22] Hobson, "Charles Lee," in Hobson, *St. George Tucker's Law Reports*, 3:1832; Letter from Henry Tazewell to Richard Cocke, January 30, 1796, in Henry Tazewell Papers, Special Collections Research Center, Swem Library, College of William and Mary, Williamsburg, VA.

[23] See Hugh F. Rankin, *Criminal Trial Proceedings in the General Court of Colonial Virginia* (Williamsburg, VA: Colonial Williamsburg, 1965), 93.

FIGURE 6.2 Charles Lee, by Cephas Thompson, c. 1810–1811

Crane's trial began on September 2, 1791, and the Crane family – John's parents, James and Lucy Crane, his younger brother Joseph, his wife Catherine, maybe his Whiting in-laws as well – probably watched with a mixture of hope and horror as the trial unfolded. Virginia did not have a history of executing its gentry, so Crane had reason to hope. The state's most famous (or infamous) case of this sort had been the 1766 case of John Chiswell, who happened to be a distant family member of Catherine Whiting Crane.[24] Chiswell had killed merchant Robert Routledge in a Cumberland County tavern.[25] The conflict began when a drunken Chiswell began liberally using oaths. Routledge rebuked him, and Chiswell then called the Scottish Routledge a "fugitive rebel, a villain who came to Virginia to cheat and defraud men of their property, and a Presbyterian fellow."[26] He called for his sword and Routledge threw a glass of wine onto him. Chiswell responded by throwing "a bowl of toddy, a candlestick, and a pair of tongs" at Routledge before brandishing his sword and telling him to leave. When the merchant refused, Chiswell ran him through, killing him instantly.[27] He then "calmly handed his weapon to his servant, called for a bowl of toddy, and continued his abuse of the dead man, saying 'He deserves his fate, damn him; I aimed at his heart, and I have hit it.' "[28]

The Chiswells were highly regarded in Virginia society and powerful in Williamsburg; Chiswell's father had been the clerk of the General Court, and his mother was a member of the Randolph family. Their social status did not stop the Cumberland justices from charging Chiswell with murder – but that was not the end of the story. The county justices sent him to Williamsburg for trial at the colonial General Court. But in Williamsburg, the Virginia Council – which, in the colonial era, also sat as the judges of the General Court – held a brief court of their own and granted him bail.[29] The unorthodox action precipitated an uproar. Letters to the *Virginia Gazette* protested and defended. As one member of the Virginia gentry, who criticized the bailment, wrote satirically in a private poem:

> The Laws, in Vulgar Hands unkind,
> The worthy Gentleman confined;
> But in the Hands of Gentlemen
> Politer, they released again.
> But then began a strange Fracas:
> Some swore it was, some 'twas not, Law.

[24] Chiswell was the father-in-law of Virginia's powerful colonial treasurer, John Robinson, who himself was the first cousin of Catherine's maternal grandfather (also named John Robinson). See Dakota Best Brown, *Data on Some Virginia Families* (Berryville, VA: Virginia Book Company, 1979), 241.

[25] There are several different treatments of the Chiswell case. One thorough example is J. A. Leo Lemay, "Robert Bolling and the Bailment of Colonel Chiswell," *Early American Literature* 6, no. 2 (1971): 99–142.

[26] Rankin, *Criminal Trial Proceedings*, 209. See Mary A. Stephenson, "Chiswell-Bucktrout House Historical Report, Colonial Williamsburg Foundation (1959/1990)," *Colonial Williamsburg Digital Library*, accessed October 12, 2016, http://research.history.org/DigitalLibrary/View/index.cfm?doc=ResearchReports\RR1018.xml.

[27] See Stephenson, "Chiswell-Bucktrout House Historical Report."

[28] Rankin, *Criminal Trial Proceedings*, 210.

[29] Cynthia A. Kierner, *Scandal at Bizarre: Rumor and Reputation in Jefferson's America* (Charlottesville, VA: University of Virginia Press, 2006), 50.

> 'Twas not for common Men, 'twas plain;
> But was it not for Gentlemen?[30]

Chiswell died of "nervous fits" before he could be tried, although most suspected he had actually committed suicide.[31]

If Chiswell's case gave the Crane family reason to hope, there was also plenty to fear. As the proceedings began, the Cranes had to watch as witness testimony aired the details of John's supposed, sordid crime before the whole community. Was Catherine Whiting Crane present in court when the men testified that she had told her husband not to "demean himself" by fighting with "such a set of negrofied puppies?" Did those ugly words echo across the courtroom, and did her neighbors send her glares of disgust or avoid her eyes altogether? Did she feel embarrassed? Or quietly justified? It was not so much the slur against the men and women the Cranes owned – the actual "negroes" – that mattered to the community, of course, but the fact that she had used the term to describe her working white neighbors, and helped to provoke such a tragic outcome. And down in Winchester, did this slur play even worse than it would have in Martinsburg? Berkeley County, after all, had a fair number of gentry from eastern Virginia. Frederick County did too, especially since the 1780s, but Winchester was an older town and Abraham Vanhorn had been known there. And the testimony was harsh, unforgiving; as one observer later remembered, "I was at his Tryal and heard the witnesses which were much prejudiced against him, and by appearance would say as much as they could against and as little in his favour."[32]

Newspapers across the country carried reports of the trial. "On Friday morning," one paper reported, "a jury from this County was empaneled, and after the evidences given, the attorneys continued pleading til twelve o'clock that night, when the jury retired to the jury room."[33] The tradition was to confine jurors without "Meat, Drink, Fire, or Candle," until they reached their verdict and a court officer ensured that directive was followed.[34] Crane's jury, confined "without refreshment of any kind," was deadlocked.[35] Winchester juries typically returned their verdicts the same day but Crane's jurors were still out at the end of September 2; as a result the court remanded John to jail for the night. The next morning, the jury continued to deliberate, but September

---

[30] Poem by Robert Bolling. See Lemay, "Robert Bolling and the Bailment of Colonel Chiswell," 100–101.

[31] Michael Ayers Trotti, *The Body in the Reservoir: Murder and Sensationalism in the South* (Chapel Hill, NC: University of North Carolina Press, 2008), 14–15; Rankin, *Criminal Trial Proceedings*, 211.

[32] "Robert Throckmorton to the Governor," June 19, 1791, *Calendar of Virginia State Papers*, 5:599.

[33] "Shepherdstown, September 5," *Mail* (Philadelphia, PA), September 17, 1791.

[34] Rankin, *Criminal Trial Proceedings*, 101–102; William Waller Hening, *The Statutes at Large ...,* vol. 2 (New York, NY: R. & W. & G. Bartow, 1823), 2:73–74.

[35] "Petition of Citizens for the Pardon of John Crane, Jr.," April 20, 1792, in *Calendar of Virginia State Papers*, 5:511.

3 progressed with still no verdict.[36] Finally, late in the evening of September 3, the jury returned. As the *Philadelphia Mail* reported, the jury "continued in the jury room, until nine o'clock on Saturday evening."[37]

They had at last reached a verdict. Given the notoriety of the case, even at this late hour, the jury probably returned to a room full of local citizens, parties, and leading members of the Bar. But if the crowd expected a full determination, they were disappointed. The exhausted and frustrated jurymen had solved their impasse by rendering a "special verdict." They had found Crane "guilty" but had not decided whether his actions were murder or manslaughter. Instead, they gave a more than 800-word account of the facts related to the fatal fight in which Crane had stabbed Vanhorn and asked the court to decide whether, on those facts, Crane was guilty of manslaughter or murder.

The jury's verdict, probably written out and signed by its foreman Gerard Alexander, gave a long and careful account of the events that had led up to Vanhorn's mortal wounds. It contained elements of the story that had appeared in the newspapers, with new additions and some careful cautions. It did not begin with Crane maiming Vanhorn's horses; in fact, the verdict did not mention anything of what might have happened earlier in the day. Instead, it began with the afternoon challenge (deletions and insertions in original):

We of the Jury find that about three o'clock on the fourth of July one Thousand seven Hundred and ninety one John Crane the Prisoner at the bar, was Informed by His Reapers that one Camples ^Reapers had sent a Challenge to his ~~Reapers~~, That in consequence of this supposed Challenge, the said John Crane went with others out of his own field into the field of ^the said Campbell which was adjoining to that of Cranes, and that the said Crane did make use of Threatening Language, such as he cou'd whip any man in the field meaning Campbells Reapers amongst which was Abraham Vanhorn but after some altercation we find all parties appear to be reconciled ...

The reconciliation was short-lived. Even "before said Crane left the field another dispute arose in which Crane challenged them to fight man for man, which Campbell's Party agreed to do, of which number the said Abraham Vanhorn was one." But they did not actually fight, and fear of Crane was the reason why:

[W]hen the parties came near together, they Parlied and disputed for some time, the Ishue of which was, that the Prisoner of the Barr, swore that if he fought any Man that Day, he would let out their Gutts, & likewise that he wou'd fight Joseph Vanhorn the next morning, for ten Dollrs, which the said Abraham Vanhorn was to bet him.

---

[36] "September 2, 1791," and "September 3, 1791," Winchester District Court Order Book.
[37] "Shepherdstown, September 5," *Mail* (Philadelphia, PA), September 17, 1791.

Crane had then left Campbell's field, but later Dawkins suspected another insult:

[T]he Prisoner of the Bar leaving Campbell's Field, after some time ^a certain John Dawkins, ^one of Crane's reapers suspected some insult given by Campbells party & going to fight any one that would insult him, the Prisoner at the Barr observing this, requested the said Dawkins to get him a club, & he would take his Knife, which Knife he took out of his Pocket, declaring they could clear their way through the whole of Campbells party.

Dawkins had wanted to fight, but Crane had again mentioned his knife and threatened to use it. After Crane made his threat, "the said Dawkins desisted from prosecuting his Intentions, and likewise the Prisoner of the Barr." Significantly, upon hearing Crane's ferocious response, Dawkins, who knew the men in Campbell's field, had backed down.[38]

But the day was not over. Apparently the men had made a bet that Crane and Joseph Vanhorn would fight the next morning, and Campbell's men came by Crane's to confirm the bet:

[W]e find that between Sunset & dark, that the said Abm Vanhorn with several others passing through ^the Field of John Crane, the Prisoner of the Barr to confirm a Bett which was to ensue the next morning, & also making a Noise and singing which the said Dawkins conceived was ^an insult to the Prisoner of the Barr & his party.

Now John Dawkins was involved again. He "haled out he cou'd whip Joseph Vanhorn, Joseph Vanhorn reply'd it would be no credit to him if he did, as he was a larger Man." Again, Dawkins instigated. This account paralleled the deposition later given by Crane's reaper Hugh McDonald (who for unknown reasons did not testify at the trial – one account said Crane was "deprived" of McDonald's testimony).[39] McDonald had also assigned John Dawkins a large role in the day's events, and attributed to him similar statements.[40]

The dispute continued. Upon hearing Dawkins and Joseph Vanhorn exchanging words, Crane emerged from his house:

[T]he Prisoner of the Barr came out, & ordered them out of his Field, or he wou'd blough them through, upon which they immediately quitted the Field, he then call'd for his Gun, which was refused by his wife; he then call'd for his Knife, & pursued them to the fence, exclaiming Abrahm Vanhorn, you've us'd me Ill, & I'll be damn'd if I dont have satisfaction then the said Abm Vanhorn reply'd not more so, than you have used me.

The verdict had not mentioned Crane's crops or Vanhorn's horses, but clearly suggested some prior dispute between the men.

---

[38] *Crane*, 3 Va. at 10–13.

[39] "Berkeley County," May 29, 1792, *Calendar of Virginia State Papers*, 5:598–599.

[40] For instance, according to McDonald, Dawkins had said that he had stated that "he was not afraid of any one man that was then in Campbell's field." "Deposition of Hugh McDonald, October 1, 1791," *Calendar of Virginia State Papers*, 5:371–372.

[T]he Prisoner then requested the said Abraham Vanhorn to come over the fence and fight Him; the said Abraham Vanhorn made answer, he the said Prisoner ^at the barr would use a Knife or Razor, the said ^Prisoner at the bar Replyed, come over the fence, and I will give a fair fight, the wife of the said Prisoner at the barr came down crying out, Mr. Crane I am supprised you shou'd demean yourself to fight with such a sett of Negrofied puppies.

After Catherine Crane's haughty, condescending statement, things escalated quickly:

[B]y this time the prisoner at the barr, and the said Abraham Vanhorn, were much Irritated, at which time ~~the prisoner~~ the said Abraham Vanhorn, and ~~the said~~ Isaac Merchant ^one of Campbell's reapers had their shirts stripped off, which the Prisoner at the bar had not.

This information indicated that Vanhorn and Merchant were ready to fight, but Crane himself had not yet stripped off his shirt – that he was not necessarily the aggressor. Next,

the prisoner at the bar and the said Abraham Vanhorn attempting to get at each other acrofs the fence, who was prevented by John Dawkins then the ^said Prisoner struck at Merchant, who struck the said ^Prisoner at the Barr, and turned Him Round, who Immediately Joined in Combat with the said Abraham Vanhorn.

Vanhorn, Merchant, and Crane were all fighting at the same time. Crane had two opponents, and he was on the losing end.

[W]e find in the combat, that the said Abraham Vanhorn threw the Prisoner at the bar on the Ground and Kept Him there for some time, at length the Prisoner at the bar seemed to gett the advantage of the said Abraham Vanhorn at which time the said Abraham Vanhorn cryed enough and sayed his Gutts were cut out. [Illegible word crossed out.] we do find, that the said Abm Vanhorn did receive several Wounds with a Knife, or some sharp Instrument, of which wounds the said Abm Vanhorn died. & that the wounds were given by the Prisoner of the Barr.[41]

With this, the jury rejected Crane's claim that someone else (his slave, another participant in the fight) had done the stabbing. Then, they concluded:

Upon the whole matter the Jury pray the advice of the Court, & if the court should be of Opinion, that the Prisoner is guilty of Murder, then we of the jury ^do find ~~him~~ ^the Prisoner is guilty of murder, ~~then we the Jury do find the Prisoner is Guilty of Murder~~, & if the Court shall be of opinion that the Prisoner is not guilty of Murder, but guilty of Manslaughter, then we of the Jury do find the Prisoner not Guilty of Murder, but guilty of Manslaughter.[42]

Was this an honest question? Had the jury been delayed because they did not know if Crane was guilty of murder or manslaughter, or was the special verdict a last-ditch tool by some jurors to find consensus amidst strongly conflicting opinions?

[41] Verdict, Commonwealth v. Crane District Court File, Library of Virginia. Also recorded on "September 3, 1791," Winchester District Court Order Book.
[42] Verdict, Commonwealth v. Crane District Court File, Library of Virginia.

Later documents would shed more light on the jury's deliberations. Seven months later, when over a hundred Berkeley citizens wrote to the Governor about Crane's case, they "beg[ged] leave to state" the "peculiar circumstances" that had led to the verdict. First, "the Jury by whom he was tried, were unable to agree upon their verdict for two whole days, and the greater part of as many nights, making the whole near forty hours." During that forty hours, "all this time they were confined without refreshment of any kind, and were by necessity driven to find the imperfect special verdict upon which the Judgement of the court has since been given." Even worse, the petitioners declared, "four or five of that very Jury have ever since their verdict, declared, and still declare that the unfortunate prisoner had not in their opinion been guilty of murder."[43]

At least three of those jurors who had insisted at the time of the jury's verdict and afterwards that Crane was guilty only of manslaughter stated that opinion publicly at this later date. In petitions sent to the Governor on Crane's behalf, they affirmed under oath that they had agreed to the special verdict only reluctantly and under hardship. Gerard Alexander certified that "myself & three more of the Jurors were of opinion that the said John Crane was guilty of manslaughter, and not of willful murder."[44] Jurors Benjamin Strother and Thomas Griggs also certified that they too "were of the opinion that the said John Crane was not guilty of willful murder – only manslaughter."[45] District Court Clerk Peyton confirmed the petition's account of events: "I am apprehensive," he wrote to the Governor, "that those in his favor were induced to acquiesce, being two days confined on the business under a full persuasion that it would finally be determined [by the court] to be manslaughter only."[46]

And just who were the jurors who had been so overpowered in the jury room? The three who would later write the governor to insist that they had believed Crane to be guilty only of manslaughter were all wealthy and important men. One was the foreman, Gerard Alexander. Originally from Fairfax County, where he was a neighbor of George Washington, in 1790, Alexander owned 712 acres of property in Berkeley, more than triple James Crane's holdings and nearly the largest in the county.[47] The second was forty-one-year-old

---

[43] "Petition of Citizens for the Pardon of John Crane, Jr.," April 20, 1792, in *Calendar of Virginia State Papers*, 5:510–513; quotation at 511.

[44] "Gerard Alexander's Certificate as to John Crane, Jr.," April 19, 1792, ibid., 495.

[45] "Certificate of Benjamin Strother and Thomas Griggs as to John Crane Jr.," April 23, 1792, ibid., 504.

[46] "J. Peyton to the Governor," April 30, 1792, ibid., 519.

[47] Berkeley County Land Tax records, East 1790, BCHS. A dispute over Gerrard Alexander, Sr.'s will helps establish the juror Gerrard Alexander's identity; the dispute involved the senior Alexander's Fairfax and Berkeley (by then Jefferson) County lands, and ended up in court in 1808; summaries of that case reveal that the senior Alexander purchased land in Frederick/Berkeley/Jefferson county from Lord Fairfax, and that he had a son named Gerrard, who would be the Crane jury foreman. Alexander's forebears were among the first landowners in the northern Virginia area. See Lyman Chalkley, *Chronicles of the Scotch-Irish Settlement of Virginia: Extracted from the Original Court Records of Augusta County 1745–1800*, vol. 2

Revolution veteran Captain Benjamin Strother, the son of a prominent Fredericksburg merchant and brother of the high sheriff of King George County. Strother likely knew the Cranes from Spotsylvania; his daughter would later marry John Crane's brother Joseph.[48] The third, Thomas Griggs, lived across the street from Crane's father, James, in Charles Town. In 1791, Juror Griggs, a transplant from Lancaster County, was forty-five, had lived in the Berkeley area since 1770, and had married into Virginia's prominent Carter family. Like James Crane, he was one of the town's founding trustees. Griggs was also patron of one of the area's first Methodist churches – a Methodist revival had swept through the area and absorbed a number of the Cranes' friends and neighbors.[49] Foreman Alexander indicated to the Governor that a fourth unnamed juror also argued for manslaughter.[50]

The jurors who argued on Crane's behalf in the jury room and later to the Governor were not the only prominent men on the jury or the only jurors who knew the Cranes. In fact, the jury resembled a "who's who" of Berkeley County. Abraham Shepherd, for instance, owned the town of Mecklenburg, renamed "Shepherdstown" in his family's honor, and was a Revolutionary War veteran who conducted business for the county and owned mills. He also soon became a leading Federalist organizer in western Virginia.[51] Magnus Tate was a lawyer and one of the "gentlemen" named a founding trustee of Charles Town with James Crane in 1787; he was also a fighter, and had appeared in court years earlier complaining that someone had bitten off his ear during a fight – Tate's ear was presented as evidence, and the clerk noted that "Magnus Tate's ear placed on record."[52] David Gray had fought in the Revolutionary War and owned land in Shepherdstown; he appears in the history of the area in 1787 as one of the sworn witnesses to inventor James Rumsey's first successful steamboat

---

(Rosslyn, VA: Daughters of the American Revolution/The Commonwealth Printing Co., 1912), 236–238.

[48] William Armstrong Crozier, *The Buckners of Virginia and the Allied Families of Strother and Ashby* (New York, NY: The Genealogical Association, 1907), 234; F. Vernon Aler, *History of Martinsburg and Berkeley County, West Virginia* (Hagerstown, MD: Mail Publishing Company, 1888), 143–144.

[49] Millard Kessler Bushong, *A History of Jefferson County West Virginia, 1719–1940* (Charles Town, WV: Jefferson Publishing Company, 1941), 51, 58, 61, 77; J. E. Norris, ed., *History of the Lower Shenandoah Valley Counties of Frederick, Berkeley, Jefferson, and Clarke* (Chicago, IL: A. Warner & Co., Publishers, 1890), 635–636, 658–660.

[50] "Gerard Alexander's Certificate as to John Crane, Jr.," April 19, 1792, in *Calendar of Virginia State Papers*, 5:495.

[51] Mabel Henshaw Gardiner and Ann Henshaw Gardiner, *Chronicles of Old Berkeley* (Durham, NC: Seeman Press, 1938) 36, 53; Bushong, *History of Jefferson County*, 70; Daniel Hackett Fischer, *The Revolution in American Conservatism: The Federalist Party in the Era of Jeffersonian Democracy* (New York, NY: Harper and Row, 1965), 377.

[52] Gardiner and Gardiner, *Chronicles of Old Berkeley*, 204 [called Mangus]; Norris, *History of the Lower Shenandoah Valley*, 258–259, 355.

ride on the Potomac.[53] John Taylor's family had been early landowners in the Berkeley area, and Taylor had served on the first Berkeley County grand jury in 1772.[54] Juror George Reynolds later won a seat in the General Assembly as a Federalist.[55] Juror William Helms owned 300 acres of land, more than John or James Crane.[56] A few other names, John Bates, William Piles, and Joseph Warnsford, left less information in the historical record.[57]

And although Crane's jury might be an extreme example (one can imagine potential jockeying to sit on the jury of this celebrated case, a jury that would condemn or possibly exonerate James Crane's son), it does not seem to be truly exceptional. Other leading figures from Berkeley County also frequently filled the rosters of the Winchester District Court's juries. Judge Tucker later complained that juries were, after the first few days of court, made up of "idle loiterers" but his complaint in its assumption proved the elite rule – that juries were expected to consist of leading citizens and that such was routinely the case during the early days of a court session.[58]

It is hard to know exactly how these men felt as they confronted Crane's case. Did they genuinely disagree based on the facts? Or did the jurors in favor of a murder conviction think that the jurors who argued for manslaughter – elites with ties to eastern Virginia – were swayed by their loyalties to James Crane? Were the jurors who were set on a murder conviction especially offended by Catherine Crane's slur? Or were the facts disputed and uncertain?

The jurors who favored Crane and Crane's attorney were not the only ones who thought that manslaughter was the appropriate result. Another observer, Berkeley's sheriff, Robert Throckmorton, later wrote that his recollection of the testimony was that Campbell's men had provoked Crane and then Crane had found himself fighting with both Merchant and Vanhorn at the same time:

I was at his Tryal ... One thing has much weight with me, which is after their [Campbell's reapers'] day's work was done, they went to Crane's house, where it do not appear they had any business but to renew a quarrel that had Ran very high the preceding day. It likewise appears that Crane was engaged with two men partly at the same time.

"A man in that situation," Throckmorton observed sympathetically, "would be likely to do all he could to defeat his adversary; for when a man is fighting, he

[53] Danske Dandridge, *Historic Shepherdstown* (Charlottesville, VA: Michie Company, Printers, 1910), 320; Bushong, *History of Jefferson County*, 42–43; Norris, *History of the Lower Shenandoah Valley*, 416.

[54] Bushong, *History of Jefferson County*, 11; Norris, *History of the Lower Shenandoah Valley*, 227.

[55] Bushong, *History of Jefferson County*, 75.

[56] Berkeley County Land Tax Records, 1790, BCHS. Thomas Kemp Cartmell, *Shenandoah Valley Pioneers and Their Descendants* (Winchester, VA: The Eddy Press, 1909), 19. A Meredith Helm had been on the first commission of the peace in Frederick in 1743.

[57] Jury list, Commonwealth v. Crane District Court File, Library of Virginia.

[58] See Tucker, *Blackstone's Commentaries*, 4:64–65.

has little time to reflect, but it seems natural for him to do all he can to extricate himself."[59]

Witnesses, jurors, and community members thus had strongly differing views about Crane and his guilt. And the Cranes seem to have believed that John would triumph at trial; John himself even petitioned for trial with Tucker instead of delaying his trial until the court's spring term. Were their hopes pinned on a different understanding of what had happened that day at Campbell's fence, or merely on their social standing and influence?

Locked in disagreement, the jury passed the buck to Judge Tucker. For his part, Tucker was exasperated that the jurors had not been able to compromise with a manslaughter verdict. Although "no man could be persuaded to find murder what he thought manslaughter," he wrote, "a departure on the side of mercy was what might with some reason to be expected in those of a different opinion."[60] But no such departure had come. The jurors set on murder had obviously felt strongly about Crane's guilt – and had worded the verdict to emphasize the higher crime.

After the jury delivered its verdict, Charles Lee, Crane's lawyer, knew immediately that whatever the intentions of some of the jurors, the verdict did not look good for Crane. In fact, he told Judge Tucker, he thought that the verdict omitted proven facts and material facts in Crane's favor.[61] Lee asked Judge Tucker to allow him to point these omissions out and ask the jury to modify their findings. The jury, he suspected, had not understood that some omitted facts were material facts, essential to the determination of the degree of Crane's guilt.[62] And because the court would make its legal decision – whether Crane would hang for murder or was guilty of manslaughter only – based on the facts provided by the jury in the verdict, it was critical that the verdict include all material facts.

Tucker at first reluctantly agreed to Lee's request.[63] But as Lee made his points, Judge Tucker became concerned that Lee was overstepping and trying

---

[59] "Robert Throckmorton to the Governor," June 19, 1791, in *Calendar of Virginia State Papers*, 5:599. On Throckmorton, see Amanda C. Gilreath, *Frederick County Virginia, Deed Books 19 and 20, 1780–1785, Abstracted* (Westminster, MD: Heritage Books, 1995), 23; W. M. Noble, "The Throckmorton Family of Virginia," *Virginia Magazine of History and Biography* 15 (1908): 81–82. Robert Throckmorton was listed as Berkeley sheriff on a July 9, 1790 bond from John Cook and Colonel William Darke to Robert Throckmorton, sheriff of Berkeley County. Miscellaneous Virginia papers, 1656–1850, Box 1, Folder 30, UVA Special Collections. Also listed as the Berkeley sheriff on papers for September 1791 Court, where he or his representatives execute the summons for Berkeley County. See "Commonwealth of Virginia to Sheriff of Berkeley County," Daniels v. Blue, April 18, 1791, Box Barcode 1117433, Frederick County Ended Causes, Frederick County District Court Records, September 1791, Folder 2, Library of Virginia.

[60] "Robert Throckmorton to the Governor," June 19, 1791, in *Calendar of Virginia State Papers*, 5:599.

[61] Letter from Charles Lee to St. George Tucker, September 4, 1791, Tucker-Coleman Papers.

[62] Ibid.

[63] Ibid.

to get the jury to modify what they had already found.[64] He interrupted, and Lee became angry. When Tucker interrupted Lee for the final time, Crane's counsel let his displeasure be known. He retorted tartly that "if the court was truly satisfied that all facts proved in favor of Crane were included in the verdict" then "judgment of death might be pronounced."[65] Since Crane had not yet been convicted of murder – the verdict had, after all, left the legal decision to the court – the meaning of Lee's hyperbole was evident. The verdict, as it stood, suggested murder, and that did not bother Tucker in the least.

The special verdict solved the jury's problems but it also created many new ones for Crane – and for the court. As Tucker left the bench on September 3, 1791, the case's key question, and Crane's fate, was now his to decide.

---

[64] Ibid.
[65] Ibid.

7

"That Stigma on My Character"

Judges, Judicial Review, and "Republican"
Interpretation of the Laws

Late in the evening of September 3, 1791, after receiving the jury's verdict, Judge Tucker adjourned court and returned to his rented lodgings. There, he scrawled a short message to attorney Charles Lee in the flickering candlelight. Reflecting on the heated exchange between the two men after Crane's jury had delivered its verdict, he demanded an apology. "In a cooler moment," he wrote, "it is not improbable you may be convinced that in my official conduct I have neither deserved the Imputation of partiality, nor of blood-thirstyness: – if so," Tucker continued, "I have a right to expect from your Candour, an acknowledgement that those expressions which you this Evening made use of at the bar, & which in my interpretation of them may have a tendency to fix that stigma on my Character, were either unmerited, or unintended."[1]

When Catherine Crane had called Campbell's men "negrofied puppies," she had used arguably the worst slur that working white farmers like Isaac Merchant and his neighbors could experience.[2] Lee's words to Tucker were similar – in some ways, the equivalent for a judge. If working white men like Merchant were conscious of maintaining their difference from the enslaved African Americans who toiled in Virginia's fields, Virginia judges like Tucker were conscious of maintaining their own distinction from the arbitrary, overweening jurists so maligned by eighteenth-century revolutionary thought. For decades, theorists had argued that judges were inherently anti-democratic figures whose power and discretion threatened the people. It was this very argument that had led Montesquieu and Beccaria, and then Jefferson, to propose stark limits on judicial power. As a result, Tucker would have been especially on guard against any

---

[1] Letter from St. George Tucker to Charles Lee, September 3, 1791, Item 2756, Tucker-Coleman Papers.
[2] See Commonwealth v. John Crane, the Younger, 3 Va. 10 (1791).

type of arbitrary or heavy-handed conduct on the bench. In the late eighteenth century, there was no honor for a judge – particularly a "republican" judge – in being "bloodthirsty." Instead, the insinuation was a serious affront.

In 1776, Jefferson and the revisors of the law had held a particular conception of republican law. If the law were to be "king," they concluded, judicial discretion should be minimized – a "mere machine," as Jefferson had described it. But now, fifteen years later, Tucker and some of his colleagues had different ideas.

Tucker may not have always loved the endless, dirty travel of his lengthy judicial circuits, or the long months spent away from his family, but he did believe in the importance of his office and its responsibility in the new nation. Only a few weeks earlier, he had lectured his law students about the importance of the judiciary to republican government – its independence and its protection of the citizen against the legislature. "Herein consists the excellence of our Constitutions," he told them, "that no Individual can be oppressed whilst this branch of the Govern't [the judiciary] remains uncorrupted."[3] For the past ten years, Tucker had been advocating for judicial review – particularly the power of the judge to consider as void legislative acts that transgressed the people's constitution. Now, fifteen years after Jefferson had adopted Beccaria's idea that judges should be "mere machines," Tucker and a few other Virginians had begun to advance a new idea of republican law: one with the judge as "guardian" of republican liberty.

As discussed in Chapter 4, the first impulse of "enlightened" legal reform had been to greatly restrain discretion, especially the judge's – an idea that had perhaps emerged most clearly in Jefferson's defeated Bill for Proportioning Crimes and Punishments. The bill's animating principle had been that writing down laws, as thinkers like Montesquieu, Beccaria, and others insisted, and having judges merely execute them, was key to attaining and maintaining a people's liberty.

But by the 1780s, Virginia's judges were beginning to fashion their power and authority into a new version of the republican role, one that made them in some sense the gatekeepers and defenders of the people's constitution. This change had begun early on, as Virginia's courts and lawmakers worked out the consequences of having a written constitution. Writing a constitution had been Virginia's first and most important revolutionary act as an independent state; as Tucker explained in his edition of Blackstone, America's written state and federal constitutions had "reduc[ed] to practice, what, before, had been supposed to exist only in the visionary speculations of theoretical writers." With these constitutions, "the world, for the first time since the annals of its inhabitants began, saw an original written compact formed by the free and

---

[3] Tucker, "Ten Notebooks of Law Lectures," 5:202, Tucker-Coleman Papers.

deliberate voices of individuals disposed to unite in the same social bonds; thus exhibiting a political phenomenon unknown to former ages." The theoretical social contract had been made concrete. These written constitutions set forth "limits, which cannot be transgressed without offending against the greater power from whom all authority, among us, is derived; to wit, the PEOPLE."[4] Writing a constitution, they supposed, would cement the people's liberties.

But the actual effects of putting a constitution in writing, as Virginians soon saw, were complicated. What happened when that written constitution conflicted with a law passed by the people's legislature? This was the issue Virginia had confronted in 1782, what Tucker called the "Grand Constitutional Question."[5] It involved a conflict between the Virginia constitution and the state's Treason Act, in a case that became known as the *Case of the Prisoners*, or *Commonwealth v. Caton*. In the process, Virginia's judges began to assert a new role for themselves, this time as guardians of republican liberty.

The case began with an indictment for treason. Three men, John Caton, Joshua Hopkins, and James Lamb, were accused of assisting the British during their invasion of the southeastern part of the state. In May and June 1782, they were charged with treason in Princess Anne County, which had been known for Tory activity throughout the Revolution. The prisoners were tried in front of an oyer and terminer session of the General Court in Richmond in June 1782, convicted of giving aid to the British, and condemned to death for treason under the Treason Act. That Act had stripped the Governor of his traditional power of pardon and moved the ability to grant clemency to the "General Assembly." Following this procedure, the convicted men had petitioned the General Assembly for pardon and the House of Delegates had granted the pardon. The Senate, however, refused to concur. Under the Treason Act, the pardon (it seemed) was incomplete.[6]

However, the Virginia constitution suggested the pardon might still be valid. The constitution provided that the Governor "shall, with the advice of the Council of State, have the power of granting Reprieves or pardons, except where the prosecution shall have been carried on by the House of Delegates, or the law shall otherwise particularly direct; in which Cases, no reprieve or

[4] St. George Tucker, *Blackstone's Commentaries with Notes of Reference to the Constitution and Laws of the Federal Government of the United States; and of the Commonwealth of Virginia*, vol. 1 (Philadelphia, PA: William Young Birch and Abraham Small, 1803), Editor's Appendix Note A, 4.

[5] Charles F. Hobson, ed., *St. George Tucker's Law Reports and Selected Papers, 1782–1825*, vol. 1 (Chapel Hill, NC: University of North Carolina Press, 2013), 21.

[6] William Michael Treanor, "The *Case of the Prisoners* and the Origins of Judicial Review," *University of Pennsylvania Law Review* 143, no. 2 (1994): 491–570, 500–501. Imogene Brown, *American Aristides: A Biography of George Wythe* (East Brunswick, NJ: Farleigh Dickinson University Press, 1981), 244–247. Hobson, *St. George Tucker's Law Reports*, 1:21–22. "An Act Declaring What Shall Be Treason," in William Waller Hening, *The Statutes at Large ...*, vol. 9 (Richmond, VA: J. & G. Cochran, 1821), 168. Commonwealth v. Caton, 8 Va. 5 (1782).

Pardon shall be granted, but by Resolve of the House of Delegates."[7] The constitution thus potentially suggested that in cases where the law explicitly took pardon power away from the Governor, it could be exercised by the House of Delegates alone. This meant the prisoners' pardon by the House of Delegates had arguably satisfied the constitution's requirements.

The question at stake was important; how should such a conflict – between the Virginia constitution and an Act of the legislature – be resolved? Attorney General Edmund Randolph explained the problem to James Madison this way: "A late incident will probably try the fortitude of our judiciary, by calling upon them to say, whether a law, contrary to the constitution, is obligatory."[8] He informed Madison that some members of the General Assembly proposed to solve the conflict by "conven[ing] a committee from the legislative, and judiciary departments who shal[l] enter into a discussion of the subject, and defin[e] the powers of each." Some had also proposed that "a council of revisi[on] shall be established, to keep the legislature in futur[e] cases within its just limits."[9] Meanwhile, the General Court passed the case on to Virginia's highest court, the Court of Appeals.[10] The question: whether the Treason Act and the Virginia constitution were indeed in conflict, and if so, "Whether a Court of Law could declare an Act of the Legislature void because it was repugnant to the Act for the Constitution of Government?"[11]

Randolph's job as Attorney General was to defend the prisoners' convictions, but when he rose for his argument, he did something astounding: he ultimately admitted that the court had the power to strike down the Treason Act if the statute and constitution were truly in conflict.[12] In Virginia, Randolph had an unflattering reputation as someone "of a character that bends according to how his interest varies, and in addition that always follows the strongest party."[13]

---

[7] Hening, *Statutes at Large*, 9:115–116.

[8] See letter from Edmund Randolph to James Madison, July 18, 1782, in *The Papers of James Madison*, vol. 4: *1 January 1782–31 July 1782*, ed. William T. Hutchinson and William M. E. Rachal (Chicago, IL: University of Chicago Press, 1965), 422–424 (quotation at n. 8).

[9] Letter from Edmund Randolph to James Madison, October 26, 1782, in *The Papers of James Madison*, vol. 5: *1 August 1782–31 December 1782*, ed. William T. Hutchinson and William M. E. Rachal (Chicago, IL: University of Chicago Press, 1967), 217–218.

[10] In 1782, the Court of Appeals consisted of the judges of the General Court, Chancery Court, and Admiralty judges together; the court heard the arguments on October 31, 1782. Brown discusses the case (and Wythe's involvement) in *American Aristides*, 244–247.

[11] David J. Mays, *The Letters and Papers of Edmund Pendleton, 1734–1803*, 2 vols. (Charlottesville, VA: University of Virginia Press for the Virginia Historical Society, 1967), 2:417.

[12] Edmund Randolph, *Edmund Randolph. Notes on Virginia laws. Includes pardons for traitors.* Series 1: General Correspondence 1723–1859, James Madison Papers, Library of Congress. www.loc.gov/item/mjmo21836/.

[13] In *The Fate of the Revolution*, Lorri Glover provides a detailed look at Randolph's many changed positions regard the federal Constitution. Letter from Martin Osler to comte de la Luzerne, February 4, 1788, in Lorri Glover, *The Fate of the Revolution: Virginians Debate the Constitution* (Baltimore, MD: Johns Hopkins University Press, 2016), 72.

Randolph's argument indicates he sensed that the wind was blowing in judicial review's favor.

Randolph conceded the court's power to invalidate an act of legislation, but argued that, in this particular case, the Treason Act and the Virginia constitution were not actually in conflict. The constitutional provision, Randolph contended, could also mean that a pardon issued by the House of Delegates was necessary, but did not have to be sufficient. He explained:

[T]he liberality, necessary to catch its spirit, must be adopted. In [the construction of a stat-ute], the masculine force of substantial sense is too often subjected to the petty tyranny of grammatical rule ... [But] the constitution cannot avoid a generality of terms, lest it should omit a part of that infinity of combination, of which the affairs of society are capable – whereas a law touches single subjects only.[14]

According to Randolph, this meant that although the constitution said that the House of Delegates must be party to the pardon, that did not necessarily mean that the legislature could not also add a requirement that the Senate sign on. In the British tradition, he explained, it was proper to deny the King power to pardon in certain instances (such as impeachment, when it might be his own officials on trial), but there was no such rationale for excluding the Virginia Senate. The constitution merely meant that the Senate was unable to issue pardons without the House of Delegates concurring; in other words, in issuing its pardons, the House of Delegates could consult any other person or body it chose.[15] But in a case where a law and the constitution did indeed conflict, Randolph boldly conceded, "any law against the constitution may be declared void."[16]

It was an important question, so the Court of Appeals had invited the Virginia Bar to offer amicus arguments. Several attorneys obliged. As Judge Edmund Pendleton noted, William Nelson, Tucker, and another "volunteer," John Mercer, differed in "several points, particularly as to the Power of the Court to declare an Act of assembly void in any case."[17]

By 1782, Tucker had been away from the practice of law for several years. He had traveled to court only to watch the proceedings, but since the case raised a critical and fascinating question, the inquisitive Tucker prepared a few notes for his friend William Nelson to use in Nelson's own argument. Nelson, however, urged Tucker to deliver his thoughts to the court himself, and so Tucker scribbled out his argument – "digested & committed to paper in a great

---

[14] See Treanor, "The Case of the Prisoners," 508.
[15] Treanor, "The Case of the Prisoners," 508–509.
[16] Randolph, *Edmund Randolph. Notes on Virginia laws.*
[17] See Pendleton's account of "The Case of the Prisoners" (*Commonwealth v. Caton*), in Mays, *Letters and Papers of Edmund Pendleton,* 2:416–427.

hurry" – and prepared to offer it to the court. It was strongly in favor of the court's power to invalidate the Treason Act.[18]

With his amicus argument, Tucker would become perhaps Virginia's foremost proponent of judicial review. He began his constitutional case by framing the question as "Whether the Judges have a right to decide on the validity or nullity of a positive Act of Assembly passed with all the Formalities used in framing or enacting laws." He answered yes, and laid out his case accordingly.[19]

Tucker's argument began with the written constitution. Unlike Britain, he contended, Virginia now had a written constitution and it was the judiciary's job to interpret it. The constitution established separate branches, including judicial and legislative arms, and specified that "neither exercise the powers properly belonging to the other." In this separation, he advised, the judiciary alone had the power to interpret laws. "Now I hold it to be uncontrovertible," he asserted, "that the power properly belonging to the Judiciary Department, is, to explain the Laws of the Land as they apply to particular Cases ... where such Cases arise, the Interpretation of the Laws of the Land is in the Judiciary alone." If the legislative branch felt that the judiciary had improperly interpreted a law, the legislature could respond after the fact by explaining their acts, so that "no further Doubts may occur in the future Construction of them in such particular Cases as shall be brought the Judiciary." But in all current cases involving particular controversies, it was the sole department of the judiciary to apply the law. Otherwise, the divided powers of the constitution would be undermined.[20]

But what about this case, where a law seemed to conflict with the constitution? Having established the judiciary's supremacy over the law and particular controversies, Tucker noted that the "judiciary alone ... can decide what is or is not Law, and consequently ... on the validity or nullity of different Laws contradicting each other." Because the constitution was established by a higher power than the civil legislature – the people, acting in what Tucker called a "political Legislature" – the civil legislature had no power to alter it. Instead, any act of the legislature contrary to the constitution would be "null and void." Unlike the traditional situation where two regular statutes conflicted, here the constitution trumped any subsequent conflicting statute, rendering the subsequent Act null and void law. "I hold," Tucker wrote, "that the judges are not bound to consider such Act as Law."[21]

---

[18] Hobson, *St. George Tucker's Law Reports*, 1:22 (quoted ibid.). See Pendleton's account of "The Case of the Prisoners" (Commonwealth v. Caton), in Mays, *Letters and Papers of Edmund Pendleton*, 2:416–427.

[19] Tucker's notes of argument in *Caton* are in Hobson, *St. George Tucker's Law Reports*, 3:1741–1746.

[20] Ibid., 1741–1742.

[21] Ibid., 1742–1745.

Why? Because the constitution was "law" too – the "first Law" by which those judges were bound. Tucker here acknowledged that the history of constitutional construction was against his reasoning. After all, he admitted, in Britain "constitutional" documents like Magna Carta had been altered over time by Acts of Parliament. But, Tucker stressed, the British situation was different. There, even foundational Acts were seen as merely "explanatory" of the constitution, which was said to exist "beyond the memory of Man" and which can "only be collected from immemorial Usages, or such Statutes as have from time to time been made to explain it or amend it." Thus, Tucker explained, "by this Fiction in Law (for it seems to deserve that name) the British Constitution may be modeled agreeable to the will of Parliament." But Virginia was different. Whereas the British constitution "partakes of the nature of their common Law," and was "constructive," Virginia's was "express." Whereas the "British is traditional … ours on the Contrary was formed with all the solemnity of an original Compact between Citizens about to establish a Government most agreeable to themselves." This meant that whereas Parliament had the power to "interpret" and thus implicitly shape and reshape the British constitution, Virginia's General Assembly had no such power. Indeed, this Virginia constitution was committed to writing and made public "to all its Citizens, who became parties thereto," precisely so that it "might not be misinterpreted." The constitution was law, applicable in particular cases as well as general principles. The judiciary was charged with interpreting the law (including the constitution) in particular cases. Therefore, the constitution could be described as those "fundamental principles of our Government of which the Judiciary Department is constituted the Guardian."[22]

The inquiry before the court, then, was this: that if an Act was "absolutely and *irreconcilably* contradictory to the Constitution, it cannot admit of a Doubt that such an act is absolutely null & void." Indeed, such an Act would be void "ab Initio." Otherwise, if every Act of the General Assembly could be opposed to the constitution and yet law, they would essentially repeal the constitution – a power which the citizens had not granted to the General Assembly when "convened for the purposes of civil legislation only."[23]

But what about the Treason Act itself? Here, Tucker admitted, to his embarrassment, that he had not actually seen a copy of the Treason Act, despite his attempts to procure one. (He would later complain in his edition of *Blackstone's Commentaries* that Virginia's statutes were "stitched together" in a "*loose* and *slovenly* manner" and "dispersed throughout the country in *unbound*, and even *uncovered sheets*, more like ephemerons than the perpetual rules of property, and of civil conduct in a state.")[24] But he relayed to the court that it had been told

[22] Ibid., 1744–1745.
[23] Ibid., 1745.
[24] St. George Tucker, *Blackstone's Commentaries*: editor's preface, I:v.

to him by a reputable source that the goal of the constitution had been "to leave as few obstacles as possible in the way to mercy." That, combined with a few of the other provisions of the constitution, led him to "the Opinion that the Spirit of our Constitution declares that the power of Pardoning in all Cases where it is not given to the Executive, is vested in the House of Delegates *alone*."[25]

After listening to Tucker's argument and those of the other lawyers, the Virginia Court of Appeals adjourned to consider the case. A couple of days later, they delivered their opinions.[26] As Judge Pendleton recorded it in his notes, the judges delivered their opinions individually, but his opinion expressed the consensus of most. He believed "the Treason Act was not at Variance with the Constitution but a proper exercise of the power reserved to the Legislature by the latter ... which it was thought preserved the Spirit of the Constitution & was the best Interpretation which the Inaccurate words of the Constitution would admit of."[27] The judges had followed Attorney General Randolph's lead and found the two not to be at odds.

But several members of the court expressed their agreement with the principle of judicial review, even if they did not find it applicable in this case. George Wythe made his views clear:

I have heard of an English chancellor who said, and it was nobly said, that it was his duty to protect the rights of the subject, against the encroachments of the crown; and that he would do it, at every hazard. But if it was his duty to protect a solitary individual against the rapacity of the sovereign, surely, it is equally mine, to protect one branch of the legislature, and, consequently, the whole community, against the usurpations of the other: and, whenever the proper occasion occurs, I shall feel the duty; and, fearlessly, perform it ... Nay more, if the whole legislature, an event to be deprecated, should attempt to overleap the bounds, prescribed to them by the people, I, in administering the public justice of the country, will meet the united powers, at my seat in this tribunal; and, pointing to the constitution, will say, to them, here is the limit of your authority; and, hither, shall you go, but no further.[28]

Although he had lost the case, Tucker may have been pleased to hear his old teacher agree with him so strongly on the principle at stake.

The Court of Appeals had taken Attorney General Randolph's suggestion and found that the constitution and Treason Act were not actually in conflict, but even Randolph thought it bordered on sophistry. As he reported to James Madison, "The judges of the court of appeals avoided a determination, whether a law, opposing the constitution, may be declared void, in their decision of Saturday last ... There surely was prudence in the path, which they

[25] Hobson, *St. George Tucker's Law Reports*, 3:1745.

[26] Mays, *Letters and Papers of Edmund Pendleton*, 2:418.

[27] Brown, *American Aristides*, 249, Mays, *Letters and Papers of Edmund Pendleton*, 2:418–426; Commonwealth v. Caton, 8 Va. 5, 13 (1782).

[28] *Caton*, 8 Va. at 7.

took. But I doubt not, that to any but lawyers the construction, by which the two were reconcile[d,] would appear unintelligible."[29]

When Tucker talked about judges as the "guardian" of republican liberty, he had come a long way from the ideas about judges that Jefferson had expressed in the Bill for Proportioning Crimes and Punishments.[30] As part of that bill, Jefferson had also adopted a Beccarian attitude towards law, arguing that it should be essentially a code clear on its face (one promulgated by the legislature), not a complicated body of tradition carried by judges. Now, as more Virginians embraced judicial review, they seemed to be taking a step in another, hybrid direction. The constitution was written, but it would be "guarded" by "republican" judges.

There was also a second dimension to the problem of republican judging in postrevolutionary Virginia, one also relevant to the concerns raised by Montesquieu and Beccaria: how should judges use precedent? And, more pressingly, what would be the role of British precedent be in the new nation? In 1787, another of Tucker's cases, *Commonwealth v. Posey*, became the focal point of this debate.

Posey had never quite been at the top of Virginia society, but he certainly drifted around its edges. His father was a neighbor and close companion of George Washington, and Posey himself became a childhood friend of John Parke Custis, Washington's stepson. He later managed Custis's New Kent County properties, and there became a justice of the peace and a representative to the General Assembly. But after Custis's death, Washington fired Posey, whom he called a "Superlative Villain," and accused him of stealing extensively from Custis's estate. Writing to Washington in 1784, the general's New Kent County brother-in-law described the problem this way: "Posey has ... long since lost all sense of shame, and altho I was guarded against him, yet I could not prevent (even with much trouble), his injuring the Estate greatly in many respects. I am still pursuing such methods as I can to bring him to Justice, but his cunning is considerable, and his villainy more than I can describe or you can conceive."[31]

---

[29] Letter from Edmund Randolph to James Madison, November 8, 1782, *Papers of James Madison*, 5:263.

[30] "A Bill for Proportioning Crimes and Punishments," in *The Papers of Thomas Jefferson*, vol. 2: 2 *January 1777 to 18 June 1779 including the Revisal of the Laws*, ed. Julian Boyd (Princeton, NJ: Princeton University Press, 1950), 492–504.

[31] For "Superlative Villain," see letter from George Washington to David Stuart, November 19, 1786, in *The Papers of George Washington, Confederation Series*, vol. 4: 2 *April 1786– 31 January 1787*, ed. W. W. Abbot (Charlottesville, VA: University Press of Virginia, 1995), 387–388. For Dandridge's description of Posey, see letter from Bartholomew Dandridge to George Washington, March 13, 1784, in *The Papers of George Washington, Confederation Series*, vol. 1: *1 January 1784–17 July 1784*, ed. W. W. Abbot (Charlottesville, VA: University Press of Virginia, 1992), 208–209 (see especially n. 3). For more on Posey, see John Thornton Posey, "A Federalist on the Frontier: General Thomas Posey," *Illinois Historical Journal* 83, no. 4 (1990): 247–258, 250; Malcolm Hart Harris, *Old New Kent County* (West Point, VA: Clearfield, 2006), 97–99; "Record of the Trial of John Price Posey," March 3, 1786, in *The*

Finally, in the summer of 1787, Posey was arrested for assaulting the county sheriff and confined to the county jail. He escaped, and three days later the jail and clerk's office caught fire. Posey, whose fall from grace was so complete that he was identified in his indictment as a "laborer," was arrested and charged with enticing two accomplices to "burn the Damn'd prison down" and set fire to the clerk's office, apparently to destroy records.[32]

People all over Virginia talked about the case, which melded fears of violent unrest with the gossip of a spectacular fall from grace. "I have heard much of threaten'd Riots, In Opposition to the payment of debts and taxes," Edmund Pendleton wrote to James Madison in 1787, "but no particular Instance of mischief of the sort, except the burning of the Court House in King William, the Prison in New Kent, and the Clerk's Offices of both. That the famous Mr. Posey was author of the latter, nobody seems to doubt, tho' they have not yet evidence sufficient to convict him."[33] Posey's accomplices, however, soon decided to testify for the state.

Posey was convicted of arson, a capital offense, by the General Court (the district court system would not be instituted until the following year) and he appealed his conviction to the Court of Appeals. When Frances Tucker heard, she wrote to St. George, who was in Richmond representing clients at the General Court. "I was asked yesterday," she told him, "how many of Poseys Guineas fell to your share, I suppose none, or you wou'd have mentioned them." Frances had heard that Posey "will be condemned, although the lawyers were highly paid for a defense."[34] Tucker replied that, in fact, Posey had not yet been condemned; his case had been adjourned to the Court of Appeals.[35] A few days later, St. George reported that to his "great mortification" he had been appointed to represent the Commonwealth on Posey's appeal – replacing the Commonwealth's attorney, Tucker's friend James Innes, who was ill and indisposed.[36]

Calendar of Virginia State Papers, vol. 1, ed. William P. Palmer and Sherwin McRae (Richmond, VA: R. U. Derr, Superintendent of Public Printing, 1884), 95.

[32] Harris, *Old New Kent County*, 97–99. For the "laborer" designation, see Indictment, in Commonwealth v. Posey File, Tucker-Coleman Papers. For Green and Posey, see "will. Clayton to the Governor of Va. In Reply," July 20, 1787, in *Calendar of Virginia State Papers*, 4:321; "will. Clayton, Clerk, to Lieut.-Gov. Randolph," August 8, 1787, in *Calendar of Virginia State Papers*, 4:329–330.

[33] Letter from Edmund Pendleton to James Madison, August 12, 1787, in *The Papers of James Madison*, vol. 17: *31 March 1797–3 March 1801*, ed. David B. Mattern, J. C. A. Stagg, Jeanne K. Cross, and Susan Holbrook Perdue (Charlottesville, VA: University of Virginia Press, 1991), 519.

[34] Letter from Frances Bland Randolph Tucker to St. George Tucker, October 9, 1787, Tucker-Coleman Papers.

[35] Letter from St. George Tucker to Frances Bland Randolph Tucker, October 27, 1787, in Tucker-Coleman Papers.

[36] Letter from St. George Tucker to Frances Bland Randolph Tucker, November 3, 1787, in Tucker-Coleman Papers.

Posey's counsel, Andrew Ronald, who had represented the prisoners in *Commonwealth v. Caton,* now argued for two days on behalf of his client. "Ronald is now speaking on the subject," Tucker wrote to Frances on November 3 from court, "having begun his argument yesterday morning. Do you not pity me for being obliged to answer so long an argument, especially, as I shall, I fear, not even gain honor from the contest?"[37] The case was controversial. Under the recently defeated Bill for Proportioning Crimes and Punishments, arson would have been punished by a mere five years forced labor; but instead the common law of crimes remained in force, and Posey was accused of a non-clergyable crime.[38] This meant that, only months after the General Assembly had failed by a single vote to abolish the death penalty for all crimes except murder and treason, a former member of the General Assembly faced execution for arson.

To make matters worse, the authority for this sentence was not any Act of the Virginia General Assembly but rather the convoluted enactments of old Parliaments and various interpretive opinions of English judges. The statutes were confusing – giving clergy, then taking it away again. Ronald urged the court to review the statutes, complicated by centuries of repeals and reinstatements, *de novo.* "The antiquity of the precedent," he insisted, "was nothing compared with the letter of the statutes."[39] Ronald argued that the statutes, read on their face, proved Posey was entitled to the benefit of clergy.[40] The problem, however, was that English judges had long read the same statutes to take *away* clergy. Ronald insisted that the precedent – including an opinion by venerated English jurist Lord Coke – was wrong. The question went far beyond Posey; it was about the reception of British precedent and the proper canons of judicial interpretation in the new nation.

When Tucker finally rose to make his own case for the Commonwealth, he relied on both the text of the statutes and precedent. Arson, he argued, even the burning of buildings like the clerk's office and the jail, was a felony at common law and one of the few offenses to which clergy was not extended. Tucker then walked the court through the English statutes in force in Virginia that had taken away clergy from various crimes or restored it.[41] English precedent was correct, he told the court; in its interpretation of these statutes, clergy was unavailable. Even before receiving his letter, Frances had already heard from other sources that St. George "spoke in Posey's case for four hours." She teased,

---

[37] Ibid.

[38] "A Bill for Proportioning Crimes and Punishments"; Kathryn Preyer, "Crime, the Criminal Law, and Reform in Post-Revolutionary Virginia," *Law and History Review* 1, no. 1 (1983): 53–85, 69–70.

[39] See Tucker's notes of Ronald's argument, Commonwealth v. Posey File, Tucker-Coleman Papers.

[40] On Ronald's participation in Caton, see Hobson, *St. George Tucker's Law Reports,* 3:1842–1843. On Ronald's Posey argument, see Tucker's notes of Ronald's argument, Commonwealth v. Posey File, Tucker-Coleman Papers.

[41] St. George Tucker, Notes of Argument in Posey, in Hobson, *St. George Tucker's Law Reports,* 3:1749–1755.

"I shall cease to wonder at your silences at home in future, for I think as loquacious as I am, it would last me for a month at least."[42]

The explicit question at hand was about arson and benefit of clergy, but a deeper issue was also at stake. What did it mean for a judge to interpret law in a republic, and, more particularly, what role did British precedent play? For some members of the court, there was a certain level of embarrassment about determining a man's fate in their new republic by being bound by the opinions of British judges on complex, ancient, and confusing Acts of Parliament. Judge Tazewell, writing in dissent, agreed with Ronald that the statutes should be read *de novo* and gave a passionate opinion on that point. He admitted that "adjudications upon statutes are often to be considered, as valuable expositions of the grounds and extent of the enactments." Despite that, he concluded, "in a case of life and death, I cannot be bound by the dictum of a British judge, upon a written law; for, although I venerate precedents, I venerate the written law more."[43] Judge Wythe may have agreed. He registered his dissent but said that it would be "tedious and unnecessary" to state the reasons for it.[44]

However, other judges were more wedded to the English authorities that had so long governed Virginia's courts. Judge Mercer argued that Coke's opinion had been the authority when Virginians settled the colony and should stay that way, "as our ancestors brought the doctrine … with them into this country, it ought to be regarded as the law of the land."[45] Judge Fleming further concluded that Coke's decision "has been so uniformly considered as the true construction of the statutes that it has become the law of the land; for precedents, so long acquiesced in, cannot be overturned, without more danger than benefit, as no point will ever be settled."[46]

By a majority, the Court of Appeals agreed with Tucker, and Posey was condemned to death. Upon hearing the sentence of death, "Posey, choked with tears, confessed his crime 'and said he hoped through the merits of his Saviour, to obtain a pardon for the sins of his past life.'" He was executed in January 1788.[47]

The veneration of written law in Ronald's argument and Tazewell's opinion indicated the dispute that was taking place in Virginia's legal thought about both the law and the judge. Blackstone had described judges as "the depositories of the laws; the living oracles, who must decide in all cases of doubt,

[42] Frances Bland Randolph Tucker to St. George Tucker, n.d. [filed with November 1787], Tucker-Coleman Papers.

[43] Commonwealth v. Posey, 8 Va.109, 115–117 (1787).

[44] Ibid., 122.

[45] Ibid., 117–119.

[46] Ibid., 127–128.

[47] Letter from James McClurg to James Madison, August 22, 1787, in *The Papers of James Madison*, vol. 10: *27 May 1787–3 March 1788*, ed. Robert A. Rutland, Charles F. Hobson, William M.E. Rachal, and Fredericka J. Teute (Chicago, IL: University of Chicago Press, 1977), 154–156, editors' note 4.

and who are bound by an oath to decide according to the laws of the land."[48]
But Ronald's argument and Tazewell's opinion – refusing to be bound by bad
precedent, even if it was old precedent, when there was written law at hand –
contained echoes of a different way of regarding law and the judge's role, one
more like Jefferson's. Blackstone had also recognized that precedents "against
reason" were not really precedents at all, but the arguments in *Posey* seemed
to go in a direction consonant with republican thoughts on law voiced by
Montesquieu and Beccaria. In this new legal world, judges were not oracles
imparting rules from "time immemorial" to a merely receptive public. Instead,
they were the agents of that public, drawing their authority and their rules
from laws promulgated by the people. In the most basic sense, this meant a law
driven by statutes, not by judicial opinions or the common law.

But as the other judges' opinions demonstrated, Tazewell's was not the only
option on the table, nor did it win out. Indeed, the majority seemed willing to
uphold even bad precedent in the name of certainty. They could have followed Tucker's argument, found that Coke was correct, and thus obviated the
biggest question raised by the case, whether they should follow longstanding,
but incorrect, English precedent. Judge James Henry did just that, concluding
that "principle and precedent unite in the interpretation" that Posey was not
eligible for clergy.[49] But other members of the court were willing to go further.
For example, as Judge Peter Lyons explained, precedent itself was important,
since "there is more danger to be apprehended from uncertainty, than from
any exposition," whether or not correct, because "when the rule is settled, men
know how to conform to it; but when all is uncertain, they are left in the dark,
and constantly liable to error." After all, "the same offence which, at one time,
was thought entitled to clergy, at another, may be deemed capital; and thus the
life or death of the citizen will be made to depend, not upon a fixt rule, but
upon the opinion of the judge, who may happen to try him, than which a more
miserable state of things cannot be conceived."[50] Judge John Tyler agreed that
"it would be dangerous to decide against such long-admitted precedents upon
statutes of such antiquity."[51] The other judges were in accord. Judge Blair even
noted that the precedent, though he thought it was wrong, was binding. "If
it were a new case," he explained, "I should be at no loss to decide in favour
of the prisoner. But the decision in Powlter's case, has prevailed so long, that
it must be submitted to; and the authority of it, for the reasons mentioned by
Judge Lyons, cannot now be shaken."[52]

---

[48] Tucker, *Blackstone's Commentaries*, 1:68.
[49] *Posey*, 8 Va. at 115.
[50] Ibid., 120.
[51] Ibid., 113.
[52] Tucker, *Blackstone's Commentaries*, 1:121–122. Judge Tyler noted, however, that his decision
was limited to a British statute, and "upon one of our acts of assembly, I shall, whenever the case
is doubtful, incline to follow the letter of the statute."

It is unclear how far Tucker himself was willing to go toward upholding incorrect English precedent. A later reporter of the case quoted Tucker as stating in his argument to the court that Coke's construction, which had "stood the test of so many ages was not, now, to be shaken."[53] Emphasizing the importance of precedent would not have been entirely out of character for Tucker; throughout his career, he combined support for the British legal tradition with a republican emphasis on written law. As historian Ellen Holmes Pearson has shown, Tucker transformed the common law into a republican institution by arguing that in America, the common law was grounded in consent, expressly adopted by individual states through reception statutes. This viewpoint gave the common law what Pearson calls a "solidly visible foundation based on consent, choice, and new customs tailored to the needs of America's vigorous republican societies."[54] However, Tucker's argument notes suggest that his *Posey* argument concerned itself more about the correctness of the precedent than its inherent binding authority. According to those notes, Tucker focused on parsing through all of the relevant statutes to conclude that Coke's opinion was actually correct. Tucker thus worked, at least primarily, within the same statutory ground as Ronald and Tazewell, although he came to a different conclusion. Tucker's statement about the importance of longstanding precedent seems to have been more about the fact that its correctness had been tested than about its authority, regardless of whether it was correct.

In such a situation, as the majority opinions indicated, there were republican reasons to support precedent. Precedent (at least as it was conceived in this era) restrained power by following known, disseminated rules.[55] Tazewell's opinion might follow the form of the "republican" jurisprudence suggested by theorists, but it also unsettled longstanding precedent to reinterpret a similarly longstanding statute. Doing so paradoxically put enormous power in the hands of judges; they might, without warning, reconfigure centuries of law – precisely the statutory construction about which the revolutionaries worried. In the legal world of the new United States, many things were up for grabs, including the meaning of republican judging. But everyone seemed to agree on one thing: it was about restraining arbitrary power – whether through known, disseminated

---

[53] Call's reporter included this argument. See *Posey*, 8 Va. at 109.

[54] Ellen Holmes Pearson, *Remaking Custom: Law and Identity in the Early American Republic* (Charlottesville, VA: University of Virginia Press, 2011), 30. Morton Horwitz also emphasizes the transformation in this era of the authority of the common law from natural law to law as consent, although he sees Tucker as a more ambiguous figure in this transition. Morton J. Horwitz, *The Transformation of American Law, 1780–1860* (Cambridge, MA: Harvard University Press, 1977), 19–23. In this essentially middle way, Tucker combined republican sentiment with, in some areas at least, precedent – precedent was valid, but for republican reasons. Moreover, the precedent for which Tucker argued in *Posey* was not merely any pronouncement by a British judge: Coke's *Institutes* had been the text of every aspiring lawyer and a primary guide to the Virginia courts in the colonial era.

[55] See Horwitz, *Transformation of American Law*, 5–9.

rules explicated in precedent or through the clarity of a statute. And again it was the judges who, although restrained by law, were also in the position to put those restraints into practice.

In both *Posey* and *Caton*, Virginia lawyers and judges of the 1780s were feeling out the meaning of republican law, and, more specifically, the proper role of a republican judiciary. By the time Tucker heard Crane's case in 1791, the judicial review he had dreamed about in *Caton* was near coming to fruition. In 1788, Edmund Randolph had taken the principle for granted, telling the Virginia ratifying convention that if "Congress wish to aggrandise themselves by oppressing the people, the Judiciary must first be corrupted."[56] Also at the convention, future US Chief Justice John Marshall had agreed; in language echoing Tucker's 1782 *Caton* argument (which he had observed), Marshall argued that if Congress "were to make a law not warranted by any of the powers enumerated, it would be considered by the Judges as an infringement of the Constitution which they are to guard."[57] Tucker now similarly instructed his law students: if the new Constitution were to be violated by a law produced by Congress – a law, for example, "prohibiting the free Exercise of Religion; or abridging the freedom of Speech; or the press; or the right of the people to assemble peaceably; or to keep and bear arms" – the judiciary would declare that the "power of the Legislature did not extend to the making of such a law" and "acquit the prisoner from any penalty which might be annexed."[58]

But despite this acceptance, judicial review was still not officially enshrined in Virginia law. In 1789, Tucker had drafted an opinion in favor of judicial review in the case of *Commonwealth v. Eldridge* but seems never to have delivered it.[59] By 1791, fully formed judicial review in Virginia was imminent; two years after Crane's case it would emerge in *Kamper v. Hawkins*, written at the district court level by Tucker himself and argued by John Marshall.[60]

Over the course of the 1780s, especially in *Caton* and *Posey*, the judge was becoming a key figure for republican liberty. In *Caton*, Virginia's lawyers and judges began to claim it as the court's job to protect the constitution from an overreaching legislature. In *Posey*, the Bar and judiciary explored the role of judicial precedent versus *de novo* readings of statutes. In both cases, Virginia's judges were both reasserting the importance of their traditional

[56] Treanor, "The Case of the Prisoners," 507.
[57] "Debates," in *The Documentary History of the Ratification of the Constitution*, vol. 10: *Ratification of the Constitution by the States: Virginia, No. 3*, ed. John P. Kaminski, Gaspare J. Saladino, Richard Leffler, and Charles H. Schoenleber (Madison, WI: Wisconsin Historical Society Press, 1988), 1431. Charles F. Hobson, *The Great Chief Justice: John Marshall and the Rule of Law* (Lawrence, KS: University Press of Kansas, 1996), 224, n. 42.
[58] Tucker, "Ten Notebooks of Law Lectures," 5:202.
[59] Hobson, "Biographical Introduction," in *St. George Tucker's Law Reports*, 1:47–49.
[60] See Hobson, *St. George Tucker's Law Reports*, 1:274–275, n. 13. I am grateful to Charles Hobson for reminding me of this fact.

common law role *and* positioning themselves as republicanism's guardians. In an atmosphere like this, where the judiciary was ascendant yet still fragile, Lee's insinuations of Tucker's partiality and "bloodthirstiness" had a special sting. This was about honor, of course, but it was honor of a particular type – Tucker's honor as a republican judge.

As Tucker wrote to Lee on the evening of September 3, challenging him on the words he had used in court, he was giving the other man a chance to apologize. Like Catherine Crane's slur, Lee's words were fighting words, words that questioned the judge's honor. Lee's words, in Tucker's opinion, had struck a nerve that required some sort of satisfaction. But Tucker was not really the dueling or fighting type, so unlike the men in his court, he would seek a way to settle the affront.

Lee replied to Tucker the next day. First, he attempted to reshape Tucker's memory of their exchange into something less extreme than calling the judge "bloodthirsty." "I am not sensible," he countered, "that at any time I used expressions which properly understood imputed to your official conduct either partiality or bloodthirstiness." Not only that, Lee added, but "I can with truth say I never either in warmth or a cooler moment entertained such a sentiment." Instead, the words that Tucker remembered must be, Lee explained, "these or some like them – 'That if the Court was satisfied that all the facts proved which were favorable to the prisoner, were found in the verdict, it must remain so and judgment of death might be pronounced.'"[61]

Having attempted to diffuse Tucker's anger, Lee went on to state his position. He believed that the jury's verdict had left out important facts – facts material to whether Crane was guilty of murder or manslaughter. He had requested Tucker's permission to address the jury on the verdict's defects, but "[h]aving been permitted to address the jury upon the defects of the verdict who were willing to hear what might be said, I was doing so in as proper a manner as then occurred to me, when I was several times interrupted and however I may be mistaken, I must declare my opinion to be that I was improperly interrupted." Lee knew why Tucker had interrupted: "It was conceived by you when you last interrupted me, that I was reflecting upon the conduct of the jury which ought not to be allowed." But he insisted that he had done no such thing. "I am sure that the jury did not so understand my remarks," he explained, "and that I did not impeach them of any misconduct but attributed the omissions to their opinion that they were not material."[62]

After Tucker's interruption, a frustrated Lee had given up. "I thought it a vain thing for me interrupted as I had been to proceed in my attempt to obtain an addition of facts in the verdict, and used the expressions before recited." Having explained himself, Lee now offered the obligatory apology: "you

---

[61] Letter from Charles Lee to St. George Tucker, September 4, 1791, Tucker-Coleman Papers.
[62] Ibid.

resented them [Lee's words] immediately in a manner unexpected to me and which then and ever since has given me pain."[63]

Tucker received Lee's letter on Sunday, September 4, and confronted the other man on his attempt to reframe the story. Still agitated, Tucker replied immediately, and in his reply insisted that Lee's words had been much more offensive than Lee was willing to admit: "I have this moment received your Letter in answer to mine … if my recollection does not deceive me your Expression was, if the Court are satisfied that all the facts favorable to the prisoner were found in the verdict, <u>let it be recorded</u> and Judgement of death pronounced." This was a serious insinuation, Tucker reminded Lee. "The Idea conveyed by such a turn of expression, I conceive, might rouse a temper less susceptible than my own to an instant reply."

But Tucker was willing to accept Lee's apology. "I am willing, Sir, however to suppose, it could not have been intended by you that I was activated by such principles as I then thought might be inferred from the Expression." The judge went on respond to Lee's concerns and to justify his own actions. "With regard to my interrupting your remarks on the verdict I then thought, and still think I was strictly in the Line of my duty in so doing, as they were at the last time particularly pointed against a fact found by the Jury, and which I thought fully proved and not against an omission." He reminded Lee, "You will do me the Justice to recollect that however I might have doubted (as I really did) the propriety of entering at large again upon the testimony you were permitted to go through every fact stated in your notes." Had he remained confined to those notes, Tucker told him, "I would have sat till this time with pleasure to have heard them."[64]

However, he did think, Tucker conceded, that Crane had done well by the version of events in the special verdict. "I own I was satisfied with the Verdict," he conceded, "as one more favorable to the prisoner than I expected, for if there were omissions of fact in his favor it appeared to me that there were much more important omissions of fact which might have operated strongly against him." He then gave several examples.

First, Tucker explained, in the jury's verdict, "the testimony of Mr. Campbell was wholly omitted." To what had Campbell, Crane's neighbor and the owner of the adjoining field, testified? Did it have something to do with the story that the newspapers had reported in the days after the murder, alleging that Crane had gouged out the horses' eyes and set their tails on fire? Whatever it was, Campbell's perspective had clearly been damaging to Crane.

Second, Tucker addressed the "particular part of the testimony" that had concerned Lee, which he had discussed with the jury – the part where Crane threatened to "let out the guts" of anyone he would fight that day. On that the verdict was, Tucker admitted, "defective in a leading feature" – but, he insisted,

---

[63] Ibid.
[64] Letter from St. George Tucker to Charles Lee, September 4, 1791, Tucker-Coleman Papers.

the defect was in Crane's favor. The defect was the "omission of the words <u>with a Knife</u> after, saying he would let out the Guts of any person he should fight with that day." The jury, it seems, had included Crane's words – that he would "let out their guts" – in the verdict, but left out that he had also said "with a knife."[65] If true, that testimony was indeed bad for Crane.

Finally, there were two additional, also critical, pieces of evidence that Tucker thought pointed to Crane's guilt. One was Vanhorn's own words, saying that he'd seen a knife in Crane's hands during the fight: "The deceased's observation as to what he thought he saw in his [Crane's] hand when he struck Merchant." And second, obviating any remaining doubt that the assailant had been Crane, Tucker emphasized the "positive proof that the Knife produced in court, tho' found upon the negro, was the one the prisoner had in the afternoon – and that the Knife was bloody and dirty when found." Taken together, with the other circumstances, these alterations in Crane's favor "appeared to me far to outweigh any fact proved on the part of the prisoner which was omitted."[66]

Regardless, Tucker was still frustrated with the special verdict. "I lament," he told Lee, "that the Jury could not be prevailed upon to find a general Verdict, as my Expectations were, that although no man would agree to find that murder, which he thought manslaughter, yet a departure on the side of mercy was what might with some reason to be expected in those of a different opinion." But the judge was satisfied with his actions in the trial. "However unfortunate," he told Lee, "I have been in deviating from your Ideas of strict propriety, as it respected the prisoner, I can not reproach myself, in the occasion, but as my Conduct may have affected your own feelings, I most sincerely regret it. Mine," he added, "have not been violated in an equal Degree for many years."[67]

As he wrote to Lee, Tucker probably already knew that he would send the case up to Virginia's General Court. After all, he was the only judge at Winchester and special verdicts often went to the General Court anyway.[68] But that did not make Lee's comments less offensive. In 1791, Tucker may have still felt a little insecure on the bench – he was only thirty-nine, and just finishing his second year as a judge. And Lee had made his remarks in public, in front of a room full of spectators and visiting lawyers. Court days were important, public events and the *Crane* case was both high stakes and high profile. In this setting, Lee had accused Tucker of being careless with a man's life, undermining the judge's authority and credibility. Tucker's honor was offended, and it was not just any honor – it was his honor as a republican judge.

Tucker had a day to cool off. He returned to court on Monday, ready to address Crane's case. The Winchester paper reported that "the court, being

---

[65] Ibid.
[66] Ibid.
[67] Ibid.
[68] For more on special verdicts, see Chapter 8 below.

comprised of only one judge" had allowed Crane "to determine ... whether the present judge should pass sentence, or be postponed to a full court." Crane decided to take the case to the General Court.[69] The court clerk entered the decision in the Order Book: "the special verdict found by the jury being seen and inspected because the Court are not advised what Judgment to give thereupon The same is by and with the assent of the said John Crane the younger adjourned to the General Court for difficulty."[70]

But there were still several days of court left. Wednesday brought yet another special verdict; in this case, the jury included Crane's neighbor and witness in his case, Thomas Campbell. As with *Crane*, Tucker adjourned both to the General Court, for "novelty and difficulty."[71] On Thursday, Tucker heard a case where the jury had given a verdict for the defendant but later claimed they had mistaken the issue. Charles Lee, arguing in the case, contended – perhaps, to Tucker, ironically – that the jurors should "not be permitted to gainsay their verdict."[72] Then, in a case on Friday, Tucker expressed an opinion and later reversed himself, after "considering the law."[73] By the next Monday, he was ready to close court and move on to his next stop, Monongalia.[74] On October 8, as he finished his last tasks at Winchester, he penned a short line to his new fiancée:

To Miss Skipwith, October 8, 1791

On her sister's wedding at which no company was invited, except what had been for several days present.

A subject fair to write a farce on;

All drest so fine! ___ to see the Parson.[75]

Now, for Tucker, Crane's case was over. Normally, Tucker would have encountered the case again at the General Court, when the whole court gathered to hear arguments on the special verdict. But this time, Crane's decision to take his case to the General Court had provided Tucker with a double out. Not only did he not rule on the case at Winchester, but because he planned to marry Lelia Skipwith Carter in October, he would skip the General Court's November session. It was one of the few courts that Tucker missed in his long career.

[69] "Shepherd's-Town, September 5," *Mail* (Philadelphia, PA), September 17, 1791.
[70] "September 5, 1791," Winchester District Court Order Book, Library of Virginia.
[71] John Sukright v. Richard Cosnyne, ejectment, Tuesday, September 6, 1791. No jury overlap. This also adjourned to the General Court "for novelty and difficulty." Sukright v. Cosnyne, September 7, 1791, Winchester District Court Order Book, Library of Virginia.
[72] Noble v. Snickers (September 8, 1791), in Hobson, *St. George Tucker's Law Reports*, 1:248.
[73] Barton v. McMullin (September 9, 1791), ibid., 250.
[74] "September 12, 1791," Winchester District Court Order Book, Library of Virginia.
[75] St. George Tucker, "Poems," Tucker-Coleman Papers.

However, he may not have minded; if nothing else, it saved him from having to consider Crane's case again, particularly after his exchange with Lee at the trial. At the District Court, Tucker had been able to avoid explicitly ruling on Crane's fate, but at the General Court, that would have been impossible.

So Judge Tucker went on his way. And John Crane and his family prepared to argue his case in Richmond.

8

Murder or Manslaughter?

Crane's Special Verdict at the General Court

Crane's case came before the General Court on November 22, 1791.[1] There was one issue for the court – applying the law to the special verdict that Charles Lee and Judge Tucker had argued about, the same verdict that Lee said had omitted material facts. Now, the General Court needed to decide the question that Crane's jury had dodged: Was it murder or manslaughter?

But for this hearing, Crane had a new lawyer: Judge Tucker's friend, John Marshall. Crane's old lawyer, Charles Lee, had been visibly frustrated by the jury's verdict at the district court trial, and the Crane family was also probably shocked. After all, even Judge Tucker, convinced as he was of Crane's guilt, had commented that he wished the jury could have agreed on manslaughter. Now, with execution looming, the Cranes were desperate. So for this argument before the General Court – the argument which would determine John's fate – the Cranes had hired yet another member of Virginia's elite Bar to try to undo the damage.

As Marshall readied himself to take Crane's case, he may have looked less polished than other Virginia lawyers, but he was arguably the very best. In 1791, Marshall was only thirty-six years old, but was already one of the most respected lawyers in the state. Born in 1755, he had grown up on the edge of the Blue Ridge Mountains in a rustic area that counted as frontier, but with the benefit of a well-connected family. Marshall's parents were well-educated, and intent on furthering his education through a combination of learning at home and formal schooling in the classics – English literature, poetry, and history. In fact, in 1772 his father had been one of the first

[1] "Novem. 22nd, Richmond," *Calendar of Virginia State Papers and Other Manuscripts*, vol. 5: *From July 2, 1789 to August 10, 1792*, ed. William P. Palmer and Sherwin McRae (Richmond, VA: Virginia State Library, 1885), 398.

American subscribers to Blackstone's new *Commentaries on the Laws of England*.[2]

As a young man, Marshall had served in the Continental Army, where he quickly developed a reputation among his fellow soldiers for his athletic abilities. He was the "only man in the army who could put a stick on the heads of two persons of his own height (six feet) and clear it at a running jump."[3] Marshall was also famous in a "foot race," as one of his biographers explains: "running in his stocking feet, [he] was nicknamed 'Silverheels' by the soldiers, from his uniform success and the color of the yarn with which his mother finished off his blue stockings at the heel."[4]

After the war, Marshall had returned to Virginia to open a law practice. Experience in the army had convinced Marshall, like many veterans, of the importance of a strong central government; as he later remembered, "I partook largely of the suffering and the feelings of the army." Then, after the war, "My immediate entrance into the state legislature opened my views to the causes which had been chiefly instrumental in augmenting those sufferings, and the general tendency of state politics convinced me that no safe and permanent remedy could be found but in a more efficient and better organized general government."[5] Although a relative newcomer on the state's political scene, Marshall had played an important role at the Virginia ratifying convention, passionately defending the proposed Constitution.[6] And, like his friend St. George Tucker, Marshall championed judicial review. He had been in the audience for Tucker's argument in *Caton* in 1782 and had asserted at the Virginia ratifying convention in 1788 that the federal judiciary would have the power to strike down laws that conflicted with the proposed federal Constitution.[7] "If," Marshall had assured the convention, in language that evoked Tucker's exact phrasing from the his 1782 *Caton* argument, federal lawmakers "were to make a law not warranted by any of the powers

---

[2] R. Kent Newmyer, *John Marshall and the Heroic Age of the Supreme Court* (Baton Rouge, LA: Louisiana State University Press, 2007), 7–9.

[3] James Bradley Thayer, *John Marshall: An Address Delivered in Sanders Theatre Cambridge before the Law School of Harvard University and the Bar Association of the City of Boston* (Cambridge, MA: The University Press, John Wilson and Sons: 1901), 16–17.

[4] Ibid., 17.

[5] Quoted in Newmyer, *John Marshall and the Heroic Age*, 28.

[6] See Lorri Glover, *The Fate of the Revolution: Virginians Debate the Constitution* (Baltimore, MD: Johns Hopkins University Press, 2016), 130.

[7] See William Michael Treanor, "The *Case of the Prisoners* and the Origins of Judicial Review," *University of Pennsylvania Law Review* 143, no. 2 (1994): 491–570, 497, citing Charles F. Hobson et al., "Introduction," in *The Papers of John Marshall*, vol. 5: *Selected Law Cases, 1784–1800*, ed. Charles F. Hobson, Fredrika J. Teute, George H. Hoemann, and Ingrid M. Hillinger (Chapel Hill, NC: University of North Carolina Press, 1987), xxiii, lvii–lviii.

FIGURE 8.1 John Marshall, by Charles Balthazar Julien Févret de Saint-Mémen, 1808

enumerated, it would be considered by the Judges as an infringement of the Constitution which they are to guard."[8]

Despite his legal prominence, Marshall had retained a bit of his frontier roughness. He tended to overlook stylish dressing and retained an "uncultivated

---

[8] "Debates," in *The Documentary History of the Ratification of the Constitution*, vol. 10: *Ratification of the Constitution by the States: Virginia, No. 3*, ed. John P. Kaminski, Gaspare J. Saladino, Richard Leffler, and Charles H. Schoenleber (Madison, WI: Wisconsin Historical Society Press, 1988), 1431.

twang" in his speech.[9] He liked to walk and sometimes favored a mule instead of the fine horse preferred by other members of the Virginia gentry. One observer early in Marshall's legal career described him as having a "careless and languid air," strolling around town in "a plain linen roundabout and shorts, his hat under his arm, from which he was eating cherries." During one stroll, an acquaintance pointed him out to a man visiting town on business, who required legal counsel. The Richmonder identified Marshall as the "best lawyer to employ," but the visitor was skeptical – until he heard Marshall in court, and promptly hired him.[10] Tucker's stepson, John Randolph (a political opponent), would later eulogize Marshall as "simple in his tastes," "social in the intercourse of life," but "inexorably just."[11] As Randolph commented, "if a clearer head & sounder heart than Mr. Justice M. be possessed be on earth, I have never found them."[12]

The Cranes, with their connections, knew a good lawyer when they saw one. It was a wise choice. The jury's verdict had been a compromise, but it used an old form that in late eighteenth century Virginia was being put to new uses. At this stage, it would not be the General Court's job to reconsider the whole case. Instead, the judges would decide whether, based on the information in the special verdict, John Crane was guilty of murder or manslaughter. And convincing the court that the jury's language pointed to manslaughter would take a good lawyer.

Special verdicts like Crane's were almost as old as the jury itself. They had appeared early in English civil cases, as far back as the thirteenth century, as a way for jurors to protect themselves from prosecution for false verdicts, called "attaint."[13] As one legal scholar has noted, when it came to attaint, it was no excuse for jurors that "their mistake was based upon a misconception of a nice point of law," even on an issue where authorities differed.[14] As a result, to

---

[9] Newmyer, *John Marshall and the Heroic Age*, 14.

[10] Thayer, *John Marshall*, 11.

[11] Randolph commented that Marshall was easily mistaken for a "modest country gentleman, without claims to attention, and ready to take the lowest part in company"; but after close observation and conversation, he displayed "winning and prepossessing talk, and just as much mind as the occasion required him to show." Randolph quoted in Evert Augustus Duyckinck and George Long Duyckinck, *Cyclopedia of American Literature, Embracing Personal and Critical Notices of Authors and Selections from their Writings from the Earliest Period to the Present Day: With Portraits, Autographs, and Other Illustrations*, vol. 1 (New York, NY: Charles Scribner, 1856), 405.

[12] *The Papers of John Marshall*, vol. 8: *Correspondence, Papers, and Selected Judicial Opinions, March 1814–December 1819*, ed. Charles F. Hobson (Chapel Hill, NC: University of North Carolina Press for the Omohundro Institute of Early American History and Culture, 1995), 147, n. 1.

[13] Frederick Pollock and Frederic William Maitland, *The History of the English Law Before the Time of Edward I*, 2nd edn., vol. 2 (Clark, NJ: The Lawbook Exchange, Ltd., 2008), 661. Originally published by Cambridge University Press, 1898.

[14] Edmund M. Morgan, "A Brief History of Special Verdicts and Special Interrogatories," *Yale Law Journal* 32, no. 6 (1923): 575–592, 576.

protect themselves, jurors sometimes returned a special verdict, recounting a long list of facts and asking "the aid of the justices" or stating both their facts and their conclusion. As long as the facts were included as well, the judges could correct their legal conclusion if it turned out to be false.[15]

This practice, of course, shifted the risk of an erroneous verdict from the jurors to the judges, who were also subject to penalties of their own. As the great English legal historians Frederick Pollock and Frederic William Maitland explained, "Neither jurors nor justices had any wish to decide dubious questions."[16] As a result, the main contest between judge and jury in medieval England was not for, as one legal scholar has put it, "enlargement of jurisdiction, but for the evasion of responsibility."[17] Judges often rejected special verdicts, forcing "the jurors into statements which explicitly answer[ed] the words of the writ, and thereby in effect require an oath about matter of law."[18] This was enough of a problem that a 1285 statute forbade the practice, and explicitly allowed jurors to return both general and special verdicts, "if they state the truth of the matter and pray the aid of the justices."[19]

Jurors also returned extensive verdicts in criminal cases. As legal historian Thomas Green has demonstrated, criminal juries in medieval England returned detailed verdicts which not only determined defendants' guilt but also their eligibility for pardons "of course," pardons granted routinely in cases that fit criteria for self-defense or other situations in which the law excused homicide. And juries used this practice to considerable effect. Comparing coroner's records with eventual verdicts in criminal cases, Green finds that juries often fudged their factual findings, usually to characterize crimes in such a way as to allow an otherwise undeserving defendant to be eligible for a royal pardon.[20] As Green demonstrates, medieval English juries often altered their factual findings to fit their understanding of the "rough justice" of the case, or, in other words, to squeeze community norms into the criteria of the law.

Green's description of a powerful medieval jury using its power to produce an outcome compatible with community norms sits alongside another history of jury fact-finding, one which has emphasized judges' use of the special verdict to control juries. By the early eighteenth century, tables had turned and judges themselves forced special verdicts in criminal as well as civil cases.

[15] Ibid., 587.
[16] Pollock and Maitland, *History of English Law*, 2:661.
[17] Morgan, "History of Special Verdicts," 586.
[18] Pollock and Maitland, *History of the English Law*, 2:631.
[19] Morgan, "History of Special Verdicts," 587; Pollock and Maitland, *History of the English Law*, 2:660–661.
[20] See Thomas Andrew Green, *Verdict According to Conscience: Perspectives on the English Criminal Trial Jury, 1200–1800* (Chicago, IL: University of Chicago Press, 1985), 35–52. For instance, crimes that appeared to be manslaughter at the coroner's stage were often later described by a jury in (sometimes strikingly different) terms that closely tracked the formula for self-defense.

As legal scholar John Langbein has shown, English judges at London's Old Bailey – the court for serious crimes – dominated the jury trial, not only examining witnesses but directing verdicts of guilty or not guilty.[21] Sometimes, when they saw "conflict looming" between jurors, judges ordered special verdicts like Crane's – containing the facts but leaving the legal decision to the court. This allowed the court itself to determine whether criminal liability would be attached.[22] Langbein reports that in some instances judges recorded verdicts with which they disagreed, while in others they "persisted in opposing fully formulated verdicts."[23] For instance, at times judges rejected guilty verdicts and required the jury to return a special verdict instead. Even if the jury did convict against the wishes of the judge, the judge might still appeal to the king for the defendant's pardon.[24]

Meanwhile, in the colonies, juries fought for control over law as well as fact. In the celebrated trial of New York printer John Peter Zenger in the 1740s, Zenger's jury had staked a broad and widely celebrated claim for itself when it refused to convict the printer for seditious libel. Zenger admitted the facts of his offense but claimed they were true and thus that he was not guilty of libel. Although the judge instructed his jury that truth was not a defense to libel, they (at the urging of Zenger's counsel) took the law into their own hands and acquitted.[25] Although its actual legal effects were limited, the case became, as historian Stanley Katz has written, "a useful symbol of the development of political freedom in America" with influence on the "hearts and minds of the people."[26] It was representative in other ways as well. For instance, Massachusetts witnessed similar cases during the colonial era, and its juries, as legal historian William Nelson has argued, routinely had control over law as well as fact. This was due at least in part because of colonial pleading practices, which tended to emphasize the "general issue," instead of pleading "specially."[27]

Against this backdrop of powerful colonial juries, the right to trial by jury became, in the prerevolutionary period, a flash-point for perceptions of British abuse and American colonists' resistance to it. From British attempts to allow

---

[21] John Langbein, "The Criminal Trial before the Lawyers," *University of Chicago Law Review* 45, no. 2 (1978): 263–316, 285–286.

[22] Ibid., 295–296.

[23] Ibid., 291.

[24] Ibid., 296.

[25] See Robert Mark Savage, "Where Subjects Were Citizens: The Emergence of a Republican Language and Polity in Colonial American Law Court Culture, 1750–1776" (Ph.D. dissertation, Columbia University, 2011), 293.

[26] James Alexander, *A Brief Narrative of the Case and Tryal of John Peter Zenger*, 2nd rev. edn., ed. Stanley N. Katz (Cambridge, MA: Harvard University Press, 1972), 34–35, n. 2; quoted in Savage, "Where Subjects Were Citizens," 293.

[27] William Edward Nelson, *Americanization of the Common Law: The Impact of Legal Change on Massachusetts Society, 1760–1830*, 2nd edn. (Athens, GA: University of Georgia Press, 1994), 22–31.

jury verdicts to be appealed in fact as well as law to Acts giving jurisdiction to jury-less vice-admiralty courts, American colonists worried that Britain was consciously attempting to subvert this treasured right. "What has America done," colonists asked during the Stamp Act Crisis, "to be thus particularized, to be disfranchised and stripped of so invaluable a privilege as the trial by jury?"[28] These measures, they worried, threatened "future generations in America with a curse tenfold worse than the Stamp Act," and changed juries into "mere machines."[29] No wonder the denial of trial by jury appeared in the Declaration of Independence in the catalogue of the mother country's misdeeds. All the original state constitutions secured this right.[30]

Over a decade later, during the ratification debates over the US Constitution, the jury remained an important issue. One of the key objections of the Constitution's opponents was that it did not sufficiently secure the right to jury trial. Because the body of the Constitution, as proposed, had only mentioned trial by jury in criminal cases, some opponents argued that it effectively abolished civil juries. Others were concerned that it threatened juries overall by giving the federal courts appellate jurisdiction in law and fact.[31] As Patrick Henry reminded Virginia's ratification convention, Blackstone had cautioned that if a people lost their right to trial by jury, all other rights would follow.[32]

In Virginia, however, concern for juries coexisted paradoxically alongside a proliferation of special verdicts. These verdicts appeared in county courts and state courts, at the initiative of judges, parties, and sometimes jurors themselves. And because these verdicts left it to judges to determine important points of law they had a curious character. On the one hand, they gave away the jury's power to the court, and gave judges, Tucker worried, "an influence in questions of fact which may become highly pernicious."[33] On the other hand, they seemed disposed to help create greater uniformity between cases, by isolating the law and leaving legal decisions to legal professionals. In some ways this fit nicely with Virginia's ambition to be, as Thomas Paine had put it succinctly in *Common Sense*, a place where "the law is king."[34]

In 1803, reflecting in his edition of *Blackstone's Commentaries* on the importance of the jury, Judge Tucker would complain that special verdicts were

---

[28] Bernard Bailyn, *The Ideological Origins of the American Revolution*, enlarged edn. (Cambridge, MA: Harvard University Press, 1992), 108–109.

[29] Ibid., 109; Steven Wilf, *Law's Imagined Republic: Popular Politics and Criminal Justice in Revolutionary America* (New York, NY: Cambridge University Press, 2010), 35.

[30] Nelson, *Americanization of the Common Law*, 96–97.

[31] See Pauline Maier, *Ratification: The People Debate the Constitution, 1787–1788* (New York, NY: Simon & Schuster, 2011), 79, 340.

[32] Ibid., 289; see also F. Thornton Miller, *Juries and Judges versus the Law: Virginia's Provincial Legal Perspective, 1783–1828* (Charlottesville, VA: University of Virginia Press, 1994), 18–19.

[33] Tucker, *Blackstone's Commentaries*, 4: Editor's Appendix Note F, 64–65.

[34] Thomas Paine, *Common Sense: Addressed to the Inhabitants of America* (Philadelphia, PA: T. Robson and Co., 1776), 31.

the "practice constantly, in difficult cases" in Virginia.[35] He blamed them on Virginia's juries, whom he deemed lazy, unqualified, or otherwise problematic, unable to fulfill their required function. He complained that Virginia's juries were so bad that parties often decided that they would rather have the jury merely find the facts in a special verdict, and allow the court to decide the case. Tucker explained:

Where the courts are held in country places, the juries, after the first day or two, instead of being composed of the most respectable freeholders in the county, men above the suspicion of improper biass [sic], or corruption; men whose understandings may be presumed to be above the common level, are made up, generally, of idle loiterers about the court, who contrive to get themselves summoned as jurors, that they may have their expenses borne: and are in every other point of view the most unfit persons to decide upon the controversies of the suitors. The parties and their attorn[e]y are unprepared for a challenge, and the trial proceeds, not unfrequently, without a fourth part of competent jurymen to decide the question. Hence the number of ... special verdicts, demurrers to evidence, and points reserved; which the parties, mutually apprehensive of a decision by an incompetent jury, are ever ready to propose, or agree to.[36]

Crane's case was, of course, a little different. Here, instead of the verdict coming at the request of the parties, the jurors had offered the verdict on their own as way to solve their impasse, much to the frustration of Lee and Tucker.[37] But the effect was still to throw the responsibility for convicting Crane – and for deciding issues such as his intent, and whether he had had time to cool off, which were essentially factual questions – from the jury to the judge. Maybe Crane's jurors were truly divided, or maybe some of Berkeley's prominent men just did not want the responsibility of condemning James Crane's son.[38]

But when Crane's jury opted for a special verdict, they also used a common form. It was one which these individual jurors had probably used in other cases in the past, had requested as litigants, or had seen used by others at court. In Virginia, use of special verdicts stretched back to the colonial era, part of the colony's long history of deference to learned opinion on the law. Although surviving records are few, Sir John Randolph and Edward Barradall's reports of General Court cases from the 1730s and 1740s include a number of civil cases arising from special verdicts, often in which the court requested the opinion of the Attorney General. These included controversies over wills, disputes

---

[35] Tucker, *Blackstone's Commentaries*, 4:376, n. 31.

[36] Tucker, *Blackstone's Commentaries*, 4: Editor's Appendix Note F, 64–65.

[37] After all, Lee thought the verdict's contents were incomplete, indicating that he did not write the special verdict (as parties sometimes seem to have); and he attributed its flaws to the jury not understanding that some facts were material, indicating the verdict came directly from the jury itself. For his part, Tucker indicated that he thought there was enough evidence to convict Crane of murder, but regretted that, given disagreement, the jurors were not able to merely agree on manslaughter. This suggests that the verdict was more or less the jury's own remedy for its impasse – it was certainly not suggested in order to isolate a point of law, etc.

[38] I am grateful to Judge Thomas Steptoe for reminding me of this important possibility.

in detinue over slaves, tax liability, debts, land ownership, and other issues originating from both county courts and General Court juries.[39] Virginia's surviving colonial county court records also show special verdicts. Legal historian William Nelson has found judges directing special verdicts in Virginia county courts in the early eighteenth century and at times granting a new trial if the jury refused to comply.[40]

Special verdicts continued after the Revolution. In 1787, a single session of Virginia's General Court reviewed cases involving at least five special verdicts appealed from other places in the Commonwealth and from trials held in the General Court itself.[41] Special verdicts were common enough that the Virginia General Assembly dealt with them explicitly by statute, giving the General Court jurisdiction to hear special verdicts arising in the various districts.[42] Further evidence suggests they or similar forms occasionally occurred in county courts as well.[43] When Tucker complained that they were the "practice, constantly," he clearly knew what he was talking about.[44]

Tucker's legal notebooks provide the most thorough record of early national Virginia law available today – there, he recorded the cases he observed as an

---

[39] Parsons v. Lee, Sheriff of Stafford, Jeff. 49, 1737 Va. Lexis 1 (April 1737); Edmonds v. Hughes, Jeff. 2, 1730 Va. Lexis 2 (April 1730); The King v. Moore, Jeff. 8, 1733 Va. Lexis 2 (Oct. 1733); Morris v. Chamberlayne, Jeff. 14, 1735 Va. Lexis 4 (April 1735); Legan, Lessee of Chew v. Stevens, Jeff. 30, 1736 Va. Lexis 3 (October 1736); Giles et ux. & Mallecote v. Mallecote, Jeff. 52, 1738 Va. Lexis 2 (April 1738); Webb v. Elligood, Jeff. 59, 1739 Va. Lexis 1 (April 1739). Due to the nature of Randolph's and Barradall's reports (used by Jefferson), in these reports the contents of the verdicts are recounted through the arguments of counsel.

[40] William Nelson, "How the Rich Got Richer and the Poor Got Enslaved: Colonial Virginia's Legal Order as Model for Repression" (NYU School of Law Golieb Research Colloquium, January 18, 2012), 92–93; William Nelson, *The Common Law in Colonial America*, vol. 3: *The Chesapeake and New England, 1660–1750* (New York, NY: Oxford University Press, 2016), 40–41.

[41] Dandridge's Executors v. Allen (April 7, 1787), Posey v. Mark (April 9, 1787), Hannah v. Davis (April 20, 1787). In Charles F. Hobson, ed., St. George Tucker's Law Reports and Selected Papers, 1782–1825, vol. 1 (Chapel Hill, NC: University of North Carolina Press, 2013), 150–168. Call's reports for this era reference even more special verdicts not recorded by Tucker – in the admiralty cases of Dawson v. Graves & Hague, 8 Va. 127 (1788), Bentley v. Roan, 8 Va. 153 (1790), and Stratton v. Hague, 8 Va. 564 (1790), for instance, and the assumpsit case of Beall v. Edmondson, 7 Va. 514 (1790), which was a seller's action to recover for the value of goods delivered to the buyer.

[42] "Act for Establishing District Courts, and for Regulating the General Court," in William Waller Hening, *The Statutes at Large ...*, vol. 12 (Richmond, VA: George Cochran, 1809), 760.

[43] For instance, an April 13, 1787 General Court case involved a decision reached "by agreement" in the county court, which created a statement of the facts of the case; the court treated the agreement like a special verdict. Bates v. Fuquay (April 13, 1787), Hobson, St. George Tucker's Law Reports, 1:160. Posey v. Marks, which involved the court's ability to "advise" a special verdict, was also a county case, from New Kent. Posey v. Marks (April 9, 1787), as was Dandridge's Ex. v. Allen (April 7, 1787), Hobson, St. George Tucker's Law Reports, 1:153, 156. The 1737 case Parsons v. Lee, Sheriff of Stafford, also came from a county court. Jeff. 49, 1737 Va. Lexis 1 (April 1737).

[44] Tucker, *Blackstone's Commentaries*, 4:376, n. 31.

attorney or over which he presided as a judge – and they are full of cases involving special verdicts. For instance, during the April 1787 term of the General Court, Tucker recorded seventeen cases heard by the court; three involved special verdicts.[45] In another, the parties had agreed on the facts and then asked the court to apply the law, another common form which created a situation similar to a special verdict.[46] And after Crane's special verdict in the 1791 Winchester Court session, another Winchester jury would issue another special verdict, this one almost six and a half pages in length.[47] Special verdicts were a persistent feature of Virginia legal practice and evidence of Virginians' willingness to use the technical legal forms to shift the decision in any individual case to the court.

These were often important cases. After all, special verdicts were especially attractive in those cases, because they isolated significant, often charged legal issues for decision by the court. For instance, Crane's new counsel, John Marshall, had played a role in the slave freedom case of *Hannah v. Davis* (1787), which arose out of a special verdict. The case had raised the question of whether the plaintiffs, who claimed Native American ancestry, could be enslaved. Virginia's position on Indian slavery had changed several times during its colonial period and the applicable Acts and repeals were confusing. The jury in the case had rendered a special verdict, finding that "Bess [ancestor of the plaintiffs] was an Indian & was brought from some Indian nation into the County of Richmond since the year 1705, viz. 1712, and *held* & claimed as a Slave to the day of her death. We find that find that plaintiffs are *Descendants* of the said Bess."[48] They, like Crane's jury, left the rest of the case to the court.

Could Native Americans be enslaved? The General Assembly's last Act on the subject had been passed in 1705, and the question was whether it repealed previous Acts allowing enslavement of Native Americans. The case thus provoked a long and learned argument by Virginia's best lawyers. Plaintiffs' counsel, Thomas Nelson, argued that making slaves of foreign subjects was "contrary to the Law of God & the Law of nature," and thus any Act to that effect was null and void. Defendant's counsel, John Tyler, father of the future president, walked through the specifics of legislative enactments on the subject and argued that the burden of proof in the matter was not on the slaveholder to prove descent from a slave, but on the slave to prove descent from a free person. James Monroe, in turn, argued for the plaintiffs based on the apparent

---

[45] See Hobson, *St. George Tucker's Law Reports*, 1:150–168.
[46] Bates v. Fuquay (April 13, 1787), Hobson, *St. George Tucker's Law Reports*, 1:160–162.
[47] John Sukright Lesee of John I Mound pl v. Richard Cornyne, September 6, 1791, Winchester District Court Order Book.
[48] *The Papers of John Marshall*, vol. 1: *Correspondence and Papers, November 10, 1775–June 23, 1788, Account Book, September 1783–June 1788*, ed. Herbert Alan Johnson, Charles T. Cullen, Nancy G. Harris (Chapel Hill, NC: University of North Carolina Press for the Omohundro Institute of Early American History and Culture, 1974), 218–219; Hobson, *St. George Tucker's Law Reports*, 1:166.

intention of the 1705 Act in question to open free trade with the Indians. (To effect that end, he maintained, it must have repealed previous Acts allowing enslavement.) Marshall, also arguing for the plaintiffs, essentially split the difference; he contended that a disputed portion of the Act of 1705 "only relates to such Indians as were already Slaves," whereas the plaintiffs' ancestor was enslaved in 1712, making her enslavement illegal. Moreover, that ancestor, "though detained in Slavery, if wrongfully detained could still transmit the right of freedom to her posterity."[49] The court sided with the plaintiffs.[50]

Other special verdict cases implicated the Virginian debate over which British statutes were in force. For instance, in 1787, the General Court grand jury indicted John Pim Herald for bigamy, and Herald's trial jury found him guilty "if the Statute of 1 James 1 ch: 11 concerning Bigamy extends to, and is now in force in this Commonwealth; otherwise we find him not guilty." Counsel argued that Virginia's ordinance of 1776 adopting certain British statutes "made in aid of the common law, of a general nature, not local to that Kingdom" did not apply to the bigamy statute, which by its own provisions applied only to "England and Wales," and was thus explicitly local. Adding a few other points, the court agreed, and Herald was discharged.[51]

Special verdicts also appeared in other types of complicated cases, especially land or other property disputes. *Kennedy v. Wallers*, for instance, raised the question of whether the owner of a slave hired to another person for a year could maintain a trespass action against a stranger who killed the slave during the period for which he was hired.[52] An occasional case also raised issues of federal power, as in the 1787 case of *Newell v. Elam*, which involved the ownership of a slave who had previously belonged to the plaintiff but escaped to the British and had later been taken by the American troops from "a party of the Enemy and sold by General orders"; the unnamed person was now in the possession of the defendant. After the Continental Army sold the slave back into slavery, the slave's former owner sued his current owner for his return; the jury found both the plaintiff's previous ownership and the defendant's ownership by purchase. The case was reargued several times, and the court eventually found for the plaintiff.[53]

Sometimes the verdicts hinged on small, but equally critical, factual details. For instance, in *Christian Carne's Case*, where Carne had forged an auditor's

---

[49] Tucker's friend William Nelson also represented the plaintiffs, as did some other prominent Virginia lawyers, and addressed perceived shortcomings in the special verdict. For an account of the case and Marshall's participation, see Hannah & others against Davis (April 20, 1787), Hobson, *St. George Tucker's Law Reports*, 1:166–168. See also *Papers of John Marshall*, 1:219–220 (Tucker's account relies on this).

[50] Hobson, *St. George Tucker's Law Reports*, 1:167–168.

[51] John Pim Herald's Case (Dec. 1787), ibid., 208.

[52] Kennedy v. Wallers (May 20, 1808), Hobson, *St. George Tucker's Law Reports*, 2:1099–1104.

[53] Newell et ux v. Elam (October 12, 1787), Hobson, *St. George Tucker's Law Reports*, 1:182, 1:221.

certificate but had misspelled the auditor's name, the Winchester District Court jury drew up a special verdict to isolate the problem of the misspelling and the court referred the case to the General Court.[54] In *John Whealand's Case*, the problem was that the counterfeiting statute, under which the indictment charged Whealand, was actually an ordinance of Virginia's revolutionary Convention, not the General Assembly, although the indictment referred to it as an Act of the Assembly. The jury found Whealand guilty of counterfeiting, "if the Court be of the opinion that the ordinance of Convention, in Law is an Act of Assembly as recited in the Indictment." On this verdict, the court gave judgment for the prisoner because of the indictment's error, demonstrating the seriousness with which Virginia's courts took such technicalities.[55]

As Herald, Carne, and Whealand's cases indicate, special verdicts appeared in criminal cases as well as civil ones, although they were rarer. In some of these cases, like John Crane's, the verdicts arose out of difficult fact patterns. Judge Tucker's notes alone name several cases of this type. For instance, in *Commonwealth v. Benjamin Humphries*, the 1787 burglary case mentioned above, Humphries and a co-conspirator had both intended to commit a burglary. When the time came, however, Humphries merely remained at a distance and then received part of the stolen goods. Was he guilty of burglary? The court found Humphries not guilty, because although the particular distance from the crime specified in the jury's verdict would have been sufficient to convict him of burglary, the jury verdict lacked the finding that he "remained there aiding and abetting, and received goods knowing them to be stolen." Absent that finding, the court discharged Humphries.[56]

But if special verdicts were common, they were also under fire. After the Revolution, Virginia's judges took concerns about summary justice to heart, and worked to protect the jury in its functions. For instance, in *Posey v. Mark* (1787), the Virginia General Court confronted a case where the county court had "advised" a special verdict. Though the judges all affirmed the judgment, they all agreed that it would have been error had the court "directed" the verdict, and Judge Carrington noted that he "doubted not that the *advice* was meant as a Direction."[57] Public opinion in Britain was also beginning to question the wisdom of allowing a judge to order or direct a special verdict, as part of the heated political contest over the role and control of the jury.[58]

Some Virginians might have wondered what all the fuss was about. After all, would not rendering special verdicts tend to make the law more predictable and orderly by letting judges decide instead of a series of random juries? Was not having a government by "laws, not men" supposed to be one of the most

---

[54] Carne's Case (April 16, 1794), ibid., 293–294.
[55] John Whealand's Case (June 22, 1789), ibid., 226.
[56] Commonwealth v. Benjamin Humphries, ibid., 169.
[57] The court, however, reached a result on other grounds. Posey v. Mark (April 9, 1787), ibid., 156.
[58] Langbein, "The Criminal Trial before the Lawyers," 296.

important tenets of republican government? If the jury decided the facts and the judge applied the law, would not that similarly constrain the legal process with the law? After all, special verdicts were not just a Virginian thing, although they may have been used more frequently in Virginia than in many other places. As Pennsylvania's Judge James Wilson advised one of his juries in 1790, "It is not unusual, and, on many occasions, it is prudent, for the jury to draw up and exhibit, in a special verdict, a particular statement of the facts of law, and to pray from the court a judgment of the law resulting from them."[59]

The problem with this view was partly picked up by *Federalist 65*, in which New York's Alexander Hamilton argued for ratification of the new federal Constitution and incidentally referenced special verdicts. In that essay, Hamilton argued that the Senate provided a better venue than the Supreme Court for impeachment trials for many reasons. One reason was that an impeachment offense would likely bring two prosecutions – one, the impeachment action itself, to remove the official from office, and the second a criminal prosecution in the courts. If the Supreme Court heard the impeachment case, then any subsequent legal prosecution against the official in the courts based on the same offense would be tainted, by making the same persons judges in both cases. Hamilton anticipated an objection that some might make: that having a jury in a criminal case would solve this problem. He advised that it would not matter – because "juries are frequently influenced by the opinions of judges." More specifically, "they are sometimes induced to find special verdicts, which refer the main question to the decision of the court. Who would be willing to stake his life and his estate upon the verdict of a jury acting under the auspices of judges who had predetermined his guilt?"[60] This was the old view of special verdicts as judicial influence over the jury, where judges took away questions from the jury in order to reach their own desired result.

With special verdicts, there was also a related but slightly different question: about the representative and protective role of the jury, regardless of undue influence. Juries were supposed to be a key part of republican government. As Tucker wrote in his edition of Blackstone, quoting his proposed bill to reform Virginia's jury system, trial by jury was "one of the most important pillars of a free government, and the preservation of it in it's [sic] purity, the greatest security to the lives, liberty, and property of the citizens." Juries were the people's direct participation in the legal system. But in Virginia, Tucker thought, that system was broken. "There is no part of our code of laws, perhaps, so defective as those which relate to this important species of trial." The

---

[59] "Judge Wilson, Charge to the Great Jury of the Circuit Court for the District." *Daily Advertiser* (Philadelphia: PA), April 20, 1790.
[60] "The Federalist Papers: No. 65," *The Avalon Project*, accessed November 11, 2016, http://avalon.law.yale.edu/18th_century/fed65.asp.

jury in Virginia, he explained, was too corrupt, too open to bribery and favoritism, absenteeism and neglect.[61]

Whatever the concerns, Judge Tucker's notes show that by 1794, Virginia courts had resumed (if they ever had truly stopped) the practice of directing special verdicts. For instance, in *Christian Carne's Case* (1794), discussed above, the district court – made up of Tucker and Judge Nelson – first directed the jury to acquit the prisoner. The jury retired, but soon came into court dissatisfied with the court's direction to acquit, "whereupon," Judge Tucker recorded in his notes, Judge "Nelson agreed that the point *should be reserved*." The jury rendered a special verdict and the judges adjourned the case to the General Court.[62] And in the case of *Williamson v. Dement* (1796), a land dispute, Tucker, presiding at the Monongalia District Court, noted that one of the parties had asked the court to instruct the jury on a matter, but "the Court directed a Special Verdict, saying the point was of too much importance to be hastily determined."[63] However, although judges might urge a special verdict, juries did not necessarily comply. In *Carne*, the court used a special verdict as a remedy for the jury's refusal to acquit outright; in the 1795 case of *Hanson v. Kirkpatrick's Executors* Judge Tucker attempted a similar result, directing a jury in the Dumfries District Court to reserve a point via a special verdict. But this jury refused and returned a general verdict instead. The court appears to have accepted the verdict.[64]

Finding a special verdict in a civil case was one thing; but in a murder case? As high as the stakes were, a special verdict leaving the decision between murder and manslaughter to the court was something that Blackstone had specifically contemplated. In the *Commentaries*, he had advised that juries could give general verdicts, like guilty or not guilty, or special verdicts "setting forth all the circumstances of the case, and praying the judgment of the court, whether, for instance, on the facts stated, it be murder, manslaughter, or no crime at all." As Blackstone stated, juries had "an unquestionable right of determining upon all the circumstances, and finding a general verdict," but if they "*doubt* the matter of law," they could "*chuse*" to "leave it to the determination of the court."[65] Crane's jury had made that choice.

Still, in Crane's case, the jury's verdict hinted at both manslaughter and murder. On the one hand, it left out any provocation by Crane. For instance, the newspaper reports omitted the claim that Crane had maimed Vanhorn's horses. Instead, the verdict began with Campbell's men challenging Crane and his men to a fight. The verdict also listed this first challenge as at three o'clock and declared the disputing had then continued on and off until "between sunset

[61] Tucker, *Blackstone's Commentaries*, 4: Editor's Appendix Note F, 64–68.
[62] Christian Carne's Case, Hobson, *St. George Tucker's Law Reports*, 1:293–294.
[63] Williamson v. Dement, ibid., 386.
[64] Hanson v. Kirkpatrick's Exors, ibid., 356.
[65] Tucker, *Blackstone's Commentaries*, 5:360.

and dark." It also said that Merchant and Vanhorn had stripped off their shirts first, *before* Crane, making them the aggressors or at least willing participants, although Crane had then struck Vanhorn first. The jury also found that Crane had been engaged with both Merchant and Vanhorn at the same time, and that Vanhorn had been holding him on the ground when Crane finally stabbed him. At the same time, the jury did solve the knife question: they found that the wounds had been given by Crane and not by anyone else. And they also suggested that Crane had threatened earlier in the day to "let out the guts" of anyone he would fight – which he did, hours later.

Was this murder, or manslaughter? One of Tucker's long, detailed jury charges from only a few years later provides some context.[66] In a May 1800 case in the Accomack District Court, Tucker addressed the case of a man who had beaten a women to death by "throwing her on a Bed, beating her with his fists, kicking her, & choaking her with his hands, in consequence of which she died on the fourth day after." The judge advised the jury, in words closely paralleling Blackstone's, that manslaughter was the "unlawful killing of another, without malice, express or implied," and could be done "voluntarily, as upon a sudden heat; or involuntarily, but in the Commission of some unlawful act." Voluntary manslaughter depended on a sudden provocation, and was committed "without any *previous intention* against the *Life* or person of him that is killed. Murder is killing with *malice aforethought*; it is the result of a willful deliberate intention to do harm to the person of him that is slain, and not the effect of a sudden quarrel, or violent passion." This malice included a design to kill the victim, or general depravity so cruel that it resulted in death, whether or not the death was intended.[67]

Once two people were fighting, Tucker explained, if a homicide resulted, manslaughter was the killer's best bet. Both murder and manslaughter were distinguished from killing in self-defense. In his charge, Tucker specified – again echoing Blackstone – that when "both parties are *actually combatting*" at the time of the killing, then it was not self-defense, but manslaughter. And, if, in a fight, someone killed his adversary when overcome by that adversary, "this is revenge, and not self defence [sic], and the slayer is guilty of Manslaughter, at the least." Plus, "if there be any previous Malice, such a slaying may amount also to Murder, according to the Circumstances of the Case."[68]

---

[66] Tucker seems to have left no notes about the Crane case. He mentioned it only in a handful of letters between him and Charles Lee, discussed below, and there are very few surviving Virginia opinions from the time that involve the distinction between murder and manslaughter, let alone explicate it.

[67] McCottrack's Case, Hobson, *St. George Tucker's Law Reports*, 1:470. By this time, Virginia had reformed its criminal law by statute, and created degrees of murder; however, Tucker's charge still dealt with the common law background before moving into the statutory changes.

[68] Ibid. It is, of course, possible that the Crane's case itself informed this charge; however, Virginia judges tended not to parse earlier Virginia cases so much as to rely on Blackstone or other English authorities.

There were elements in Crane's special verdict that suggested that the jury thought that he had intended to kill (or at least stab) Vanhorn. According to their verdict, earlier in the day Crane had said that if he fought anyone that day he would "let out their guts." (And, according to comments Tucker made about the case, the testimony had actually been that he would "let out their guts with a knife.") Crane had also told Dawkins that he would take his knife and "clear … through" Campbell's party. Then, right before they began to fight, and after Catherine Crane had refused to give her husband a gun, the jury found that Vanhorn had protested that Crane "would use a knife or a razor." Crane had assured him that no, he would "give a fair fight." However, when pinned to the ground, Crane had then pulled out a knife and stabbed Vanhorn. He had arguably enticed Vanhorn to fight, then used the knife he had promised not to use.[69]

But there was another potential reading of the verdict, a reading that made Crane seem less culpable: one that had to do with the rules of fighting in the late eighteenth century. The verdict said that Crane had promised Vanhorn a "fair fight." To modern eyes, the phrase seems self-explanatory. However, as discussed in Chapter 1, historian Elliott Gorn has identified two distinct types of fights in this period: "fair fights" and "rough and tumble."[70] "Fair fights" were traditional fist fights, conducted according to the rules of English boxing. A "rough and tumble" fight, also called "boxing" or "gouging," was the free-for-all match for which Virginians were famous. It included eye-gouging, biting, castration, and all sorts of other physical indignities, and terminated only when one party essentially cried "uncle," normally when someone's eye was gouged out, the "rough and tumble" equivalent of the knockout punch. According to Gorn, the brawlers set the rules ahead of time:

Before two bruisers attacked each other, spectators might demand whether they proposed to fight fair – according to Broughton's Rules – or rough-and-tumble. Honor dictated that all techniques be permitted. Except for a ban on weapons, most men chose to fight "no holts barred," doing what they wished to each other without interference, until one gave up or was incapacitated.[71]

Read in this context, the emphasis in the *Crane* case on a "fair fight" takes on a much fuller meaning. Rather than an assurance that he would not use a weapon, it could mean that he agreed to a traditional fistfight, as opposed to more brutal "boxing" or "rough-and-tumble" fighting. Vanhorn said that he feared that Crane would use a weapon and Crane had replied that he would give a fair fight – a fight according to the rules of English boxing. The jury then found that after Vanhorn pinned Crane to the ground, he held him there for some time. This is particularly important. Merchant and Vanhorn were clearly

---

[69] See, e.g., *Crane*, 3 Va. at 10–13.
[70] Elliott T. Gorn, "'Gouge, Bite, Pull Hair and Scratch': The Social Significance of Fighting in the Southern Backcountry," *American Historical Review* 90 no. 1 (1985): 18–43, 20.
[71] Ibid.

very angry – is it possible that at that moment, when Crane expected the fight to be over, for Vanhorn it was just beginning? That he had clawed at Crane, or otherwise assaulted him beyond the rules of the fight? Perhaps Crane, the gentleman's son, knew tales of the rougher fights involving ear-biting and eye-gouging, and he had brought along the knife for self-defense. Pinned and defending himself against a roughness to which he did not agree, maybe Crane pulled out the knife to protect himself. In such a situation, he might indeed protest his innocence, as he repeatedly did throughout the case.

Contrasts between the jury's verdict and newspapers reports can be read to support the inference that these questions of "fair fighting" were important to determining whether Crane had committed murder or manslaughter. One widely reprinted newspaper report, from just days after Vanhorn's death, explained that "the deceased and Crane mutually agreed to box," which Gorn identifies as a synonym for a "no holts barred" fight.[72] According to this reading, Crane and Vanhorn agreed to a "no holts barred" fight and "a short time after the commencement of the conflict, the deceased cried out 'enough' and that his guts were cut."[73] The jury's verdict modifies this in two respects. First, the term "box" nowhere appears in the verdict, only "fight." And, second, the verdict specifies that "Abraham Vanhorn threw the prisoner at the bar on the ground and held him there for some time" before Crane finally used his knife.[74] Perhaps the jury meant to suggest that it was Abraham Vanhorn, not John Crane, who had broken the rules of the fair fight.

There was also the fact that two men, not just one, had assailed Crane. The verdict particularly emphasized this last point:

[T]he said Abraham Vanhorn, and Isaac Merchant one of Campbell's reapers, had their shirts stripped off, which the prisoner at the bar had not: the prisoner at the bar and the said Abraham Vanhorn attempting to get at each other across the fence, who was prevented by John Dawkins. Then the said prisoner struck at Merchant, who struck the said prisoner at the bar, and turned him round, who immediately joined in combat with the said Abraham Vanhorn. We find in the combat that the said Abraham Vanhorn threw the prisoner at the bar on the ground, and kept him there for some time ...[75]

Crane had not pulled out the knife until held on the ground for some time, after being engaged with both Vanhorn *and* Merchant. With these details, perhaps

---

[72] *ClayPoole's Daily Advertiser* (Philadelphia: PA), July 19, 1791, 2. See also *Essex Journal* (Newburyport, MA, August 3, 1791, 3); *Western Star* (Stockbridge, MA), August 2, 1791, 2; *Connecticut Journal* (New Haven, CT), July 27, 1791, 2; *Freeman's Journal, or the North American Intelligencer* (Philadelphia: PA), July 20, 1791, 3; *Burlington Advertiser* (Burlington, New Jersey), July 26, 1791, 2.

[73] See *Burlington Advertiser, or Agricultural and Political Intelligencer* (Burlington, NJ), July 26, 1791.

[74] *Crane*, 3 Va. at 13.

[75] Ibid.

at least some members of the jury felt – or maybe hoped – they had laid the groundwork for manslaughter.

Moreover, the fight had been the culmination of a long day of hostilities that, according to the verdict, were largely provoked by Campbell's men. For instance, the verdict traced the start of the conflict to actions by Vanhorn and Campbell's reapers, who had cut through Crane's fields and issued a challenge. Their taunts were enough to draw a hostile response from John Dawkins, who had said that he could "whip Joseph Vanhorn." After that confrontation cooled, the verdict again pinned its revival on Campbell's men and on Crane's reaper, John Dawkins. "We find that between sunset and dark," the jury wrote, "that the said Abraham Vanhorn with several others passing through the field of John Crane, the prisoner at the bar, to confirm a bet which was to ensue the next morning, and also making a noise and singing, which the said Dawkins conceived was an insult to the prisoner at the bar and his party." After that, Dawkins involved Crane in the fight.

Finally, the verdict painted the picture of a situation that had quickly escalated. As Crane and Vanhorn engaged in a standoff – Crane telling Vanhorn to fight, Vanhorn worried that Crane would use a knife – Mrs. Crane had entered the fray, yelling, "Mr. Crane I am surprised that you would demean yourself to fight with such a set of negrofied puppies." The insult was important enough, and memorable enough, that it appeared in the men's testimony, and made its way into the jury verdict. And after this insult – which was itself enough to provoke a fight – according to the verdict, Vanhorn and Crane became "much irritated; at which the said Abraham Vanhorn, and Isaac Merchant one of Campbell's reapers, had their shirts stripped off, which the prisoner at the bar had not."[76] As the fight started, Crane may have indeed faced serious threat.

The intensity of the conflict as well as any potential "cooling off" moments in-between were essential in determining Crane's guilt. In a similar 1796 case from nearby North Carolina – one also involving multiple conflicts that eventually escalated into a stabbing – the court observed, "The great distinction between murder and manslaughter is this, manslaughter is committed under the operation of furious anger, that suspends for a time the proper exercise of reason and reflection, and which hath been stirred up by some great provocation: for there are some provocations that are not indulged with an allowance of exciting the passions to such excess, and thus a distinction is formed between the different degrees of provocation." Moreover, if sufficient time passed between the provocation and the killing, it became murder, unless there was "fresh provocation." Even then, however, the response needed to be proportional to the offense.[77] As Crane's jury detailed the long day's events, it had

[76] Ibid.
[77] State v. Norris, 2 N.C. 429 (1796).

described not one conflict but multiple conflicts, each with its own importance and circumstances. In doing so, the jury left room for new conflicts, and new provocation – for manslaughter. The question, however, was how provoking those events were seen to be, and the extent to which those several heated incidents related to each other. Now that was the General Court's problem.

What did Marshall – the man who would become America's "Great Chief Justice" – argue on Crane's behalf? Unfortunately, no records survive. Virginia's General Court records were burned during the US Civil War, and accounts of the early court during this time often rely on Tucker's thorough notebooks, carefully preserved by his descendants (who were themselves lawyers) and other members of Virginia's legal profession. But Tucker was absent in November 1791, so his notes provide no help. As a result, what Marshall argued on Crane's behalf, what the judges said and asked, and the Commonwealth's case, are lost to history.[78]

The sole record of Crane's case in the General Court comes from an early Virginia volume of case reports, which included the court's short order. It provided no analysis of Crane's claims or the jury's verdict, or any indication of the views of the various judges. Instead, the reporter merely recorded:

The District Court not being advised what judgment to give on this verdict, adjourned the question, with the consent of the prisoner, to the General Court for difficulty.

On the 21st November, 1791, the General Court, consisting of Judges Prentis, Tyler, Henry, Jones, Roane and Nelson, entered the following judgment. "This day came as well, the Attorney General as [well as] the Council [sic] for the said Crane, and thereupon the question of Law arising upon the special verdict in the transcript of the record of the said case mentioned, to wit: whether the said Crane be guilty of murder or manslaughter, being argued, it is the opinion of the court that the said Crane is guilty of murder, which is ordered to be certified to the District Court of Winchester.[79]

Two later petitions in favor of Crane add slightly to this story. The entirety of this information is less than two sentences: "your petitioners are informed that the [General] court was divided, and that even there two of the Judges thought that Judgement ought not to be against the Prisoner."[80] As the Berkeley sheriff confirmed, the "Judges were ... divided."[81]

---

78 The case was likely argued for the Commonwealth by James Innes, Virginia's Attorney General and Judge Tucker's close friend. Innes was a very large man, and renowned for his oratory – even compared to Patrick Henry. Jane Carson, *James Innes and his Brothers of the F.H.C.* (Williamsburg, VA: Colonial Williamsburg, 1965), 9.

79 *Crane*, 3 Va. at 14. See also "The Ruling of the General Court," *Calendar of Virginia State Papers*, 5:507. The judges were Joseph Prentis, John Tyler, James Henry, Joseph Jones, Spencer Roane, and William Nelson. See Hobson, *St. George Tucker's Law Reports*, 3:1821–1854.

80 "Petition of the Citizens for the Pardon of John Crane, Jr.," *Calendar of Virginia State Papers*, 5:510–513.

81 "Robert Throckmorton to the Governor," 19 June 1791, ibid., 599.

The special verdict had left Marshall with an uphill battle. He had done his job well and had even carried two judges, but it was not enough. The Crane family had hired one of the best lawyers in the state, but they lost. The General Court pronounced its order, and Marshall noted in his November 1791 account book that he had charged Crane £14, "for murder."[82]

No matter how they had felt at each step along the way, the Cranes and the Whitings likely felt stunned in November 1791 as they stepped back and contemplated John's fate. Virginia just did not have a history of executing its gentry. When historian Kathryn Preyer examined the actions of Virginia's examining courts from 1789 to 1800, she found that only one "planter" had been prosecuted, and he was acquitted of negro-stealing.[83] As John Crane's case indicates, of course, designating a defendant's class could be complicated. Crane, after all, was identified as a "yeoman" despite his family's background. But even taking these designations with more latitude, it is clear that there had been reason to hope that Crane's social status would work in his favor. But if John's family had hoped that the General Court would be more sympathetic than the county and district, they were disappointed.

One last possibility remained. After the decision, Marshall performed a final task for the Cranes.[84] On December 2, 1791, he drew up a pardon petition for James Crane, asking that the Governor and Council of State show John mercy. The Council of State was the executive council created by the Virginia constitution to advise the Governor on various matters, including pardons. And in this case, the Council was not some remote body; instead, its President was Winchester native James Wood, brother of Crane's grand juror, Robert Wood.[85]

"To his Excellency the Governor & the Honbles the members of the Privy counsel," Marshall wrote, "the petition of James Crane humbly sheweth":

That John Crane son of your petitioner was arraignd in the Honble the district court holden at Winchester for killing a certain Abraham Vanhorn in a fight & a special verdict was found thereon which was referd to the Honble. the General court for difficulty. On the hearing of the said special verdict it was by a majority of the court determind to be murder & judgement of death will be pronouncd at the next term unless Your

[82] *The Papers of John Marshall*, vol. 2: *Correspondence and Papers, July 1788–December 1795, Account Book, July 1788–December 1795*, ed. Herbert Alan Johnson, Charles T. Cullen, and Nancy G. Harris (Chapel Hill, NC: University of North Carolina Press for the Omohundro Institute of Early American History and Culture, 1977), 427.

[83] Kathryn Preyer, "Crime, the Criminal Law and Reform in Post-Revolutionary Virginia," *Law and History Review* 1, no. 1 (1983): 53–85, 72.

[84] *Papers of John Marshall*, 2:100.

[85] See *Journals of the Council of the State of Virginia*, vol. 5, ed. Sandra Giola Treadway (Richmond, VA: Virginia State Library, 1982), 409–410; see also Guide to the James Wood Executive Papers, Accession Number 40844, Library of Virginia. Guide available at "A Guide to the Governor James Wood Executive Papers, 1796–1799," *Library of Virginia*, accessed November 17, 2016, http://ead.lib.virginia.edu/vivaxtf/view?docId=lva/vi00867.xml.

Excellency & your Honors will interpose with mercy. Your petitioner humbly prays that the case may be considerd & if it shall appear to be a proper case for pardon your petitioner prays that your Excellency & Honors will extend your mercy to the son of your petitioner.[86]

This was the Cranes' last option. And here, with a murder conviction, there were no complications – no conflicting statutes – as there had been in *Caton*. Instead, the Governor, "with the advice of the council of state," had the explicit power of granting reprieves or pardons.[87] But would he save John Crane?

[86] *Papers of John Marshall*, 2:100 (see also n. 4).
[87] *The Revised Code of the Laws of Virginia* ... (Richmond, VA: Thomas Ritchie, 1819), 35.

9

Pardon Request

Mercy and Crane's "Lunatic Fits"

The Council deferred the petition until after Crane's final sentencing, at the spring session of the Winchester District Court. In April, the judges assigned to the Winchester circuit that spring, Joseph Prentis and Joseph Jones, recited the order of the General Court and sentenced Crane to death.[1] A few days later, John Crane filed his own petition, requesting a one-month reprieve.[2]

In the meantime, letters supporting Crane poured in from Berkeley County. Requests came from family members, neighbors, friends, acquaintances, even leading members of the county and the region.[3] Some were from the very men who had helped condemn Crane, including witnesses, justices of the peace, members of the grand jury and jury. Some letters were long and detailed, others short; some talked about the crime, others about the character of Crane and his family. And, from the letters, a new story also emerged, and brought to light something that had long been whispered about among certain members of Berkeley's elite: John Crane had "lunatic" fits.

As supporting documents flooded the Richmond offices of the Governor and the Council of State, writers asked for Crane's pardon on two principal grounds. First, they argued that justice, particularly the circumstances of the

---

[1] "April 26, 1792," Winchester District Court Order Book, Library of Virginia. See also "Indictment of John Crane Jun.", April 26, 1792, *Calendar of Virginia State Papers and Other Manuscripts*, vol. 5: *From July 2, 1789 to August 10, 1792*, ed. William P. Palmer and Sherwin McRae (Richmond, VA: Virginia State Library, 1885), 507.

[2] "Petition of John Crane," *Calendar of Virginia State Papers*, 5:541. James Crane's petition for his son also survives in Governor Henry Lee's official papers and in John Marshall's papers. But for the other pardon petitions in Crane's case, *The Calendar of Virginia State Papers* seems to be the only remaining record. A comparison reveals that James Crane's petition is abbreviated in those papers, indicating that the other petitions, including John Crane's, may be abbreviated there as well.

[3] "Petition of Citizens for the Pardon of John Crane Jr.," 28 April 1791, ibid., 511.

crime and its verdict, required that Crane not be put to death for his crime. Second, they argued that Crane was not even responsible for the crime because he had not been mentally competent at the time of its commission. And finally, they added an important detail, reminding the governor that John Crane came from a good, "respectable" family, one that ran in the same social circles as the best men in the county.

A number of the letters emphasized that the crime was much closer to manslaughter than to premeditated murder. On April 19, after the General Court remanded the case and seven days before the Winchester District Court formally pronounced the judgment of death on Crane, the foreman of Crane's jury certified before the Winchester clerk:

I, Gerard Alexander, foreman of the Jury on the trial of John Crane the younger, for the death of Abr'm Vanhorne, do hereby certify that myself & three more of the Jurors were of opinion that the said John Crane was guilty of manslaughter and not of willful murder.[4]

Four days later, two other jurors certified the same, before a Berkeley County justice of the peace: "We, Benjamin Strother and Thomas Griggs ... were of opinion that the said John Crane was not guilty of willful murder – only manslaughter."[5]

On top of the jurors' certifications, the clerk of the Winchester District Court sent his own letter to the Governor, emphasizing that the jurors' letters were not a post-conviction change of heart. "The Jurors upon his trial were much divided in their opinion with respect to the matter of the crime," clerk John Peyton reported. Peyton was "apprehensive that those in his favor were induced to acquiesce, being two days confined on the business under a full persuasion that it would finally be determined to be manslaughter only."[6] A petition signed by a long list of Berkeley citizens stressed the same thing. Because the jury, confined for "near forty hours," had been "by necessity driven to find the imperfect special verdict upon which the Judgement of the court has been since given ... four or five of that very Jury have ever since their verdict, declared and still declare that the unfortunate prisoner had not in their opinion been guilty of murder." The case was of "such difficulty" and "so peculiarly circumstanced" that the petitioners hoped the Governor would intervene.[7]

The petitioners' arguments for manslaughter, however, reached beyond the jury's unusual verdict and its own inner conflict, to emphasize the evidence on

---

[4] "Gerard Alexander's Certificate as to John Crane, Jr.," April 19, 1791, ibid., 495.
[5] "Certificate of Benjamin Strother and Thomas Griggs, as to John Crane, Jr.," April 23, 1791, ibid., 504.
[6] "J. Peyton to the Governor," April 30, 1791, ibid., 519.
[7] "Petition of Citizens for the Pardon of John Crane Jr."

the crime itself. Berkeley's Sheriff Robert Throckmorton, for instance, wrote to the Governor that Crane deserved pardon:

I have taken the Liberty of wrigthing [sic] to you and your Honorable Council concerning young John Crane, who is now under sentence of Death, and none but you can save him. I was at his Tryal and heard the witnesses which were much prejudiced against him, and by appearance would say as much as they could against and as little in his favour. One thing has much weight with me, which is after their day's work was done, they went to Crane's House, where it do not appear they had any business but to renew a quarrel that had Ran very high the preceding day. It likewise appears that Crane was Ingaged [sic] with two men partly at the same time. A man in that situation would be likely to do all he could to defeat his adversary; for when a man is fighting, he has little time to reflect, but it seems natural for him to do all he can to extricate himself.

Several witnesses, Throckmorton emphasized, supported "the two men being in contact with him at the same time."[8] In addition, "the Jury were divided and could not agree; that the foreman and four others, perhaps the ablest of them, were in his favour – the Judges were also divided." Under these circumstances – the ambiguity of the crime itself and the unease of the jurors – Crane, Throckmorton concluded, "ought not to suffer death."[9]

A letter from Berkeley County Court clerk and grand juror Moses Hunter, and justice of the peace Andrew Waggener, who also served as Berkeley's member of the House of Delegates, emphasized similar details:

We believe that passion was one great cause of this misfortune ... We do not wish to reflect upon the deceased, nor can we presume to Justify what the prisoner has been guilty of, but we beg leave to remark that if the party who were going home from Campbell's harvest field, one of which Mr. Vanhorn was, had have taken the nearest and common rout [sic], and had not called upon Crane, he would not have been thrown into this violent passion, which so frequently deprived him of his reason, and the melancholy event could not have happened.

Hunter and Waggener begged the Governor to grant Crane a pardon, and gave the opinion "that if the languishing prisoner could be so happy as to receive your merciful interference in his favor, he would in future become a peaceable, orderly and valuable citizen."[10]

---

[8] "Robert Throckmorton to the Governor," 19 June 1791, *Calendar of Virginia State Papers*, 5:599. For Throckmorton as sheriff, see "June 16, 1789," Berkeley County Court Minute Book, BCHS; Throckmorton is still listed as the Berkeley sheriff on papers for September 1791 Court, where he or his representatives are noted to have executed the summons for Berkeley County. See "Commonwealth of Virginia to Sheriff of Berkeley County," *Daniels v. Blue*, April 18, 1791, Box Barcode 1117433, Frederick County Ended Causes, Frederick County District Court Records, September 1791, Folder 2, Library of Virginia.

[9] "Robert Throckmorton to the Governor."

[10] "A. Waggener and Moses Hunter to the Governor," June 14, 1792, *Calendar of Virginia State Papers*, 5:598. On Waggener, see Virgil Anson Lewis, *A History of West Virginia in Two Parts* (Philadelphia, PA: Hubbard Brothers, 1889), 499–500; Willis F. Evans, *History of Berkeley County West Virginia* (Westminster, MD: Heritage Books, 1928), 279.

But the letter's reference to "violent passion" and Crane's deprivation of his "reason" also invoked the second factor in the petitions flooding the governor: lunacy. Whereas Crane himself protested his innocence, his supporters – seemingly spurred on by his father – informed the Governor that Crane had been known to have "fits" since at least the 1780s. Richard Ransom certified under oath that in 1788, when the young John Crane and Catherine had visited Ransom's house for the night, "some short time after [their arrival] I discovered a great alteration in Mr. Crane appearing to look very wild out of his eyes." Crane insisted that he needed to go home, and he and Catherine left despite their previous plans to stay. Concerned, Ransom sent his son along with them, "for fear of his meeting with some accident; in a very short time or sooner than I expected he had got home, and a messenger came for me, informing me Mr. Crane had a fit." Ransom himself immediately traveled to the Cranes', "where I saw Mr. Crane Quite Insensible of his complaint – ravin Distracted; at times took several people to hold him. He continued in this way of madness for six or seven hours quite out of reason." Ransom concluded, "These fits of madness has followed him ever since at times."[11]

Other letters gave their own first-hand accounts. Members of Catherine's Whiting family, along with Robert Throckmorton, Giles Cooke, and others certified:

[W]e, the subscribers, do hereby certify that we have seen Mr. John Crane ... seized with uncommon fits; at which time appeared to be a kind of madness for some time before he was confined to his bed, & after his recovery, which was generally three or four days before he came to his reason; & when that was obtained, he often mentioned that he did not remember anything of his being disordered, tho' felt himself very sore, weak, and light-headed – the first of his seizure was late in the year 1786.[12]

Dr. Robert Henry also certified that he had treated Crane during these fits, and "found him labouring under a violent Nervous complaint, attended with great agitation of the whole frame, a considerable degree of Phrensy, and perfectly insensible of his situation."[13] He was not informed then that Crane had had a "fit," because the family wished to "keep it a secret."[14] He treated Crane on this and subsequent occasions, but each time the symptoms returned and were accompanied with "stronger appearances of Real Madness." Henry related that his own wife had suffered similar fits, and that he suspected that Crane's were of the same sort, "that suffocating or strangling kind, which people of an unhappy passionate temper, and over heated animal spirits are liable to, and which often ends in total madness." They had "always been occasioned by

[11] "Rich'rd Ransom's Certificate as to John Crane Jr.," April 14, 1792, *Calendar of Virginia State Papers*, 5:491.

[12] "Judith Whiting, William Howard, Robert Throckmorton, Daniel Duffield, Susanah Whiting, Giles Cooke, certify as to John Crane, Jr.," April 14, 1792, ibid., 491.

[13] "Certificate of Dr. Robert Henry," April 20, 1792, ibid., 496.

[14] Ibid., 496.

his overheating himself, either by the ardent use of spirits, too much exercise, or something Ruffling his temper."[15] Henry certified that he had subsequently attended Crane for the same complaint in 1789, "always had the same symptoms of phrensy, with this difference that it bordered more on madness & continued longer and more alarming, that it was preceded by a Fit, as the family informed me."[16]

Henry's account was seconded by the testimony of another area physician, Edward Tiffin, Crane's neighbor in Charles Town and, later, the first Governor of Ohio. Tiffin's family had emigrated to America from England in the 1780s; there he had married into the Worthington family, who were friends and in-laws of the Cranes.[17] The Crane family had called upon Tiffin to attend John Crane on June 24, 1786. Tiffin related to the Governor that Crane had been "seized with Fits, of what kind I cannot say, as the violence of them was over before I got to him. But I found him perfectly insensible of his situation, and his whole frame in violent agitations. His situation in great measure resembled a mania while it lasted." He had again attended Crane for the same complaint, "which was more violent than the others – from what cause they originated I cannot say; but they have returned at times ever since, & every time I have had opportunity of knowing anything about them, have deprived him of the use of his reason."[18]

Even the keeper of the Winchester jail chimed in. Jailor Edward Powers wrote two separate petitions on behalf of John Crane, relating that during Crane's confinement he had witnessed "violent fits, which I am not able to determine; they appeared to be a kind of madness, at which time was under the necessity of calling on my next door neighbor to assist me in keeping him confined, to prevent him from doing injury to himself." Then, according to Powers, Crane's "hard struggles so weakened him, and his nerves so affected, that he would be very black in the face, followed with a choking that I expected every moment to be his last, tho' still recovered by three of four days before he would come to his natural reason." Once back to his senses, Crane, according to Powers, "often mentioned that he did not remember anything of his being disordered, but felt himself very sore, weak, and light-headed."[19] Otherwise, Crane had "behaved himself as an honest, well disposed man." Powers also mysteriously

---

[15] "Dr. Robert Henry to Dr. James McClurg," April 14, 1792, ibid., 492.

[16] "Robert Henry's Certificate as to John Crane Jr."

[17] Tiffin's home is now a historic site in Charles Town, West Virginia, just a few lots away from the lot owned by James Crane (purchased from Charles Washington). For more on Tiffin, see William Edward Gilmore, *Life of Edward Tiffin, First Governor of Ohio* (Chillicothe, OH: Horney & Son, 1897). For the Crane–Worthington connection, see Dakota Best Brown, *Data on Some Virginia Families* (Berryville, VA: Virginia Book Company, 1979), 263.

[18] "Edward Tiffin's Certificate at to John Crane Jr.," April 20, 1792, *Calendar of Virginia State Papers*, 5:497.

[19] "Edw'd J. Power's Certificate as to John Crane Jr.," April 20, 1792, ibid., 497.

reported that "many reports have been propagated to his prejudices sinse [sic] the said prisoner has been in my custody, which I must say is false."[20]

In all, the Governor received pages and pages of documents relating to the Crane case. Those who had not personally witnessed John Crane's fits and spells vouched for the character of those who had, or spoke more generally of the character of the young man and his family. As Winchester District Court Clerk John Peyton told the Governor, the furor against Crane had subsided, "and mercy seems now on all hands to have taken place thereof."[21]

Peyton affirmed that the crime was of such a horrible nature that pardon was seldom granted, but he expressed his wish that Crane would be an exception. Mercy to Crane, he wrote, "I am conscious would gratify the wishes of many respectable citizens of this County, and would not only restore to the community a member once thought to be useful, but to an amiable woman, and ancient and respectable parents, a husband and son."[22]

Peyton was not the only person to reference Crane's "ancient and respectable parents." Indeed, the distress of James and Lucy Minor Crane permeates the state's records. Many of the missives begin with a notation about the information having been solicited by James Crane: "Being called on by Mr. James Crane"; "I have just been applied to by Mr. James Crane"; "Mr. James Crain ... has solicited my signature to a petition which prays a pardon for his son." One gets the impression of James Crane himself going door to door, house to house, and to the Winchester jail, trying desperately to free his son. One letter came from John Smith of Frederick County, a veteran of the Revolution who was now a representative to the General Assembly, later a US Congressman.[23] Smith explained that James Crane himself had approached him to sign the petition and though he did not know John Crane, "if the favourable representations of others should in any manner engage the Executive to the prayers of a mild and benevolent Father and those of a mother whose goodness is exceeded by few of her sex; permit me to add those of, Sir, your m'st obed. & Hum. Serv't."[24]

Letter after letter echoed the concern for Crane's parents. One also ended with a dire prediction; the letter expressed the hope that Crane's pardon would "lengthen the days of his venerable parents, his mother especially, who is thought will not surmount the shock, should he be executed."[25] Crane's execution, they warned, would also kill his mother. And the Berkeley County citizens' petition, which focused primarily on Crane's spells of lunacy and the fact that

---

[20] "Edward Powers' Certificat, April 30, 1792," ibid., 520.
[21] "J. Peyton to the Governor."
[22] Ibid.
[23] *History of the Lower Shenandoah Valley Counties of Frederick, Berkeley, Jefferson, and Clarke*, ed. J. E. Norris (Chicago, IL: A. Warner & Co., Publishers, 1890), 667–668. See also "John Smith," *Biographical Dictionary of the United States Congress*, accessed January 10, 2017, http://bioguide.congress.gov/scripts/biodisplay.pl?index=S000564.
[24] "John Smith to the Governor," April 23, 1792, *Calendar of Virginia State Papers*, 5:503–504.
[25] "Robert Throckmorton to the Governor," June 19, 1792, ibid., 599.

his jurors were forced into the special verdict by deprivation and now disavowed it, also ended by adding that "the situation of this unhappy man is in itself truly pitiable, but that their consideration and concern are greatly heightened by the distresses of his affectionate wife, and his aged and much respected Parents."[26]

In the early 1790s, pardons were still an important part of making sure that Anglo-American criminal law, including in Virginia, functioned in a way that was tailored to the crime and its circumstances. In the *Commentaries*, Blackstone had written that the magistrate essentially held "a court of equity in his own breast, to soften the rigour of the general law, in such criminal cases as merit an exemption from punishment."[27] This reflected the belief that law "cannot be framed on principles of compassion to guilt: yet justice, by the constitution of England, is bound to be administered in mercy." The power to pardon was, Blackstone asserted, one of the great advantages of monarchies. In democracies, he cautioned, this "power of pardon can never subsist; for there nothing higher is acknowledged than the magistrate who administers the laws."[28]

Blackstone's words echoed a common maxim, the one that Judge Tucker's grand jury charge had set forth, "in a republic, there is no sovereign but the laws." Blackstone's observations about the incompatibility of pardon and democracy merely took this maxim to its logical conclusion: if authority stopped with the law, then there was, he reasoned, no room for the kind of personal equity exercised by the king through a pardon. Other writers agreed about the incompatibility, even if they disagreed about the desirability of pardons. For instance, Cesare Beccaria, whom Blackstone cited as an authority disfavoring pardons, argued that clemency "is the virtue of the lawgiver and not of the executor of the law." At the base of Beccaria's objection was both a distrust of what he called "private judgment," and also its tendency to, he contended, undermine the law. "When the prince grants a pardon," he wrote, he "with a private act of enlightened benevolence, lays down a public decree of impunity." Instead, Beccaria argued: "Let the laws therefore be inexorable and those who enforce them be inexorable in individual cases," but the lawgiver – the legislator – be "gentle, indulgent, and humane."[29] If legislators created new laws, mild and suited to the crime, he concluded, clemency would no longer be necessary.[30]

---

[26] "Petition of Citizens for the Pardon of John Crane, Jr.," ibid., 511.
[27] St. George Tucker, *Blackstone's Commentaries with Notes of Reference to the Constitution and Laws of the Federal Government of the United States; and of the Commonwealth of Virginia*, vol. 5 (Philadelphia, PA: William Young Birch and Abraham Small, 1803), 396.
[28] Ibid.
[29] Cesare Beccaria, *On Crimes and Punishments*, trans. David Young (Indianapolis, IN: Hackett Publishing Company, 1986), 80.
[30] Ibid.

Jefferson had set forth similar sentiments in his draft of the unsuccessful Bill for Proportioning Crimes and Punishments. There, he had declared that it was "a duty in the legislature to arrange in a proper scale the crimes which it may be necessary for them to repress, and to adjust thereto a corresponding gradation of punishments," and that "if the punishment were only proportioned to the injury, men would feel it their inclination as well as their duty to see the laws observed."[31] Proper punishment should, in general, be determined by the legislature in a uniform manner and not adjusted to the offender on a case-by-case basis. As he had written to Edmund Pendleton, "Let mercy be the character of the law-giver, but let the judge be a mere machine. The mercies of the law will be dispensed equally and impartially to every description of men; those of the judge, or of the executive power, will be the eccentric impulses of whimsical, capricious designing man."[32]

In his argument to the court in *Caton*, Judge Tucker had seemed to evince a similar positivism: the previous, multiple sources of law – tradition, precedent, theory – had been replaced by legislation. In talking about the Virginia constitution, Tucker had emphasized that it was "written, that it might not be misunderstood," and that it "settled the controversy between speculative writers."[33] For Tucker, it was about the legislation of the most supreme assembly, the convention of the people that had formed the constitution; for Beccaria and Jefferson, it was about the normal civil legislature, which was able to have the final word on penal laws. Both suggested that justice was best done by compact and, in the case of Beccaria and Jefferson, in bulk – by treating like cases alike, with no room for adjustment.

But when it came to pardons, Tucker parted company. When editing Blackstone, he added a note to the jurist's laudatory discussion of pardons: "This boasted advantage is not excluded from democratic governments, witness the constitution of Virginia; that of the federal government, and those of every republic in the American union."[34] And, as previously discussed in Chapter 4, Tucker explained to his students that the revisors' attempt to eliminate pardons in the Bill for Proportioning Crimes and Punishments had been a mistake. If, he explained, a jury knew that their verdict against a criminal would be final – that there would be no appeal for a pardon based on factors that might not be taken account of in the law, but which would have moved for clemency – then the jury would likely render a verdict based on their desired

---

[31] "A Bill for Proportioning Crimes and Punishments in Cases Heretofore Capital," in *The Papers of Thomas Jefferson*, vol. 2: *2 January 1777 to 18 June 1779 including the Revisal of the Laws*, ed. Julian Boyd (Princeton, NJ: Princeton University Press, 1950), 493.

[32] Letter from Thomas Jefferson to Edmund Pendleton, August 26, 1776, in *The Papers of Thomas Jefferson*, vol. 1: *1760–1776*, ed. Julian P. Boyd (Princeton, NJ: Princeton University Press, 1950), 505.

[33] St. George Tucker, "On the Study of the Law," in *View of the Constitution of the United States: With Selected Writings* (Indianapolis, IN: Liberty Fund, 1999), 6.

[34] Tucker, *Blackstone's Commentaries*, 5:397, n. 2.

outcome, not the law and the facts. If they did so, the jury would have been "transformed into a kind of criminal Court of Equity; they would no longer have been triers of fact."[35] "The power of pardon," he told his students, "seems, then to be necessary, to be entrusted somewhere, so long as the frailties of human nature continue to subject us to the influence of momentary passion, of misguided zeal, or other causes impelling us to Error."[36] Mercy, Tucker explained, should continue in democracy as well.

Many Virginians seemed to feel the same way. In the last decades of the eighteenth century, pardons played a crucial role in the administration of Virginia's criminal law. They were used for all sorts of reasons and matters, often to take into account factors not easily considered by the law itself. Surviving records of Virginia's Council of State list forty-five pardons granted between October 1788 and Crane's General Court hearing in 1791. *The Calendar of Virginia State Papers*, moreover, indicates other pardons were granted that do not appear in the Council's Journals. Pardons were issued to all sorts of people, including whites, free blacks, and slaves, although the whites were usually denoted as "laborers" if class was mentioned. Offenses spanned the spectrum of felonies – horse-stealing, murder, theft, and other crimes – often with little explanation in surviving records, only that the convicted was an appropriate object for "mercy."

Some types of pardons were used systemically. Because criminal law reform was pending but not yet completed, Virginia's governors routinely used pardons to commute death sentences for all crimes except murder to a term of years laboring in the public works. These "conditional" pardons both buffered the sanguinity of the criminal law and traded death for labor, one of the small steps recommended by Beccaria.[37] But these pardons also made some Virginia legal officials uncomfortable. It was unclear if the Governor held the constitutional power to pardon in this manner – adjusting the sentence, without absolving of the crime. Some argued that it merely required an act of the legislature, authorizing the practice; others had deeper concerns about constitutionality. Finally, in 1786, the Virginia Court of Appeals ruled that conditional pardons issued by the executive were indeed unconstitutional under the state constitution.[38]

At other times, pardons were used not to reduce a sentence itself, but to procure testimony in a particular case. For instance, in 1782 Attorney General Edmund Randolph advised the Governor that pardons were particularly useful for conspirators whose testimony the Commonwealth wanted to use in

---

[35] St. George Tucker, "Ten Notebooks of Law Lectures," Notebook 5:179–180, Tucker-Coleman Papers. Blackstone raised a similar concern. Tucker, *Blackstone's Commentaries*, 5:396.

[36] St. George Tucker, "Ten Notebooks of Law Lectures," Notebook 5:179–180.

[37] Kathryn Preyer, "Crime, the Criminal Law and Reform in Post-Revolutionary Virginia," *Law and History Review* 1, no. 1 (1983): 53–85, 68–69.

[38] Commonwealth v. Fowler, 8 Va. 35 (1785).

court against their confederates. Randolph felt that the fact that these witnesses were already pardoned, before their testimony, made that testimony more credible. Otherwise the jury would think that they were saying whatever the Commonwealth wanted them to say, in hopes of achieving goodwill and leniency later. Or, as Randolph put it, they would think that the witness was "making court to government for his life by the virulence of evidence against his accused brother."[39] Randolph advised that without a prior pardon, the witness's credibility could be "very much suspected."[40]

But pardons were used for more than administrative or prosecutorial purposes. Sometimes petitions informed the governor of a legal error which had taken place during the trial, when there was no other recourse. For instance, in the case of Phil, an enslaved man who had been convicted of an unspecified felony in the New Kent County Court, the Commonwealth's attorney for the county and the county justices informed the Governor that the court had sentenced Phil to death only after being shown a law that Attorney General Edmund Randolph had later informed them was no longer in effect. According to the correct law, however, the defendant had been eligible for the benefit of clergy. Unable to correct their error, the petitioners asked the Governor to pardon Phil.[41] In a similar letter, the Rockingham County Commonwealth's Attorney asked for pardon for another slave named Jack, whose conviction had arisen solely because the petitioner had "carelessly, not willfully" allowed Jack's accomplice to testify against him, in direct contravention of an Act passed in October 1789.[42]

In other cases, legal officials, especially justices of the peace, requested pardon for more general considerations of justice. In late eighteenth-century Virginia, justices of the peace, witnesses, and other court personnel filed petition after petition asking for pardon for someone whom they had helped to convict. For instance, in one case, justices of the Nansemond County Court recommended that the Governor pardon Coff, a slave who had been sentenced to death for an unspecified felony, because they believed that another slave – an accomplice whose testimony resulted in Coff's conviction – had actually

---

[39] "Ed'wd Randolph to Gov: Harrison," in *Calendar of Virginia State Papers and Other Manuscripts*, vol. 3: *From January 1, 1782 to December 31, 1784*, ed. William P. Palmer (Richmond, VA: James E. Goode, 1883), 193. The "Edward" is a typographical error – Edmund Randolph was the attorney general at the time, and the letter appears to be advising about events related to the treason prosecution in the *Case of the Prisoners*.

[40] "Ed: Randolph Atty: General, to the Governor," ibid., 395. Randolph mentions this technique twice within a ten-month period, suggesting that it was a normal practice.

[41] "Letter from Bartlett Williams, Attorney for the County and the Members of the Court to the Governor and the Honorable, the Council of State," January 18, 1790, *Calendar of Virginia State Papers*, 5:101.

[42] "O. Towles, Commonwealth's Attorney for Rockingham, to the Governor," July 20, 1790, ibid., 189.

been the "principal" offender in committing the crime.[43] In another case, the justices of the Mathews County Court recommended that the Governor pardon Cornell, an enslaved man belonging to Benjamin Marable, for breaking and entering into the storehouse of Lewis Gan, citing his "good character previous to his committing the aforesaid offence."[44] And in Petersburg District Court, court clerk William Whitlock forwarded to the Governor petitions for the pardon of a man named Martin, whose friends and the jury requested his pardon, citing "Martin's youth and subsequent good behavior since the felony was committed."[45] The justices of New Kent County similarly unanimously recommended for pardon the slave Hercules, who had been sentenced to death for assisting John Price Posey to burn down the county jail and clerk's office.[46]

Pardons like these – especially involving slaves – could make it seem as if there was a struggle between different components of the court system. Did local justices convict slaves of crimes, only to have their masters seek state intervention to protect their property? And sometimes conflicting petitions even arrived at the capitol, revealing fractures in community opinion. For instance, Thomas Gatewood contradicted other pardon petitions when he asked Governor Lee not to pardon Argyle, a slave who had been sentenced to death for robbing him, claiming that Argyle was "a notorious villain, & an old offender."[47]

But pardons also occurred in all sorts of cases, and in circumstances that showed the *same* decision-makers both convicting and then appealing for leniency. For instance, a letter from General Court judges Tazewell and Nelson sheds particular light on the ways in which law and justice interacted not just at the county but also in cases at the state district courts. In 1792, at the same time as the Governor considered Crane's pardon, judges Tazewell and Nelson recommended that William Cheetwood of Powhatan County – found guilty of arson for burning the county jail – be pardoned for his crime. They related that immediately after convicting Cheetwood – who was "of a fair character" but had a "weak mind" and had sometimes been "deprived of reason" – the jurors had delivered to the court a statement requesting his pardon. Because there was a question whether Cheetwood's crime was a capital one, the judge had referred the case to the General Court, but the judges asked the Governor to

---

[43] "Willis Riddick, A. Richardson, Albert M. Riddick, and Josiah Riddick to the Governor," March 21, 1792, ibid., 472.

[44] "Recommendation for Cornell," April 17, 1795, *Calendar of Virginia State Papers and Other Manuscripts*, vol. 7: *From January 1, 1794 to May 16, 1795* …, ed. Sherwin McRae and Raleigh Colston (Richmond, VA: J. H. O'Bannon, 1888), 468.

[45] "William Whitlock, Clerk of the Court, to the Governor," April 26, 1790, *Calendar of Virginia State Papers*, 5:144.

[46] "Negro Slave, Hercules," December 12, 1787, *Calendar of Virginia State Papers and Other Manuscripts*, vol. 4: *From January 1, 1785, to July 2, 1789* …, ed. William P. Palmer (Richmond, VA: R. U. Derr, 1884), 367.

[47] Thomas Gatewood to the Governor, May 13, 1792. *Calendar of Virginia State Papers*, 5:543.

pardon Cheetwood even before the General Court had made his condemnation final to save him from "a severe imprisonment" in the meantime.[48]

Petitions like these made clear both Virginians' respect for the letter of the law and their concern that justice be done appropriately to each case. The jury's conduct in the Cheetwood case made explicit the fact that they had followed the law, even though they then immediately prayed that its sentence would not be carried out. With the one immediately following the other, no possible lapse of time or alteration in community sentiment could account for the change between verdict and pardon petition, nor were different actors involved. The many surviving petitions from justices of the peace suggest a similar attitude – justices (who had final jurisdiction in cases concerning slaves) seem to have routinely delivered guilty verdicts in cases and then quickly petitioned for the condemned slave's pardon.

To be sure, at other times the justices convicted a defendant of a lesser crime than that with which he had been charged, thus adjusting the punishment up front to what they considered to be appropriate. But the many pardon petitions that inundated Virginia's governors also indicate that Tucker had it right: in the courts, Virginians tended to follow the law. Whether it was concern about whether a defendant had taken the fall for a co-conspirator, qualms about his age or responsibility, a belief that he had repented, or the fact that evidence had subsequently come to light which made the propriety of the result less certain, Virginia's magistrates, jurors, witnesses, and judges did their own jobs, then turned to the executive, requesting pardon to do justice in ways that the law had not. In petition after petition, a picture emerged – of fact-finders who had made decisions according to law, then asked the Governor to mitigate the sentence. In 1792, it seems, the harsh sanctions that remained the law were buffered – by the legal inheritance of clergy, and by the discretion of the executive. If the pardon were taken away, juries might indeed function more as courts of "equity" themselves.

Opinion was not unanimous in John Crane's case, but his father did a good job of making it look that way. On behalf of his son, James Crane mounted what seems to have been the most extensive pardon campaign of late eighteenth-century Virginia. But as Crane's friends and family petitioned, they knew that his chances were slim. As Winchester District Court Clerk John Peyton admitted in his letter to Governor Lee, murder was a crime for which mercy was "seldom interposed."[49]

But seldom did not mean never. Indeed, only two years earlier, Catherine Crull, who had been convicted of murdering her husband, had been pardoned and committed instead to the lunatic asylum in Williamsburg.[50] As Virginia

---

[48] "Judges Henry Tazewell and William Nelson to the Governor," April 13, 1792, *Calendar of Virginia State Papers*, 5:529.

[49] "J. Peyton to the Governor."

[50] The asylum, also called the "Public Hospital" or the "Eastern State Hospital," was established in 1770 by an Act of the House of Burgesses, and the first patients were admitted in 1773. See

Attorney General Joseph Jones had written to then-Governor Edmund Randolph: "The conduct of this ill-fated woman brought strongly to mind the case of one Phillips, from the county of Hanover, who, during the regal government, was tried and convicted for shooting his wife. He was pardoned on suggestion of lunacy and committed to the lunatic Hospital, where I remember frequently to have seen and conversed with him."[51] And in May 1792, as Crane's petitions piled up on Governor Lee's desk, two other condemned defendants raised the same claims, men named Ralph Crawforth Anderson, convicted of murder, and Isaac VanMiter, convicted of horse-stealing. Anderson had been convicted of murder in the Richmond District Court and in May 1792, his brothers wrote a letter to the Governor that claimed that their brother suffered from "interruptions of his reason," that he had never borne any "resentment" toward the victim before killing him, and asked for his pardon on this account.[52] Judges Henry Tazewell and William Nelson also wrote, seconding the pardon request: "The state of the prisoners [sic] mind was offered to the Court and Jury as an apology for his conduct, and some testimony as to his insanity was examined, but it was not considered as sufficient in the opinion of either. Since the judgment, several papers on that subject have been sent to us. We take the liberty to enclose them to your Excellency."[53] Anderson's mental state had been raised at both the trial and pardon stage, and the request seems to have been successful.[54]

William Waller Hening's *The New Virginia Justice*, a handbook produced only a few years later to aid justices of the peace, indicated the ways in which an insanity defense could be handled. According to Hening, "ideots [sic] and lunatics who are under natural disability of distinguishing between good and evil, are not punishable by any criminal prosecution." Hening defined lunatics as those "who sometimes have their understanding and sometimes not." Whether a criminal was actually a lunatic or not was to be determined by an inquest, returned by the sheriff, with evidence presented either to the court

Granville Lillard Jones, *The History and Founding of the Eastern State Hospital in Virginia* (Williamsburg, VA: n.p., 1954); Norman Dain, *Disordered Minds: The First Century of Eastern State Hospital in Virginia, 1766–1866* (Williamsburg, VA: Colonial Williamsburg Foundation, 1971); "Public Hospital," *Colonial Williamsburg*, accessed November 26, 2016, www.history. org/almanack/places/hb/hbhos.cfm. I am grateful to my research assistant Amelia Nemitz for gathering this information.

[51] "Jos. Jones, Attorney General, to Governor Beverley Randolph," January 28, 1789, *Calendar of Virginia State Papers*, 4:554.

[52] "Petition to the Hon'ble Henry Tazewell & William Nelson, Esquires, Judges of the General Court sitting in the District of Richmond," May 2, 1792, *Calendar of Virginia State Papers*, 5:521.

[53] "Judges Henry Tazewell and William Nelson to the Governor."

[54] A "Ralph C. Anderson" appears again in Virginia records only a couple of years later, in Chesterfield County – near the Richmond District Court where Anderson had been convicted. "Petition for Jack," *Calendar of Virginia State Papers*, 7:30. I am grateful to my research assistant Amelia Nemitz for this discovery.

or to the trial jury.[55] Although practice may have varied from the straight-forward dictates of Hening's manual, these sources indicate that Crane could have raised an insanity defense in the examining court or in the district court, although he seems to have chosen not to make this case during his trial.

Tucker and Lee made no reference to lunacy evidence in their letters, and there is no evidence of this argument having been presented before the court. Since the petitioners stated that the Crane family had attempted to keep John's condition a secret, this is no surprise – perhaps because they felt certain of their manslaughter defense and thought airing John's condition unnecessarily laid bare their family shame. Or perhaps it was only later, after John's conviction, when they attempted to connect his "fits" to the crime. Saving lunacy until then allowed the Cranes to continue to conceal John's illness, a goal the letters written on Crane's behalf suggest was of great value to his family. Here one glimpses another face of "honor." Often seen in the study of the South as an enabling force, giving license to touchy behavior and extraordinary reactions to minor slights, honor also had a constraining side, one that necessitated the maintenance of one's reputation. Indeed, here class may have played against Crane, making him less likely to reveal his instabilities.

And if the Cranes, or John himself, were at first reluctant to air the full extent of his ailments, it is possible that the extraordinarily passionate outpouring of the letters begging his pardon, and what Court Clerk John Peyton described as a change in community sentiment, came in the face of a full disclosure of his mental illness in the months after the trial and General Court's decision. And it makes sense that these revelations accounted for the dramatic turn in public opinion. At this eleventh hour, as James Crane traveled around the Valley gathering signatures for his son, the desperate Cranes probably regretted not having raised the issue of John's lunacy earlier.

In these waning days of the Crane case, perhaps the community began to understand more of the secret that the Cranes had carried all along. Perhaps Catherine Whiting Crane's ugly slur – telling her husband that she was "surprised" that he would "demean himself to fight with such a set of negrofied puppies" – now seemed less like the vicious words of a haughty woman, and more like the desperate cry of a terrified wife. "Mr. Crane, I am surprised you would demean yourself" she had called out, as she tried to appeal to his pride and his honor in a futile attempt to stop the fight. Maybe she had seen before the unbalanced anger in his behavior at the fence – maybe even directed towards her, others he fought, or the people they owned.

So how did Catherine feel as she watched her father-in-law desperately try to save his son? Was she stunned that it had come to this? Or was she not stunned at all? Maybe it was her worst fear, her persistent dread, come to life.

[55] William Waller Hening, *The Virginia Justice: Comprising the Office and Authority of a Justice of the Peace in the Commonwealth of Virginia* (Richmond, VA: Johnson & Warner, 1810), 380.

Or maybe it was the public expurgation of a burden that she had carried privately for far too long.

At the last stage of Crane's proceedings, as at the beginning, Berkeley County was against telling stories – stories about him and his crime. Crane's petitions stand out, even amongst hundreds of other surviving petitions amidst Virginia state papers. They are striking first for their sheer volume: whether because of strong feeling about John's case or because of James Crane's clout and status, the family procured at least thirteen petitions on John's behalf. They are also notable for their comprehensiveness. The letters provided detail, personal observations, and medical expertise to back up their pleas for pardon.

But the truth behind these stories is elusive. Why did so many of Berkeley's citizens petition for Crane's pardon? Was it out of sympathy for James and Lucy Crane, or because they really thought that justice demanded it? Did they suspect that, given the nature of the crime, it was a futile enterprise, and thus see no harm in attempting to help the Cranes? Did they feel obligated, given James Crane's status, or did they genuinely seek to help the young, condemned man?

And what of John Crane himself? Even with the wealth of information in Crane's pardon petitions, it is still hard to grasp the reality behind the formulations. Was Crane's the case of a privileged, mentally ill man whose parents had for years sought to keep his affliction secret, a man now sentenced to die for something he could not control? Or was it a last-minute defense made possible by his parents' clout and connections? Was Crane's illness unrelated to his stabbing of Vanhorn? Or had it driven him to commit a crime that, as some accounts suggested, he might not even remember?[56]

If the pardon petitions suggest that Berkeley's inhabitants had united behind Crane's cause, a closer look makes things more complicated. True, no petitions were submitted that flatly opposed Crane's pardon, as sometimes happened in other cases. But if many signatures appeared in Crane's support, others were conspicuously missing. Three of Crane's jurors wrote to say they thought Crane guilty only of manslaughter, but no other jurors wrote to the Governor about their verdict. Thomas Campbell signed the petition on Crane's behalf, but John Dawkins and Isaac Merchant did not. If Berkeley feeling had swung towards Crane, there were stubborn, if officially silent, dissenters. These citizens, particularly those who had witnessed Vanhorn's death in Campbell's fields, may have seen John's "ungovernable disposition" – as the Shepherdstown paper had called it almost a year earlier, when it first ran the story of Vanhorn's death – less as an excuse, and more as the "barbarous" heart behind his crime.

In the end, the Governor and Council denied Crane's request. Had his credible case of manslaughter actually lessened his case for pardon? Or was it the lack of support from legal authorities like Judge Tucker, or the Attorney General, or any judges of the General Court? In any case, Crane's pardon did not materialize. John Crane would face the gallows.

[56] See "Edw'd J. Power's Certificate as to John Crane Jr."

Conclusion

Making Law Sovereign in Revolutionary Virginia

James Crane's friends and neighbors may have written to Richmond, but in the end it was the ordinary farmers and laborers – the "negrofied puppies" – who were vindicated by the state machinery. The Governor and Council denied Crane's pardon request. This was despite the fact that Governor Henry Lee was the older brother of Crane's lawyer, and that the President of the Virginia Council, which deliberated on Crane's pardon application and made recommendations to the Governor, was James Wood of Winchester, brother of Crane's grand juror Robert Wood, whose signature appeared at the top of Crane's longest pardon petition.[1] When it mattered, those elite networks had not worked for John (or James) Crane.

The Frederick County sheriff executed Crane alongside a horse thief named Robert Johnston at Winchester on July 6, 1792, almost a year to the day from his fight with Vanhorn.[2] Executions in the eighteenth century followed a ritual – confession, apology, and exhortation of others to follow a better path.[3] Johnston complied with this ritual to the letter. The

---

[1] See *Journals of the Council of the State of Virginia*, vol. 5, ed. Sandra Giola Treadway (Richmond, VA: Virginia State Library, 1982), 409–410; see also Guide to the James Wood Executive Papers, Accession Number 40844, Library of Virginia. Guide available at "A Guide to the Governor James Wood Executive Papers, 1796–1799," *Library of Virginia*, accessed November 17, 2016, http://ead.lib.virginia.edu/vivaxtf/view?docId=lva/vi00867.xml.

[2] See *The Herald of Vermont, or, Rutland Courier* (Rutland, MD), August 13, 1792; see also family Bible that appears to have belonged to Catherine Whiting Crane ("Bible in possession of the Slaughter family") listing his death date, in Dakota Best Brown, *Data on Some Virginia Families* (Berryville, VA: Virginia Book Company, 1979), 251–252. Incidentally, the Bible lists all of Catherine's family's dates but not her own death date, further suggesting that it belonged to her.

[3] See Steven Wilf, *Law's Imagined Republic: Popular Politics and Criminal Justice in Revolutionary America* (New York, NY: Cambridge University Press, 2010), 83–104.

newspapers reported that his "behavior at the place of execution was suited to his unhappy situation, and he died apparently satisfied of having made his peace with the Supreme Governor of the Universe." However, Crane "met his fate with reluctance," the paper euphemistically reported, "persisting in his innocence to the last."[4]

John Crane's refusal to go along with the execution ritual is, to the historian, both deviant and endearingly real in its unconcealed anguish. Why did Crane insist he was innocent? Was it because, as he may have claimed early in the case, he had not stabbed Vanhorn at all? Because he had done so in self-defense? Or because, despite full knowledge that he had committed the crime, Crane simply felt that his execution – so unexpected to him and his family – was unjust? Was he defying ritual because he could – because class made him seem above it? Or because his fragile mind had shattered under the stress of execution, showing the full tragedy of what the newspapers had early identified as his "ungovernable disposition"?

Of course, as family and friends watched in horror as John Crane was dragged to the gallows in 1792, their thoughts may have centered on the past. The world was changing, and James and Lucy Crane and the Whiting family surely felt their impotence in its wake. Perhaps the Frederick County sheriff also questioned the new reality of independent, republican government as he executed John Crane – despite John's connections, and the many pleas for pardon from the community. But whether Crane's execution was a triumph or a tragedy probably depended on who you asked, on that gruesome July day – one that came almost exactly a year after an equally gruesome day the year before.

Crane died, but his special verdict – and through it, his case – lived on in Virginia's court records, providing a glimpse into the chaotic, jumbled world of late eighteenth-century America. Crane's experience, and his fate, was a motley combination of intentional change and unintended consequence. Years of failed efforts at reforming Virginia's laws, the newly leveled postwar society, and big principles combined with small, individual decisions; intention intersected with accident and bad timing. The legal world that Crane encountered in 1791–1792 was a work in progress, part of the attempted creation of, and engagement with, republican legal principles and institutions – the tense discussion about what it meant to make law "king."

In 1792, legal reform could be seen on the horizon, though it came too late for John Crane. As Crane's family and friends had petitioned for John's pardon, Judge Tucker had continued to work on Virginia's revisal of the laws. Although he had pushed to be able to propose substantive reforms, he failed.[5] In the

---

[4] *Baltimore Evening Post* (Baltimore, MD), July 26, 1792.
[5] Charles T. Cullen, "Completing the Revisal of the Laws in Post-Revolutionary Virginia," *Virginia Magazine of History and Biography* 82, no. 1 (1974): 84–99, 93–99.

spring of 1792, as John's execution neared, the revisors submitted the fruit of their efforts, mostly a restatement of longstanding statutes, to the General Assembly. There were some criminal provisions in the document, which summarized existing statutes on things like maiming and disfiguring, unlawful gaming, hog-stealing, "divulging of false news," and more.[6] But the common law of crimes remained intact.

Tucker had pushed for one type of reform, however: reform of the jury. Tucked into the leaves of his copy of the revisal, Tucker attached his proposal, and noted that it had been submitted to the legislature but "did not meet their approbation." His recommendations would have provided for comprehensive lists of eligible jurors and a blind system for selecting jury venires and rotating amongst eligible men.[7] A few years later, in his edition of *Blackstone's Commentaries*, Tucker expanded his concerns, complaining that the jury selection process was too open to corruption (for instance, for juries empaneled in order to stack the cause for a defendant). Tucker speculated that such might be the cause of "the number of acquittals against positive evidence" that Tucker claimed to have seen in his time on the bench.[8] Did he have Crane's jury in mind, and its frustrating special verdict?

Finally, reform arrived four years later, in 1796. That year, the General Assembly passed a sweeping alternation of the state's criminal laws. It combined Jefferson's old concerns about efficacy with a new focus on individualized punishment and rehabilitation. In this, the reforms recalled Tucker's concern that the Bill for Proportioning Crimes and Punishments had been too long on uniformity, and too short on taking account of individual foibles.

The new bill's strongest proponent, Assemblyman George Keith Taylor, first built on the same concerns that Jefferson had raised twenty years earlier. He reminded the General Assembly that "[p]receding legislatures" were "sensible that British regulations were in many instances improper in a republican government," and had adopted reforms, especially of property laws and forfeiture provisions. "But much," Taylor asserted, "remains to be done." Like reformers before him, Taylor argued that the existing system aroused sympathy for the accused, and that the wide use of pardon and clergy made it too unpredictable to effectively deter wrongdoing. He also echoed the longstanding concern that wide use of the death penalty violated the natural rights of the criminal.[9]

---

6 Virginia Revisors of the Law, *Draughts of Such Bills as Have Been Presented by the Committee Appointed under the Act …* (Richmond, VA: Augustine Davis, 1792); Ch. 44, "To prevent malicious maiming and disfiguring"; Ch. 42, "Reducing into one, the several acts to prevent unlawful gaming"; Ch. 49, "Against hog-stealing"; Ch. 59 "A Bill against Divulgers of false News."
7 Ibid., 68, St. George Tucker's copy, Tucker-Coleman Papers.
8 St. George Tucker, *Blackstone's Commentaries with Notes of Reference to the Constitution and Laws of the Federal Government of the United States; and of the Commonwealth of Virginia*, vol. 3 (Philadelphia, PA: William Young Birch and Abraham Small, 1803), appendix F, 66.
9 George Keith Taylor, *Substance of a Speech Delivered in the House of Delegates in Virginia, on the Bill to Amend the Penal Laws of the Commonwealth* (Richmond, VA: Samuel Pleasants, 1796), 7.

But Taylor was optimistic about preventing crime and reforming criminals. He emphasized that law-breakers often became such because of insufficient education, which was society's failing. Before punishing a criminal, he lectured, the General Assembly and society should "remember that he is their fellow man, and be cautious how they consign to destruction a character which might have been virtuous had they done their duty."[10] Here, Taylor's proposal demonstrated the shift in thought about punishment that had taken place even within the past two decades. As historian Louis Masur has noted, the years after the Revolution saw an increasing influence of both liberal Christian theology (specifically the idea that the individual had free will and could bring about his own reformation) and John Locke's theories on education, which defined the personality as a creature of environment.[11] These developments combined to make Americans more receptive to types of punishment that sought reformation, not execution.[12] The result was a change in the conception of the criminal. In the words of historian Holly Brewer, criminals were not "irredeemably evil." Instead, they could and should be reformed, and turned into a "better human beings."[13]

Next, Taylor set about the means for that reformation. The new bill assigned a sentencing range for each crime, so the sentence could be tailored to the individual defendant. To deal with these indeterminate sentences, markedly different from the Beccarian scheme of fixed, definite sentences that Jefferson had proposed, Taylor prescribed that the jury would now decide not just the offender's guilt, but would also fix the period of imprisonment.[14] Next, most sentences would then involve imprisonment in the new penitentiary. In the twenty years since independence, Pennsylvania had begun experimenting with substituting confinement and labor as a punishment, aiming to reshape the mind, instead of executing the body. (In his annotations to *Blackstone*, Tucker would describe the use of the penitentiary as worthy "of the imitation of every other government.")[15] Like so many of the changes that had occurred in Virginia's legal system over the past decade, the 1796 reforms blended old theory with new ideas and a healthy dose of common law tradition. They combined a reduction of the death penalty (as Beccaria, Montesquieu, and Blackstone had advised) with a new sentencing scheme that both tailored the

[10] Ibid., 6.

[11] Louis Masur, "The Revision of the Criminal Law in Post-Revolutionary America," *Criminal Justice History* 8 (1987): 21–36, 30–32.

[12] Ibid.

[13] Holly Brewer, *By Birth or Consent: Children, Law, and the Anglo-American Revolution in Authority* (Chapel Hill, NC: University of North Carolina Press for the Omohundro Institute of Early American History and Culture, 2005), 229.

[14] Tucker, *Blackstone's Commentaries*, 5:18, n. 2. The jury would fix the period of imprisonment "in all cases," and the court would determine the period of solitary confinement, within certain limits.

[15] Ibid.

punishment to the crime and assigned that discretion to the democratic jury, not the judge. In addition, a new, optimistic and republican mode of punishment – imprisonment – captured the hope that punishment could reform human behavior (although experience would demonstrate that those methods carried their own brand of savagery).[16]

But the law also did one more thing, something that would have spared John Crane: the 1796 reforms broke down the category of murder. In addition to first-degree murder, there was now also second-degree murder, punished by imprisonment for a term of years instead of death. In a society increasingly concerned about the subjective state of mind of the criminal, these changes further parsed the degree of intent.[17] As Tucker explained it, first-degree murder was murder by poison or lying in wait, or "any other kind of willful, deliberate killing," including killing that occurred during the commission of arson, rape, robbery, or burglary.[18] "All other kinds of murder," Tucker explained, "are deemed murder in the second degree." The degree of murder would be ascertained by the jury, like the term of imprisonment.[19]

Had John Crane's sensational case made Virginia's General Assembly ready – finally – to adjust the laws? Perhaps. Second-degree murder was emerging at this moment as a popular category elsewhere.[20] But Crane's case had at the very least spotlighted the need for some middle way, something between manslaughter (committed in the heat of passion) and capital murder.

Criminal law reform came too late for John Crane, but another type of reform had clearly impacted his case: court reform. Thanks to those changes from the late 1780s, Crane's trial and execution were carried out locally, instead of at the capital.[21] As a result, the people who watched Crane as he was dragged to the gallows and who heard his final protestations of innocence were his friends, neighbors, and family, and those of his victim, Abraham Vanhorn. Because the Commonwealth's

---

[16] There is a vast and excellent literature on the rise of imprisonment in America. See, e.g., Brewer, *By Birth or Consent*, 181–229 (especially for discussion of changing ideas of culpability and Blackstone's role in English reform); David Rothman, *Discovery of the Asylum: Social Order and Disorder in the New Republic* (New Brunswick, NJ: Rutgers University Press, repr. 2006); Edward L. Ayers, *Vengeance and Justice* (New York, NY: Oxford University Press, 1984) (for discussion of the penitentiary in the South).

[17] On the rising concern with parsing intent and state of mind, see Brewer, *By Birth or Consent*, 181–229.

[18] Tucker, *Blackstone's Commentaries*, 5:18, n. 2.

[19] Ibid. For the actual Act, see Samuel Shepherd, *The Statutes at Large of Virginia, from October Session 1792 to December Session 1806, Being a Continuation of Hening Statutes at Large*, vol. 2 (Richmond, VA: S. Shepherd, 1835–1836), 5–16, 243–244.

[20] See Masur, "The Revision of the Criminal Law," 21–22.

[21] Sentencing of John Crane on remand from the General Court in "Indictment of John Crane, Jr.," April 26, 1792, *Calendar of Virginia State Papers and Other Manuscripts*, vol. 5: *From July 2, 1789 to August 10, 1792*, ed. William P. Palmer and Sherwin McRae (Richmond, VA: Virginia State Library, 1885), 507.

new legal reforms had delegated the authority of the General Court to the new district courts, the case which had begun locally essentially ended that way as well.

Local punishment was one of the newest aspects of Virginia's remodeled court system.[22] The district courts brought the state's jurisdiction into the localities, decentralizing the state's judicial system in important ways, while at the same time cementing a pyramid of tribunals from the district level to the Court of Appeals. In the old system, the burdens of court proceedings had been placed primarily on local people including litigants, witnesses, jurors, and other officials, who had to spend days traveling from their homes in order to litigate a case in the General Court in Williamsburg and then Richmond.[23] But, in the new system, that burden was shifted to state officials – especially to judges like Tucker, who spent a good portion of the calendar year trudging from place to place, bringing the courts to the people. This made being a judge onerous. (Years later, St. George Tucker would advise his son-in-law against taking a judicial appointment, based on years of "painful observation & experience."[24]) For cases like Crane's, however, court reform had made law more local than defendants had known in the past.

Of course, moving the courts to the people also brought state jurisdiction to local places, invading the physical territory of the county courts. This state penetration of local communities has led some commentators to see legal reforms like Virginia's as a centralizing move, despite their apparent decentralization – as an attempt to eradicate legal diversity by replacing varying local courts with state tribunals. In *The People and Their Peace*, historian Laura Edwards argues that during this era, state courts and local courts were very different tribunals run by individuals with distinct ways of doing law.[25] Local courts were (in their own, flawed way) communitarian and democratic. They sought to do justice broadly, unconstrained by the niceties of law and legal practice, by relying on community will and case-by-case, contextualized determinations. State courts, on the other hand, were staffed with professionalized lawyers and judges more interested in procedure than context and invested in conceptions of individual rights that "turned people into legal abstractions."[26] According to Edwards, beginning in the late eighteenth century, state-level courts – through reforms like Virginia's – began to strip authority from local courts and people and vest it in centralized state courts; in the process the local voices were lost amidst the confining state jurisprudence of rights. Edwards paints local areas

[22] For a description of the colonial process, see Hugh F. Rankin, *Criminal Trial Proceedings in the General Court of Colonial Virginia* (Williamsburg, VA: Colonial Williamsburg, 1965), 116.

[23] Ibid., 92.

[24] Letter from St. George Tucker to John Coalter, June 3, 1811, Item 5470, Tucker-Coleman Papers.

[25] Laura Edwards, *The People and Their Peace: Legal Culture and the Transformation of Inequality in the Post-Revolutionary South* (Chapel Hill, NC: University of North Carolina Press, 2009).

[26] See generally ibid.; see also Jessica K. Lowe, "A Separate Peace? The Politics of Localized Law in the Revolutionary Era," *Journal of Law and Social Inquiry* 36, no. 3 (2011): 788–817.

as democratic and pluralistic and state courts as professionalized bastions of the elite dedicated to the rule of law.[27]

John Crane's case, however, cautions that reforms sometimes put more power back in local hands, and that the same prominent men often wielded power at *both* the state and local levels. For instance, several of Crane's jurors and grand jurors would later be federal or state officeholders. Daniel Morgan was not only a nationally renowned general, but later represented Berkeley in Congress; Moses Hunter, Thomas Rutherford, George Reynolds, and Magnus Tate would all later serve in the General Assembly; and Magnus Tate also became a US Congressman.[28] These same men who participated in the state courts held powerful local positions as well. Thomas Rutherford appears occasionally as a Berkeley County justice of the peace, and his father had been the first high sheriff of Frederick County.[29] The examples go on. These men were chosen to sit on Crane's jury and grand jury because of their local prominence, demonstrating that their prominence simultaneously led to and sometimes came from ties across the state.

Thomas Rutherford's brother Robert exemplifies the ways in which state and local power overlapped – and how prominent individuals moved easily from one sphere to another. Robert Rutherford was a member of the colonial House of Burgesses but resigned his term and became Frederick County's coroner.[30] He then returned to the House of Burgesses in 1775, and, when relations between the General Assembly and Governor began to deteriorate, became a member of the Virginia Convention and then served in the state senate from 1777 to 1790.[31] In 1793 he would be elected a US Congressman of the "republican" persuasion, although in this last characteristic he differed from many other elected officials in the Berkeley area, many of whom became Federalists, including Daniel Morgan, Abraham Shepherd, George Reynolds, and Magnus

---

[27] Edwards, *The People and Their Peace*; Lowe, "A Separate Peace?"

[28] For General Assembly, see Earl G. Swem and John W. Williams, *A Register of the General Assembly of Virginia and of the Constitutional Conventions* (Richmond, VA: Davis Bottom, Superintendent of Public Printing, 1918), 23 (Rutherford), 50 (Tate), 96 (Reynolds – by then, the eastern part of Berkeley had become Jefferson County). For Morgan and Tate as Congressmen, see "Daniel Morgan," *Biographical Directory of the United States Congress, 1774–Present*, accessed December 7, 2016, http://bioguide.congress.gov/scripts/biodisplay.pl?index=M000946; "Magnus Tate," *Biographical Directory of the United States Congress, 1774–Present*, accessed December 7, 2016, http://bioguide.congress.gov/scripts/biodisplay.pl?index=T000047.

[29] Thomas Kemp Cartmell, *Shenandoah Valley Pioneers and Their Descendants* (Winchester, VA: The Eddy Press Corporation, 1909), 19.

[30] On Rutherford, see Everard Kidder Meade, "Notes on the History of the Lower Shenandoah Valley," *Proceedings of the Clarke County (W. Va.) Historical Association* 14 (1956–1957), various, and John Pendleton Kennedy, ed., *Journals of the Virginia House of Burgesses, 1773–1776* (Richmond, VA: Virginia State Library, 1905), 8.

[31] Millard Kessler Bushong, *A History of Jefferson County, West Virginia, 1719–1940* (Westminster, MD: Heritage Books, 1941), 80; Don Higginbotham, *Daniel Morgan: Revolutionary Rifleman* (Chapel Hill, NC: University of North Carolina Press, 1961), 195–196.

Tate.[32] Rutherford lived near Charles Town and was appointed a Charles Town trustee with James Crane in 1786, in the midst of his political career.[33]

In an age where political participation was still tied to property ownership, and where population was sparse, local and state power networks were bound to be connected. This was perhaps even more apparent in a newly settled area like Berkeley, which had fewer people to choose from when leaders were elected for positions in local and state governments. When choosing individuals to serve as justices, as members of the General Assembly, and in other capacities, Berkeley people and leaders chose over and over from the same pool of men, men like Robert Rutherford, Magnus Tate, Daniel Morgan, and others.

Local and state connections, however, were not merely generated by the scarcity of life in the old west, but also followed it there. Although some men like Daniel Morgan were self-made, some like Abraham Shepherd were wealthy but with out-of-state origins, while others were products of Virginia's old gentry. Just as John Crane's family carried its old Spotsylvania connections to Berkeley, and Catherine Crane's family carried connections to the powerful Robinson and Whiting clans, the Page brothers who sat on John Crane's grand jury were first cousins of Tucker's good friend, John Page of Rosewell, who at the time of the case was a US Congressman and would later be elected Virginia's Governor. Although they lived in what was technically "the west," they were descendants of a well-connected and important Virginia family. When defendants like Crane faced county and district courts, they simultaneously faced forms of state, local, and sometimes national power.

In this way, John Crane's case shows that despite being physically west in the eighteenth century, Berkeley was ruled by many of the same families and represented by the same names one might find elsewhere in the Commonwealth. They often had different interests, but not always. They married each other, visited each other, and maintained connections that can be lost on historians who assume that Winchester or Martinsburg (in the lower Valley where the case takes place) comprised a different world from the Tidewater. Over time, the families in Berkeley developed their own identities as western elites – identities shaped, no doubt, by the introduction of new families – but they never forgot their connections to, for instance, Robert "King" Carter or other elite forebears, as the names they gave their children demonstrate.

This was true not just for the wealthy families with Virginia roots who moved west, but also for other Berkeley settlers who had moved into Virginia from the North or overseas. As historian Warren Hofstra has noted, the Virginians who moved to the Valley from the east "became models for a group of prosperous, self-made men with origins not in the Tidewater but in the Valley" who "purchased slaves, built large and impressive homes, and lived much as the

[32] "Rutherford, Robert," *Biographical Directory of the United States Congress, 1774–Present,* accessed December 7, 2016, http://bioguide.congress.gov/scripts/biodisplay.pl?index=R000548.
[33] Bushong, *A History of Jefferson County, West Virginia,* 17.

affluent and cultured."[34] The Valley's immigrants established large plantations, owned many slaves, and sometimes married into Virginia's prominent families. For instance, the daughter of Martinsburg's General Adam Stephen married Alexander Spotswood Dandridge (grandson of the former governor, second cousin of Martha Washington, and brother-in-law of Patrick Henry), and early German settler Jost Hite's grandson married James Madison's sister, Nelly.[35] By the 1790s, many of Berkeley's wealthy families, regardless of origin, were already intertwined in the region and embraced the identities and values of the Old Dominion. Similarly, the alliances in John Crane's case do not fit neatly into an east-versus-west framework. At the trial, the three jurors who argued for manslaughter *did* have roots in lower Virginia. But many of Crane's pardon petitioners, including those who sent individual letters, were from the Valley's German stock. By the 1790s, regional and ethnic origins remained, but there was also the sense of an elite who seem to have paid more attention to money than heritage.[36]

The one constant that transcended regional origin or other variables was reliance on slaves. Land ownership was important, but Berkeley's records indicate it was not sufficient for achieving genteel status. One could be a small-ish landholder like James Crane and, with the right family connections and enough slaves, be a gentleman. It was this distinction that drew a line across the different areas of the Valley, separating the area west of the Opequon, which was organized more along the lines of individual farms, from the slave labor plantations in the east.[37] And, in the next few years, Berkeley gentlemen who chose to manumit their slaves, like Crane's friends and Methodist converts Thomas Worthington (a Crane neighbor and in-law) and Dr. Edward Tiffin (who had testified to Crane's lunacy), moved to Ohio, where they eventually became governors, instead of remaining slaveless masters in the Valley.[38] In this way, Virginia mores were defining Berkeley, at the same time as Berkeley was participating in the definition of Virginia. As in the rest of the nation, however, the prevailing slave-owning order was not uncontested; leading gentlemen still lamented the corruptions and brutality of the slave system. Only a few years later, Judge Tucker, who already criticized slavery in his law lectures, would

---

[34] Warren R. Hofstra, *A Separate Place: The Formation of Clarke County, Virginia* (Lanham, MD: Rowman and Littlefield, 1999), 12.

[35] For Dandridge, see Harry M. Ward, *Major General Adam Stephen and the Cause of Liberty* (Charlottesville, VA: University of Virginia Press, 1988), 219–221; for Nelly Madison, see "Belle Grove History," accessed December 2, 2016, *Belle Grove Plantation*, www.bellegrove.org/index.php?/about/history.

[36] Higginbotham reaches a similar conclusion about absence of serious east–west issues in Higginbotham, *Daniel Morgan*, 17–19.

[37] Hofstra, *A Separate Place*, 13–24.

[38] See William Lang, "Governor Edward Tiffin – A Biography," in *The History of Seneca County* (Springfield, OH: Transcript Printing Co., 1880), 196–207, which relies on interviews with Tiffin's daughters and memoirs and letters of Tiffin and his family.

publish an emancipation scheme and retain his respectability, even if his ideas provoked great controversy.[39]

The many connections between state and local elites are important for thinking about the meaning of law in late eighteenth-century Virginia, but *what* these men did in Virginia's courts – how they *thought* about the law – is just as important. Edwards argues, looking at the Carolinas, that local people (both elites and non-elites) had different ideas about law from legal professionals – that they were members of a different legal culture, which she terms "localized law." These non-professionals, she contends, tended to absorb law into the realm of fact, deciding what the law was on a case-by-case basis, and not hewing closely to statutes or case law.[40] But in Crane's case, the jury drew a bold line between law and fact, and punted the legal question – murder or manslaughter – to the court. And although the Crane case could be seen as an exception – perhaps the jury's way of avoiding an uncomfortable duty – special verdicts were very common in Virginia. As seen in Chapter 8, Judge Tucker complained that they were the "practice, constantly, in difficult cases."[41] In Virginia at this moment, they were often proposed by counsel, at the prompting of parties seeking the judge's ruling on the law in lieu of a jury verdict. Moreover, Virginia special verdicts appeared in all types of cases, in both state courts and county courts. This is important, because it shows that even in areas where Edwards finds localized law in North and South Carolina, Virginia parties, lawyers, and juries were drawing lines between law and fact – and seeking the courts' opinion on the law. And, when it came to pardon, they were sometimes, as seen in Chapter 9, even convicting individuals whom they then hoped to have pardoned.

Of course, as we have seen, this does not mean that all people – especially non-elites – liked the *content* of the law. Tucker himself complained about "partial" juries, and Virginia in the 1780s was rife with conflict over law and courts. But this was less about vague cultural divide between elite lawyers and local people than about the political and economic strife of the era. At first, it was that middling and lower-class Virginians were unwilling to bear the brunt of the war effort without proper compensation. After attempts to draft poor Virginians into the defense of the state resulted in riots, the General Assembly laid high taxes on the wealthy in order to fund bounties for new recruits.[42]

---

[39] St. George Tucker, *A Dissertation on Slavery, with a Proposal for the Gradual Abolition of it in the State of Virginia* (Philadelphia, PA: Matthew Carey, 1796). For more on Tucker and his complicated relationship to slavery, see Alan Taylor, *The Internal Enemy: Slavery and War in Virginia 1772–1832* (New York, NY: W. W. Norton, 2013), especially 86–89, 107, 229–230, 419–420, but also throughout.

[40] Edwards, *The People and Their Peace*, 65.

[41] Tucker, *Blackstone's Commentaries*, 4:376–377, n. 31.

[42] For a helpful discussion of class and Virginia's military recruitment efforts, see Michael A. McDonnell, "Class War? Class Struggles During the American Revolution in Virginia," *William and Mary Quarterly*, 3rd Series, 63, no. 2 (2006): 305–344.

St. George Tucker's father-in-law, Theodorick Bland, complained that he had paid £1,435 for himself, and £524 for his son in one county and around £600 in another, to pay their portion towards the hire of soldiers for revolutionary service. "Such laws," Bland complained, "I believe will soon reduce the most opulent fortune to a level with that of the inferior class of people, especially if the assembly continues to put the power of taxation into the hands of the very lowest class of people, which they have done in this instance."[43] A year later, he described the General Assembly as "enemies of America, or fools or knaves" who, he suspected, were attempting to bring on "a [social] revolution in this state."[44] As the marquis de Chastellux remarked during his 1782 travels through Virginia, "In the present revolution, the ancient families have seen, with pain, new men occupying distinguished stations in the army and in the magistracy." This "popular party have maintained their ground," and had struck at the old elite with a vengeance. As Chastellux noted, "it is only to be regretted that they have not displayed the same activity in combating the English, as in disputing precedence," by which he meant social rank.[45] By the early 1780s, even strong democrat St. George Tucker had begun to doubt the wisdom of the lower-status General Assembly. After a new election in 1782, he wrote that he hoped that the new house would show "more wisdom, foresight, and stability of conduct," than its predecessor. But he feared that "a general misconception of the people, originating partly in their own inattention," and partly in the "studied fallacy in the arguments of those who court popularity" would repeal a tax that Tucker thought would have produced much benefit.[46] By this time, as discussed in Chapter 3, the tables had turned, as Virginians protested the oppressive taxes laid on them to pay war bonds and wealthy speculators. Dissatisfied, they delayed courts and sometimes burned courthouses – but this was not about expressing an alternative legal culture. Instead, it was about protesting the laws as they were, and their perceived effects – wanting the laws to work for them.

Local Virginians did not wish for a bygone day where local grandees lorded over them and demanded paternalistic deference. Instead, they wanted to have control of their institutions and, in the General Assembly, to make that law themselves. Rather than exemplifying a cohesive culture of localized law, Virginia's courts were fraught with politics and protest while steeped in legal ideas and forms. These Virginians wanted to be heard, to be included – to govern.

---

[43] Letter from Theodorick Bland, Sr. to Dr. Theodorick Bland, October 21, 1780, in *The Bland Papers* ..., vol. 2, ed. Charles Campbell (Petersburg, VA: n.p., 1843), 37.

[44] Letter from Theodorick Bland, Sr. to Dr. Theodorick Bland, January 8, 1781, ibid., 51.

[45] François-Jean, marquis de Chastellux, *Travels in North America in the Years 1780–81–82* (New York, NY: n.p., 1828), 291.

[46] Letter from St. George Tucker to Dr. Theodorick Bland, May 2, 1782, in *Bland Papers*, 2:79.

And in John Crane's case, they did – sort of. The conflict at the fence between Crane's and Campbell's fields in some ways embodied the class conflict that had so pervaded Virginia only a few years earlier. Then, angry farmers had burned courthouses and pledged to resist collection of their taxes – and Crane's own father was, as deputy sheriff, one of those tax collectors. The perceived class discrepancy between Crane and the other harvesters is what led Catherine Crane to yell to her husband not to fight with "such a sett of negrofied puppies." Men like Crane, Catherine inferred, did not jump into a field to fight with their neighbor's reapers.

But Crane's class was complicated. Indeed, the ambiguous nature of his class provides one of the case's most fascinating and elusive aspects. On one hand, a first perusal of the case – of John Crane, "yeoman," fighting with the men who worked in Campbell's fields on July 4, 1791 – conjures up a picture of middling western farmers. But John Crane was something different – the son of one of the county's most prominent men, and well connected to the Virginia gentry who ruled the colony and then the state. He was, also, an elite.

Or was he? Despite John's connections, on July 4, 1791, he owned less land than many of the men who worked in his fields. Isaac Merchant surpassed him by almost a hundred acres; Abraham Vanhorn's father owned more slaves. By this measure, John Crane was, indeed, just another yeoman – making Catherine's slur all the more ridiculous, and all the more infuriating. No wonder that, with her words, Vanhorn became "much irritated," as the verdict reported, and he and Merchant stripped off their shirts to face Crane. In that light, the words of this desperate, perhaps haughty woman appeared ridiculous. At the same time, the words and signatories of Crane's many pardon petitions reminded the Governor and Council that John Crane *was* different – that he was not just any defendant.

In this way, class in *Commonwealth v. Crane* is both rigid and surprisingly flexible. On one hand, as notions of class play out in the case, names, families, and people seem to carry more weight than wealth and property. Catherine Crane, for instance, clearly felt that, despite her husband's middling property ownership status, she and he were better than the men who worked in his fields. And, at this, the frustration of Campbell's workers is palpable. Perhaps this rigidity – this ceiling – on Virginia advancement was partly what was prompting so many people like Isaac Merchant's brother and John Dawkins's parents to relocate farther west.

At the same time, class in *Crane* emerges as, in law, dependent entirely on wealth. Crane is classified as a yeoman – despite his "gentleman" father, and his "esquire" grandfather. Crane's abrupt fall in the world brings to mind the class fragility about which Virginia leader George Mason worried extensively; Mason lamented that no matter how great a "Man's Rank or Fortune," his "posterity must quickly be distributed among the different Classes of Mankind, and blended with the Mass of the People." While contemplating a new government at the Constitutional Convention in Philadelphia, he wrote that he "often wondered at the indifference of the superior classes of society" to the importance of a broad electorate, when "the course of a few years, not only might but certainly would, distribute their posterity throughout the lowest classes of society."[47] A rapid descent down the social ladder is also apparent in *Commonwealth v. Posey*; in his indictment, defendant Posey, former justice of the peace in New Kent County and former member of the General Assembly, was designated a "laborer."[48] On the other hand, when one looks closely at Posey, companion and friend of John Parke Custis, one also gets the feeling that Virginia's gentry may have never felt that he belonged – not quite.

As some fell in status, others rose. When St. George Tucker entered Virginia in 1772, he was from a genteel Bermuda family, but he had few connections in the mainland colonies. He and his brother, Thomas Tudor Tucker, who moved to South Carolina, managed to climb their way through America's social structure. In South Carolina, the Edinburgh-trained Thomas initially struggled. St. George fared better, making friends with leading Virginians, but still found himself on the periphery until the Revolution came and he began to run the family's smuggling operation. And while the social standing of Tucker's Bermuda background was a necessary foundation for his later incorporation into the Virginia elite, it was Tucker's marriage to Frances Bland Randolph, and thus into Virginia's kinocracy, that integrated him most fully into the life of the new state.

In Virginia after the Revolution, class was thus both fluid and rigid. It was fluid in the falls down the social scale, like John Crane's and John Price Posey's, and the climbs up it, like those of St. George Tucker or, more dramatically, of men like Daniel Morgan – or like the new men who began to exercise power in the General Assembly and sometimes, the county courts. There were also, of course, thanks to the Revolution, formerly powerful families who opted out of the new order – men like James Wormeley, who moved to Britain, or the Loyalists who relocated to Nova Scotia.[49] At the same time, Virginia's dense kin networks – those who complained about some of the changes in the type of "new" men who led Virginia's government – continued to

---

[47] Jack Rakove, *Revolutionaries* (New York, NY: Houghton Mifflin, 2010), 163.

[48] See Indictment, Commonwealth v. John Price Posey, on file with St. George Tucker's General Court Cases, Tucker-Coleman Papers. For more information on the Posey affair, see A. G. Roeber, *Faithful Magistrates and Republican Lawyers: Creators of Virginia Legal Culture, 1680–1810* (Chapel Hill, NC: University of North Carolina Press, 1981), 191–192; Malcolm Hart Harris, M.D., *Old Kent County Virginia* (Baltimore, MD: Genealogical Publishing Co., 2006), 97–99.

[49] See Maya Jasanoff, *Liberty's Exiles: American Loyalists in the Revolutionary World* (New York, NY: Knopf, 2011); *The Recollections of Ralph Randolph Wormeley, Written Down by His Three Daughters*, ed. Katharine Prescott Wormeley, Elizabeth Wormeley Latimer, and Ariana Wormeley Curtis (New York, NY: Privately Printed, 1879), in UVA Special Collections; Alan Taylor, *The Internal Enemy: Slavery and War in Virginia 1772–1832* (New York, NY: W. W. Norton, 2013), 29.

dominate, making it hard for some to fall too far or climb too high. This may have crossed the mind of Isaac Merchant, as he worked in the fields for his neighbor, Campbell, and yet was called a "negrofied puppy" by the wife of a man who owned far less land than he did. And Catherine Crane may have taken the safeguards of her name for granted when, a couple of years after John's execution, she married Smith Slaughter, a man who had served as Berkeley's high sheriff, the same office her kinsmen had also held on and off since the colonial era. They had no children, and lived at a Berkeley estate called "Richwood Hall."[50] When she died in 1822, her second husband was a delegate to the General Assembly; the General Assembly, which was in session, marked her passing, offering its sympathy for the "loss sustained by Smith Slaughter," and adjourned early in Catherine's memory.[51] John Crane's ignominious end did not send her into the darkness outside of acceptable society – but perhaps she expected that.

The inner contradictions of Virginia's class structure can be easy to miss, especially when using sources created and preserved by the gentry themselves in the antebellum period. As many historians of the South have noted, available sources are heavily biased toward the planter class, who, though a minority, employed forced laborers who enabled them to philosophize, correspond, and serve in public office. Not only are their accounts of life in the South as a whole (and perhaps especially in Virginia) predominant, their accounts of class also overshadow all others. Their depictions of their less fortunate neighbors, employees, and enslaved workers as people fundamentally different often stand alone, such that observations about one segment of the population, and about the dissipation or laziness of other segments, black or white, are taken at face value as evidence for the character and manners of those who did not have the learning or leisure to themselves reflect on paper.

But these aristocratic accounts concealed messy realities – not only the many relationships between masters and the slaves who, as historian Annette Gordon-Reed has so eloquently and incisively shown, were often their concubines, children, and siblings, but also the white families who had climbed up and fallen down the social ladder, or who were far less different than their depicters might wish to think.[52] All too often, gentry accounts of their "neighbors" – whether Catherine Crane's crude slur or other descriptions couched in more sophisticated language – have been taken for granted as definitive. As much as later upper-class Virginians liked to see their status as an inborn

---

[50] Catherine's marriage to Smith Slaughter is listed in Brown, *Data on Some Virginia Families*, 264. Slaughter was named as Berkeley sheriff in September 1789 records. For Richwood Hall, see ibid., 252.

[51] Ibid., 264; "Virginia Legislature: Proceedings of the House of Delegates," *Richmond Enquirer* (Richmond, VA), January 17, 1822.

[52] See Annette Gordon-Reed, *The Hemingses of Monticello: An American Family* (New York, NY: W. W. Norton, 2008).

commodity, it was (at least for whites) constantly in the process of being constructed and reconstructed, both inside and outside the courtroom.

In this way, Catherine Crane's statement is arguably, for the historian, the most revealing moment of the jury's arrestingly vivid verdict. Later observers argued that Southern slavery led to the association of manual labor with bondage and blackness, and made the South's non-slaveholding whites unwilling to toil in the fields.[53] Historians have largely accepted this claim. But although Merchant and Vanhorn reacted strongly when Catherine called them "negrofied puppies," the statement in many ways said more about her prejudices than theirs. Crane's and Campbell's reapers had toiled in fields for their whole lives, and many of them – perhaps all – would continue to do so. But Catherine, raised among Virginia's most privileged class, saw things differently – for her, manual labor was something that only slaves did. Any idea that labor was "negrofied" and should be shunned was, at least that day in Crane's and Campbell's fields in 1791, more about the prejudices of Virginia's slaveholding elite than those white men who actually worked. Perhaps this is why Hugh McDonald's deposition, which Crane's supporters presented to the General Court and Governor on John's behalf, not only emphasized that Crane had been provoked and then ambushed by Merchant and Vanhorn, but also that he had spent at least part of the day reclining – not in the field.[54] Was he ill, exhausted, or "conspicuously lounging," as historian Alan Taylor has called it, in order to separate himself from the men who worked in his fields?[55]

Crane's case thus cuts through the glossy images of class, wealth, heritage and Virginia life offered by the elite as the definitive word on their society, and offers an important window, albeit an imperfect one, onto the South at its demographically most typical – a picture of white landowners with few or no slaves toiling in each other's fields on a hot July day, and of individuals in the process of rising or falling in class status, persons with no property who would later have some, and sons of gentlemen settlers who now worked with their hands. Several of the men listed in Crane's case – like Isaac Merchant, who spent the rest of his life reacquiring his family's property – at the time of the fight owned some land but would themselves be larger landowners several years later. (Isaac would die in 1814, and leave his estate to his widow, with instructions to use it to bring up their remaining children in "principles of religion and godliness.")[56] Others, like John Dawkins, whose family had long

---

[53] Upton Sinclair succinctly captured this common view, which became an oft-repeated anti-slavery argument, in his novel *Manassas*: "You hear slavery justified ... because the negroes are inferior, but it is not only the negroes it degrades – look at the working classes of the whites ... A poor man in the South will not work besides negroes, and he cannot compete for the good soil with the great planters; so he squats on used-up lands and sinks lower every year." Upton Sinclair, *Manassas: A Novel of the War* (New York, NY: Macmillan & Co., 1904), 72.

[54] See "Deposition of Hugh McDonald, October 1, 1791," *Calendar of Virginia State Papers*, 5:372.

[55] Taylor, *The Internal Enemy*, 65.

[56] See will of Isaac Merchant, Probated September 1814, Berkeley County Will Book, 5:151, BCHS.

owned land and was descended from early settlers in the area, nonetheless toiled with their hands in a neighbor's harvest field, and were in the process of relocating even further west.[57] Finally others, like John Crane, were raised as gentlemen but for this moment were spending at least part of the day in the fields.

Like these individuals – like John Crane and Abraham Vanhorn and Isaac Merchant and John Dawkins – the Virginia of Crane's case was a Virginia *in motion*, in the process of becoming and of departing, of encompassing and excluding. Whatever Virginia may have become by 1830, 1865, or 1890, in 1791 it was a place old by North American standards but still being born, still in the process of generating its new, free polity, still assimilating new migrants from the northeast and overseas, still stretching and redefining its boundaries as its white inhabitants claimed and settled new areas, and as other areas, like Kentucky, broke off to become new states. When one looks more closely at the characters, the landscape, and the hues and textures, the portrait becomes fluid – a blended, complex swirl of meaning and motion, much of which is beyond our grasp.

This Virginia in motion is lost, however, if one focuses on the law as it was eventually pronounced, rather than how it worked – from court to court, and from participant to participant. Given the paucity of records that exist for the period – not many cases offer records even as complete as Crane's, which is thin compared to records left by cases of later eras – this motion is often hard to catch in full. But part of the exercise is not just about historical sources, but also about methodological orientation – about seeing the case as a moment in an unfolding drama about the law and its application to life.

Using legal materials presents a particular challenge, for those materials are at once more credible and more suspicious. On one hand, they are produced either by or for a body charged with truth and justice. Crane's jury verdict, for instance, is not the account of a random witness or potentially agenda-driven newspaper, but instead the reasoned conclusion of some of the "best" men in the community as to what happened that day in Crane's field. On the other hand, these same indicia of trustworthiness also mean that the documents require greater scrutiny. The jury verdict, as the later letters supporting Crane's pardon so plainly show, was a product of compromise, in a time where feelings about the event in question ran strong. Likewise, the letters are written with an end in mind, and the behavior they describe tracks almost perfectly the legal descriptions of the temporary "lunatic" in legal treatises of the era. Without trivializing the importance of oaths to those who gave their certified testimonies about Crane's condition, how much had that testimony been fashioned to correspond with prevailing views about insanity and legal responsibility?

[57] The Dawkins family identifies the John Dawkins of the Crane case as John Dawkins, Jr. Lela Wolfe Prewitt, *The Dawkins and Stewart Families of Virginia and Kentucky* (N.p: 1968), 5.

Legal materials are difficult, however, not just because they are adapted to the demands of the often particular legal process, but also because they are by nature decontextualized. When, in the nineteenth century, General Court judges William Brockenbrough and Hugh Holmes compiled a collection of criminal case reports, they included *Commonwealth v. Crane* – both the General Court's short order and the jury's elaborate special verdict, thus preserving for posterity its riveting account of a fight in early national Virginia.[58] But although a simple reading of the verdict in Crane's case gives much information, for the historian it leaves out many important details. For instance, it lists Crane as a yeoman, and of course does not mention his prominent father or the fact that he was a brand-new landowner. It omits that there were any slaves in the field, including the "negro man of Mr. Crane's" who was mentioned in the case – likely the man on whom Crane had planted his knife – and probably others, since both Crane and Campbell (at least) were slave owners; there must have been other men and maybe women toiling next to the white men whose names ended up recorded in the verdict, other witnesses to the fight who were not allowed to testify. And because the case involves an area now included in West Virginia, it evokes an ethos of rugged hills and frontier justice; the verdict leaves the impression of two rival groups of young, backcountry laborers and lower-status yeoman, fighting in the rough style so famous in accounts of lower-class brawls.[59] But such assumptions are far from the truth – the men in the field that day varied from the enslaved to the white laborer to the prosperous yeoman to the gentleman's son, all at work amid large plantations nestled in the soft, rolling hills of the Shenandoah Valley.

The many blanks left by legal materials make it tempting to fill them in with what we, the modern readers, think we know. This is a particular problem in the South, where hindsight is so strong and stereotypes so deep, that it is easy to read pat answers from the antebellum and postbellum periods, when fatal violence was rampant and unchecked, back into the early days of the states that would later make up the Confederacy and border region. It is easy to attribute this willingness to condone violence and refusal to convict to Southerners across time, but this was certainly not the reality that young John Crane encountered in 1791, as he was tried, convicted, and then hanged – despite his father's best efforts – for the murder of fellow combatant in a harvest field. Seeing the complicated and intricate reality of *Commonwealth v. Crane* actually *requires* one to trace the historical context – context that would have been obvious to those involved, but is frustratingly elusive to the modern reader.

---

[58] William Brockenbrough and Hugh Holmes, *A Collection of Cases Decided by the General Court of Virginia, Chiefly Relating to the Penal Laws of the Commonwealth* (Philadelphia, PA: James Webster, 1815), 10–14.

[59] See Elliott T. Gorn, "'Gouge, Bite, Pull Hair and Scratch': The Social Significance of Fighting in the Southern Backcountry," *American Historical Review* 90, no. 1 (1985): 18–43.

It also requires an understanding of how courts operated – legal strategies, the meanings and processes of examination, trial, and appeal. For much of the meaning and drama of the Crane case comes out not just in the case itself, but from the context of the new court system, built on reformers' desires to perfect the legal system of their recently independent commonwealth. Courts were being moved to localities in order to expedite the legal process and make state adjudication more accessible and available throughout Virginia.[60] Pardons had been out of favor with some as relics of a monarchical system where the sovereign's will (individual and extra-legal, and thus despotic to republican reformers) was allowed to have the last word, but they were still in use, and were regaining a foothold. And problems with criminal punishment, especially the common law's overreliance on the death penalty, had been noted by Virginia's legal reformers as early as 1776, but attempted reforms had not yet been enacted when Crane faced his death in 1791.

But watching the motion of the Crane case is important not just for history, but also for how we conceive of the law. Crane's experience with the law was not just about the outcome, but also about the exhausting, overwhelming, and uncertain process that brought it about. At each stage, that process was shaped by all the resources his father could marshal, by Crane's own vehement protestations of innocence, and the decisions he made – like pressing for immediate trial. But also at each stage, representatives of the legal system were charged with reaching behind the many varying stories to determine the truth. Crane, like many defendants after him, faced not just a legal outcome, but also an extended encounter with the legal process.

And, as with many criminal cases, even with the wealth of documents available about John Crane the truth is still beyond reach. Did having Vanhorn's horses trample his wheat trigger a nervous "fit" in John Crane, who then maimed them, and in doing so provoked Merchant and Vanhorn? If that story was merely fiction invented by distant newspapers, did the hoots of Vanhorn and his companions as they left work for the evening evoke Crane's affliction? Or was Crane completely lucid at the time of the crime? Were the "fits" an invention of his family and friends to procure his pardon? Did he carry the knife into the field intending to stab Vanhorn, or did he pull it out in self-defense when trapped on the ground and besieged by two assailants? Or did someone else in the tumble – Merchant or another – actually stab Vanhorn by accident?

It is difficult to untangle all the threads – anger, violence, class, and mental illness – to judge if John Crane's execution was a victory or a tragedy for the legal system. A wagoner died, and a gentleman's son was executed. But it may also have meant the execution of a man who was not culpable for his actions.[61]

---

[60] See Roeber, *Faithful Magistrates*; Charles T. Cullen, *St. George Tucker and Law in Virginia, 1772–1804* (New York, NY: Garland Publishing, 1987).

[61] "Edw'd J. Power's Certificate as to John Crane Jr.," April 20, 1792, *Calendar of Virginia State Papers*, 5:497.

In a sense, the frustrations that confound us reading the *Crane* case are the same ones that confounded the many individuals who addressed it at the time.

Judge Tucker liked to think of law as a science, but the truth was that law-making and judging were messy. This was certainly true literally, as Tucker and other judges trudged around the state on their circuits to sit at district courts dispersed throughout Virginia's vast territory. But it was also the case jurisprudentially. On one hand, the Commonwealth's laws and legal system were rapidly changing; independence had brought new structures of power, new statutes, and new legal questions. On the other hand, many things had stayed the same, and Virginia's judges confronted the disjunction between these two realities every time they dealt with a common-law case or precedent based on a British statute. Virginia's law, like its judges, was on the move – transitioning from the colonial to the "republican," as they called it; from the inherited to the created.

And it was still moving. Although it is easy to see the Old Dominion in light of its subsequent history – the capital of the Confederacy, the seat of "Lost Cause" nostalgia – in the 1790s this future was far from assured. The new president, Washington, was an advocate of nationalism; many of the prominent individuals involved in Crane's case – Henry Lee, Charles Lee, Abraham Shepherd, Daniel Morgan, Magnus Tate, and others – would soon identify themselves as Federalists. As Crane fought with Vanhorn in the summer of 1791, political disagreements – over Alexander Hamilton's economic proposals, the Jay Treaty, the Alien and Sedition Acts, and more – were just beginning or still in the future. In 1800, writing from Washington, John Marshall, the new Chief Justice, received his friend Tucker's letter with relief, and put into words the terrible tensions that had gripped the new nation: "No man regrets more than I do, that intolerant & persecuting spirit which allows of no worth out of its own pale, & breaks off all social intercourse as a penalty on an honest avowal of honest opinions."[62]

The partisan split would reframe American politics and jurisprudence; in the decades that followed, Marshall and his legal theory would become identified as Federalist, and with New England.[63] In 1803, Marshall would write his famous opinion in *Marbury v. Madison*, in which the Supreme Court established the power of judicial review. Jefferson, then president, was still criticizing the case a whole seven years later in 1810, griping to James Madison about Marshall's "twistifications" in *Marbury* and alleging that those and other decisions "shew how dexterously he can reconcile law to his personal biases."[64]

---

[62] Letter from John Marshall to St. George Tucker, November 18, 1800, Tucker-Coleman Papers.
[63] Kent Newmyer, "Harvard Law School, New England Legal Culture, and the Antebellum Origins of American Jurisprudence," *Journal of American History* 74, no. 3 (1987): 814–835.
[64] Letter from Thomas Jefferson to James Madison, May 5, 1810, *The Papers of Thomas Jefferson, Retirement Series*, vol. 2: *16 November 1809 to 11 August 1810*, ed. J. Jefferson Looney (Princeton, NJ: Princeton University Press, 2005), 417.

But Marshall's opinion – which echoed aspects of Tucker's 1782 argument in the *Case of the Prisoners* almost verbatim – was largely an outgrowth of his training as a Virginia lawyer. Marshall and Tucker both had a long history with judicial review. Not only had Marshall observed Tucker's 1782 argument, but in 1793, two years after Crane's case, they had cooperated in *Kamper v. Hawkins* to make judicial review official in Virginia – in an opinion written by Judge Tucker (later a staunch Jeffersonian, and whose son became one of the first theorists of states' rights and secession), and argued by Marshall himself.[65] In this way, *Marbury* (whose lawyer, incidentally, was Charles Lee) was a culmination of a principle that had seemed so logical in the *Case of the Prisoners* in 1782 that even Attorney General Randolph, against whose client it operated, had conceded the power.[66]

Like judicial review, other legal ideas already formulated in Virginia also made their appearance on the national stage as Virginians took leading roles in shaping the nascent federal government. Most notably, James Madison had drafted the Constitution, and George Washington shaped the executive (and was the man for whom it was shaped). And when Jefferson returned from his sojourn in France – where he had been for much of the 1780s – he began with Madison to offer an oppositional constitutional theory, one resembling the strict construction he had advocated years earlier during the Virginia revisal. Marshall and Jefferson battled, but both were Virginians; and while Jefferson drew on some of the greatest Enlightenment thinkers – and took many Virginians' political allegiance with him – Marshall's approach was, arguably, more faithful to the legal culture that had developed in Virginia

[65] See St. George Tucker's notes of counsel's argument in Kamper v. Hawkins, in St. George Tucker, "1793 General Court Docket book" in Tucker-Coleman Papers. See also Charles F. Hobson, ed., *St. George Tucker's Law Reports and Selected Papers, 1782–1825*, vol. 1 (Chapel Hill, NC: University of North Carolina Press, 2013), 274–275. (I am grateful to Charles Hobson for reminding me of this fact.) Some scholars have suggested that Virginians may have been somewhat exceptional in their insistence on and acceptance of judicial review. William Treanor ascribes this difference to the dominance of Virginia's gentry over both the legal profession and the legislature, resulting in greater respect for lawyers and less friction between the bar and the General Assembly. A. G. Roeber's work on colonial Virginia lawyers suggests a similar explanation, one based on the adept ways in which those lawyers, traditionally conceived as (in the parlance of the time) a "court" interest, repositioned themselves as advocates for independence and republican government, or for the country as a whole. William Michael Treanor, "The *Case of the Prisoners* and the Origins of Judicial Review," *University of Pennsylvania Law Review* 143 (1994): 491–570, 500. Roeber, *Faithful Magistrates*. On Beverley Tucker's complex life and his fraught relationship with his father see Robert J. Brugger's excellent *Beverley Tucker: Heart over Head in the Old South* (Baltimore, MD: Johns Hopkins University Press, 1978).

[66] See Marbury v. Madison, 5 U.S. 137 (1803). For an excellent and lengthy discussion of *Marbury*, situating judicial review in the larger context of the case and national attitudes, see G. Edward White, *Law in American History*, vol. 1: *From the Colonial Years through the Civil War* (New York, NY: Oxford University Press, 2012), 210–220.

during Jefferson's absence in the 1780s.[67] Both represented the different ideas that Virginians had debated and considered while pondering what it meant to have a state where "law is king."

Virginia litigants, counsel, and juries had their own influence. These Virginians took their own legal habits into federal court, making the special verdicts that were the "practice, constantly," in Virginia's courts also a federal matter. In the first twenty years of the new US Supreme Court, that court would hear at least thirty-three cases involving special verdicts – about a third from Virginia and the District of Columbia Circuit, which sat in Alexandria.[68] Eighteenth-century Virginians were certainly Virginians first, but through their power, proximity, and participation, they were also in many ways defining, and would continue to define, what it meant to be American.

St. George Tucker never achieved the profile of Washington, Marshall, Jefferson, or Madison, but still exercised substantial influence in his own way. Tucker became both a judge of Virginia's Court of Appeals, its highest court, and the US District Court, but his greatest influence came from his edition of *Blackstone's Commentaries*, published in 1803, which became the most important legal treatise of the next thirty years. As legal scholar Robert M. Cover would later note, Tucker's "singular example of an attempt to translate Jeffersonian political theory into law" would make him an important authority on American law, in an era before a general American commentary existed; Tucker would be "quoted and cited as a master until after the Civil War."[69]

---

[67] See Charles F. Hobson, *The Great Chief Justice: John Marshall and the Rule of Law* (Lawrence, KS: University Press of Kansas, 1996), 30–46.

[68] See Bingham v. Cabot, 3 U.S. 19 (1795); Penhallow v. Doane's Adm'rs, 3 U.S. 54 (1795); Hills v. Ross, 3 U.S. 184 (1796); Wiscart v. D'Auchy, 3 U.S. 321 (1796); Brown v. Barry, 3 U.S. 365 (1797); Fenemore v. U.S., 3 U.S. 357 (1797); Sims Lessee v. Irvine, 3 U.S. 425 (1799); Talbot v. Seeman, 5 U.S. 1 (1801); Wilson v. Mason, 5 U.S. 45 (1801); Wood v. Owings, 5 U.S. 239 (1803); Clark v. Young & Co., 5 U.S. 181 (1803); Hooe & Co. v. Groverman, 5 U.S. 214 (1803); M'Ilvaine v. Coxe's Lessee, 6 U.S. 280 (1805); Lambert's Lessee v. Paine, 7 U.S. 97 (1805); Hallet v. Jenks, 7 U.S. 210 (1805); U.S. v. Kid, 8 U.S. 1 (1807); Alexander v. Baltimore Ins. Co., 8 U.S. 370 (1808); Croudson v. Leonard, 8 U.S. 434 (1808); Fitzsimmons v. Newport Ins. Co., 8 U.S. 185 (1808); Kempe's Lessee v. Kennedy, 9 U.S. 173 (1809); McKeen v. Delancy's Lessee, 9 U.S. 22 (1809); Tucker v. Oxley, 9 U.S. 34 (1809); Matthews v. Zane's Lessee, 9 U.S. 92 (1809); Slacum v. Simms, 9 U.S. 363 (1809); Pierce v. Turner, 9 U.S. 154 (1809); Marine Ins. Co. v. Hodgson, 10 U.S. 206 (1810); Hudson & Smith v. Guestier, 10 U.S. 281 (1810); Maryland Ins. Co. v. Ruden's Adm'r, 10 U.S. 338 (1810); Stewart v. Anderson, 10 U.S. 203 (1810); Fletcher v. Peck, 10 U.S. 87 (1810); Livingston v. Maryland Ins. Co., 10 U.S. 274 (1810); King v. Delaware Ins. Co., 10 U.S. 71 (1810); Chesapeake Marine Ins. Co. v. Stark, 10 U.S. 268 (1810).

[69] Robert M. Cover, review of *St. George Tucker's Blackstone's Commentaries*, Paper 2696, *Faculty Scholarship Series*, http://digitalcommons.law.yale.edu/fss_papers/2696, accessed January 11, 2017. See also Charles F. Hobson, "St. George Tucker's Law Papers," *William and Mary Law Review* 47, no. 4 (2006): 1245–1278.

But while Tucker's professional life flourished, his private life was more difficult. His stepson Theodorick Randolph died in February 1792, around the
same time that James Crane desperately advocated for his own son's pardon.[70]
Soon, Tucker would find himself at the center of another Virginia scandal: his
difficult stepson Richard, living wildly at his late parents' Matoax plantation,
was accused of fathering an illegitimate child with his sister-in-law, Nancy
Randolph (Richard's wife's sister – and, in Virginia's close kin circles, Richard's
own cousin). Nancy had allegedly been delivered of the child in secret while
visiting friends; slaves reported that they had found it dead, concealed in a
woodpile. By the time anyone investigated the claims, the evidence was long
gone, but the scandal remained: was there a child? Was the father Richard, or
his dead brother, Theodorick? And had Richard killed it? Richard was brought
to the Cumberland County Court to face charges, as John Crane had been
in Berkeley a year earlier. Tucker engaged John Marshall and Patrick Henry
as part of Richard's defense team. Despite conflicting evidence, the justices
decided to release Richard, and Tucker followed the verdict with a passionate,
thorough defense of his stepson in the *Virginia Gazette*.[71] Tucker had been
hard on James Crane's son, but he soon found himself defending his own. He
would remain a staunch defender of both Richard and the embattled Nancy for
the rest of their lives, although Richard's was brief: Richard Randolph died on
June 14, 1796, at the age of twenty-six, leaving his brother John Randolph –
increasingly troubled and bitter – as the sole survivor of the three young boys
whom Tucker had adopted as his own upon his marriage to Frances.[72]

Despite these events, however, the resilient Tucker again landed on his feet,
and his legal reputation continued to rise. As Tucker continued to champion
the power of the judiciary as the defender of the people's written constitution, his private writings about the judicial role became more cynical. In 1819,
he jokingly penned the "Judge with the Sore Rump" for his son-in-law John
Coalter (also now a judge). In the poem, a judge decrees a death sentence and
attempts to prepare the defendant to die. The defendant ("Aquinas") responds
in a less than respectful manner:

> *Serva tibi minas!* [Keep your threats to yourself!]
>   To a judge who was seated on high;
> As (for some fatal crime)
> He devoted some time
>   To prepare the poor culprit to die.
> "What's that about mine a--e?"
> (Says the judge to Aquinas,
>   And turned up his rump as he spoke)

---

[70] Cynthia A. Kierner, *Scandal at Bizarre: Rumor and Reputation in Jefferson's America*
(Charlottesville, VA: University of Virginia Press, 2006), 28.
[71] Ibid., 77.
[72] Ibid., 88–89.

> "I've a boil on my bum,
> Thrice as large as my thumb:
>   And, see here! – The boil has just broke!"
> Says Aquinas – "I find
> That your tortures behind
>   Are more than you threaten, by far:
> So here's the end of your farce,
> And take care of your a-- e:
> And let me get out of the bar."[73]

There were causes for his deepening cynicism, not least the General Assembly's vehement rejection of his 1796 proposal for the gradual emancipation of Virginia's slaves.[74] Aware that some might see his many reform proposals, on this and other subjects, as meddlesome, Tucker eventually began to conceal his authorship on his various reform initiatives.[75] Over time, his enthusiasm for reform declined and, as historian Alan Taylor has shown, Tucker ultimately fundamentally embraced the slave system he had once criticized, both for Virginia and for himself.[76]

But it was not the end of his association with Winchester. Not only did Tucker continue to return there on circuit, but a decade later, he sent his son, new lawyer Henry St. George Tucker, to Winchester to start a law practice.[77] Winchester had lots of litigation and because of its western location, fewer lawyers than the east, and therefore plentiful opportunities for a new attorney, Judge Tucker thought. But Henry was lonely and unhappy.[78] Over time, he began to settle into life in Winchester; in 1806, he married Martinsburg's Ann Evelina Hunter – the daughter of Berkeley County Clerk Moses Hunter, who had served on Crane's grand jury.[79] Hunter had already died by the time of the marriage, but now some of the history of Crane's case was embedded in Tucker's own family.[80]

---

73 "The Judge with the Sore Rump," January 27, 1819, in St. George Tucker, *The Poems of St. George Tucker of Williamsburg – 1752–1827*, ed. William S. Prince (New York, NY: Vantage Press, 1977), 145.

74 Tucker, *A Dissertation on Slavery*. This proposal was, admittedly, quite problematic, calling for extensive relocation of previously enslaved men and women. See also Hobson, *St. George Tucker's Law Reports*, 1:10–12.

75 Hobson, *St. George Tucker's Law Reports*, 1:54–55.

76 Taylor, *The Internal Enemy*, especially 86–89, 107, 229–230, 419–420, but also throughout.

77 Hofstra, *A Separate Place*, 36–37.

78 Ibid.

79 Phillip Hamilton, *The Making and Unmaking of a Revolutionary Family: The Tuckers of Virginia, 1752–1830* (Charlottesville, VA: University of Virginia Press, 2003), 112–113.

80 For Tucker–Hunter genealogy, see "Letter from Patrick Henry to General Adam Stephen" (with accompanying notes), *Virginia Magazine of History and Biography* 11, no. 1 (1903): 216–218; Hamilton, *Making and Unmaking of a Revolutionary Family*, 112. For Moses Hunter's death date of 1798, see "National Register of Historic Places Continuation Sheet for Stone House Mansion (Martinsburg, WV)," US Department of the Interior (1990), 15, accessed January 6, 2017, https://focus.nps.gov/pdfhost/docs/NRHP/Text/94001297.pdf.

In the spring of 1796, only four years after Crane's execution and just before Virginia's new, reformed criminal law took effect, Tucker heard another Winchester case like Crane's, one which also resulted in a special verdict. Robert Mitchell stood charged with the murder of Frederick Becktoll, a boarder in his home who had tried to intervene in a fight between Mitchell and his wife.[81] The case also occurred in Berkeley County and came out of the Winchester District Court, where Tucker and Paul Carrington, Jr., were the judges. Like *Crane*, the jury rendered a lengthy special verdict, detailing the facts of the fight – which included a physical altercation, acquisition of a weapon, and then pursuit of the fleeing boarder by Mitchell, as well as the damning finding that Mitchell "did intentionally shoot" Becktoll and then attempted to arrange the scene to cover up the crime. As with *Crane*, the jury left the question of murder or manslaughter up to the court, and Tucker and Carrington referred the case to the General Court. This time, Tucker commented positively that "this Special Verdict," he recorded, "was with the Assent of the prisoner adjourned to the General Court for the Law thereupon to be settled, as it seemed to us that it would prove a very leading case to determine the Limits between Murder and Manslaughter."[82] And this time, the General Court, which included Tucker, determined unanimously that Mitchell was "not guilty" of murder, but only of manslaughter.[83] One has to wonder what the remaining family of John Crane – his widow Catherine, now remarried, and John's brother, Joseph Crane – and their neighbors thought of that decision.

In the year that spanned the fatal July 4, 1791 fight at the fence between Crane's and Campbell's fields and John Crane's execution on July 6, 1792, John Crane was caught in a particular moment in history – that of an unfolding and as yet unfinished republican legal world. That year, John's experience of the law was, like St. George Tucker's, messy. It involved courts that were new and authority figures who were both new and old. It reflected his social standing but also defied it – and even recast it as his case progressed through the courts. It involved law that was old, so old that Virginia's lawyers and judges – as John Price Posey had discovered – turned to reports written by England's long-dead judges to explain it, and a political reality that was in many ways new, or at least unmoored from old restraints. If Crane, with his family connections, might have benefited from the deference of the prerevolutionary period, he would have also benefited from the republican reforms which were yet to come.

The world that John Crane encountered was perhaps both too republican, and not republican enough.

---

[81] Commonwealth v. Mitchell, 3 Va. 116 (1796).

[82] "Robert Mitchel's Case for Murder," April 16, 1796, in Hobson, *St. George Tucker's Law Reports*, 1:373–374.

[83] Ibid. Tucker indicated in his notebook that he gave an opinion, but filed it with a different collection of court papers – now lost.

Index